Riders in the Night

Books by Harry Harrison Kroll

The Cabin in the Cotton   I Was a Share-Cropper
The Ghosts of Slave Driver's Bend   The Keepers of the House
           Rogues' Company (A novel of John A. Murrell)
           Perilous Journey *(with C. M. Sublette)*
Three Brothers and Seven Daddies   The Mountainy Singer
           Return Not Again *(with Annette Heard)*
Fury in the Earth   Darker Grows the Valley
           Waters Over the Dam
The Usurper   Lost Homecoming
The Rider on the Bronze Horse   Their Ancient Grudge
           No Romance, No Moonlight (Play)
           The Smouldering Fire
           The Long Quest
           Summer Gold
           My Heart's in the Hills
           For Chloe — With Love
           The Brazen Dream
           Riders in the Night

Riders in the Night

Harry Harrison Kroll

Emeritus Professor of English
University of Tennessee

PHILADELPHIA
UNIVERSITY OF PENNSYLVANIA PRESS

7466
Printed in the United States of America

For Calia

Contents

Contents

Riders in the Night

Chapter One

The Land and Its Tribes

THIS KENTUCKY TOBACCO COUNTRY IS GRACIOUS LAND. IF you are sensitive to *place,* it charms you immediately. I remember the first time I saw the wide levels of tobacco plantation west of Murray, Kentucky, and how I thought the scene looked like a steel engraving out of an old book with tarnished leather covers. There were fields of tobacco running back against a wall of oak woods in the autumn afternoon. The old, log tobacco barns rose out of the levels here and there. The Negro cabins up and down — quiet weathered dwellings wearing that intangible clutter and cleanliness black folk so often contrive — stood within easy going of the big stock barns, for tobacco was in its day a man-and-mule crop. There was the big house. It was rather a large comfortable domicile than a mansion; and it was painted white and hedged in by old yard trees and many out buildings. And over all this pleasant picture was the tranquil haze of harvest.

This was a quarter century after the tobacco wars in the Black Patch of Kentucky and Tennessee, and I found it

11

hard to believe the legends and folk tales of hate, barn burnings, shootings, floggings and murder in this peaceful land.

Harry Harrison Kroll

Plantation of a well-to-do planter.

Concrete highways and blacktops now criss-cross the region. One can drive from one end of the Black Patch to the other in three or four hours of average travel. The roads are not crowded except perhaps on week-ends when the modern leisure class slithers along on fast rubber to Kentucky Lake, to speed-boat and fish for crappie and bream and drink Kentucky bourbon — with likely a woman now and then to spice the adventure. But one can dally along looking for the old roads that once carried four-mule freight wagons of rich fragrant leaf from the farms and plantations to the market towns of Murray, Hopkinsville, Russellville, Princeton and Eddyville, Mayfield and Fulton — to name a few in Kentucky; and Clarksville and Nashville, to name two in Tennessee. These old dirt roads more often than not followed landlines and took about twice as far to go from farm to market as a crow would fly. Nobody complained about this, for a crooked road was part of the leisure and patience of filling the world's pipe, its snuff bottle and cigarette pack, and its plug-twist pocket. When everybody chewed Star Navy and spat ham gravy, who cared whether the road was straight or crooked?

After you leave Murray you drive eastward along Highway 80 across Kentucky Lake. Men who have never known the old years or been moved by the nostalgia and romance of them, hoist their cigars at an angle and fleetingly admire the green-blue waters of this "inland gem." Not discounting the charm of a large body of fresh water where speed boats foam the lake to suds and now and then one sees a shapely wench water-skiing, I like to go back to the region when it was Tennessee River, with grim limestone banks, eroded by countless centuries of drifting current, overhung by hackberry and scrub oaks and now and then a pine; dotted up and down in the sleepy summer sunshine by the scows of mussel fishermen. I've seen scores of them on an afternoon in the idle current, the languid men drawing up their lines with hog liver tied to the ends and knocking the mussels off in the bottom of the scows. These fellows smelled of fish, sweat and tobacco. They were often the small farmers from back in the gravelly hills between the Tennessee and Cumberland Rivers, fishing for mussel shells for the button manufacturers between days of working their tobacco crops.

They were poor and dirty and warty. But the strip where they grew tobacco made some of the choicest dark-fired leaf to be found anywhere.

Times have changed. The tobacco-farmer fishermen have disappeared. But their log tobacco barns still stand on desolate hillsides, leaning awry over the erosions, with sedge-grass waving brown around them in the autumn sunshine. Today the tobacco barrens are mostly overgrown with persimmon and sassafras. Legend will tell you about a band of infuriated farmers gathering at a lonely, plank school house up the hollers from Golden Pond (now a halfway pause for cokes and gas between the rivers), and one of the half-crazed growers shouting, "Down with the Trust!" and leading the way with twenty followers to put the torch to the tobacco factory at Golden Pond. Masking their faces with their shirt-tails, they watched gleefully while twenty thousand dollars of the American Tobacco Company's leaf went up in flame.

But these passionate and often illiterate men had a streak of aesthetic in them. It was hidden deep under the dried sweat and tobacco tars of their leathery hides. I was struck by the example of how Golden Pond, a poetic name for a squalid little tobacco village, got its name. Long ago when rural post offices were being established in the back hills of Kentucky, a government man came to establish a post office here. He asked the old fellow who kept the crossroads general store to suggest a name. One would never have thought of this one-suspender tobacco-eating character as a poet, even less as a man with something of the eye of a painter. The sun was just setting and its last light fell upon a horsepond in the barnlot across the road.

"Golden Pond," he said immediately.

The store is long gone and the pond is almost filled. It

has a fringe of willows around its gold. I walked around this brushy locality one hot summer afternoon. My companion was the village historian. I said, "Wordsworth could not have named it better."

"Who's he?" my companion asked.

Harry Harrison Kroll '64

A century-old tobacco barn still in use.

We're still on Highway 80. We cross the Cumberland River on a high modern steel-and-concrete bridge. Miles

upriver and miles downriver there is a slumbering ribbon
of flood plain. The corn here was growing as tall as a man-
and-mule. It's rich dirt, and corn was everywhere, not a
leaf of tobacco in sight. I could see some of the faded
two-story houses where lived a past breed of affluent farmers who cultivated this land. I missed the plank-and-log
cabins of the croppers. But only a mile east, where the tall
hills set in, the shacks began to show themselves in the
sharp narrow valleys. Tobacco barns began mushrooming
again. Though many have collapsed into rotten logs and
rubble, a surprising number still remain in use. My visits
have often taken me through the tobacco country just after
cutting-time, and lacy smoke from sawdust in the firebins
issues from around the eaves to tantalize one's nose with
the mixed fragrance of hickory and tobacco. These are the
poverty-stricken shacks of the marginal farmers. Their cut-
over patches rise gray-green on every hill slope. They mat
on the floors of the valleys. You see ugly old women and
young females with flat bosoms stare at you as you drive
past, and the steam and smoke of outdoor wash pots is in
their hair. Each yard is a junkpile of old rusty cars and
trucks and tires, and maybe the man of the place is potter-
ing among them, making something run. There are children,
dogs, chickens, mules, a cow or two, and ducks on the
horsepond.

Then you come out on the plateau on the road to
Clarksville. Or if you take the fork of the road, Highway
193, you'll come to Cadiz, the hotbed of Night Riding, or
Hopkinsville and Russellville, scenes of the great raids. All
this level land is rich tobacco country. The dwellings are
mixed "Old-Kentucky-Home" types and modern ramblers.
You see leathery men driving tobacco trucks. You meet
big-girthed, landed men with sunsquinted eyes in red faces

driving new Fords and Chevrolets. There are poor whites and Negroes rattling along in vintage jalopies. There are handsome wives working in pretty yards, and now and then a bourbon-fed beauty will snap past you in a VW. You turn in at the gas station where all the men around the place are filling her tank, cleaning her windshield, checking her air, and eyeing her "charms," while you cool your heels and go up and down her comely figure and listen to their talk. The semi-literates have a language of their own, mostly grammarless. The smart young lady has another dialect, crisp and pleasant but solid Kentucky. A stranger can't make much of any of these jargons, beyond their lazy softness, slurred *r's* and dropped *g's*. If you happen to be a Yankee carpetbagging down in these parts, you might wish at times you'd picked up an interpreter at the Illinois state line. Their languor, their unhurried mannerisms, suggest the land and its inheritance. A lot of Kentuckians still use the language of their ancestors, when no man needed to read, let alone write; and they gummed their language with their cornpone and peas, washing it down with forthright homemade whisky.

So on to Hopkinsville, scene of the greatest civilian resistance movement known in America short of the Revolution and the Civil War.

The land is still changing, but the people remain pretty much the same. There are lovely semi-levels between Russellville and Hopkinsville, floors of shallow valleys with wooded ridges on either hand; and back from the highways there are half-hidden, comfortable homes, long-established and reached through parallel lines of trees: it was a convention of the old days to escape the dust and traffic of the dirt roads. Horses and whiteface cattle graze on the slopes.

A long yesterday ago there was little here save the fields of tobacco.

I had a companion on one of my junkets over the tobacco lands, and she would wave her hand. "I miss the woods most. When I was a child all the hills were covered with big trees." Now the limestone boulders rise out of many wastelands. "I miss the Negro cabins. The blacks have moved to town, or gone North. But there used to be thousands and thousands of acres of dark tobacco."

She told me when the early settlers came into what became the Black Patch, they found the valleys as treeless as today. They called them "barrens." The people settled on the hills, cut the timber and cleared the land, thinking that dirt in the valleys that didn't grow trees wouldn't grow crops. They didn't know the Indians burnt the meadows off every year for grazing for buffalo. Wild clover and buffalo grass will still spring up where the land is not grazed or cultivated.

These early comers had brought along from Virginia and North Carolina their tobacco seed. When they found their mistake about the barrens, they set out tobacco to find a type different from the light leaf of the coast country. The weed grew rank and dark and strong. It made a stout chew, filled a hearty pipe, rolled into a goodly cigar, and could be ground into prime snuff. No one remembers now how this type of tobacco found its way to England, Italy, Russia, Germany; and how almost before the close of the Revolutionary War, when Kentucky and Tennessee were already settled, the demand had begun. Nowhere else than in the Black Patch was such flavored tobacco known. A day came when dark fired tobacco covered all of the 22 counties of

Now there are ghost towns in this once thriving region.
the area. Men got rich, men got poor, growing it.

Guthrie, Kentucky, is one of the saddest, making you think of the village belle with a glowing future marrying the village drunkard and winding up taking in washing. Here the main line of the Louisville & Nashville railroad crosses the Memphis Branch going to Bowling Green, and shipping facilities were described as "unsurpassed." In its prime it was a busy mart, with huge warehouses for storing leaf tobacco, tobacco factories, bustling merchandise stores, three banks, and scores of old Victorian brick houses, where dealt the merchants who wore gold chains across their vests with Masonic charms, and bankers with their hip pockets stuffed with notes and mortgages on the surrounding farms. One can wander up and down its quiet streets today and stare at the fine old trees and yards and rusty iron fences, and the neglected graveyard back of a brick church with a mossgrown roof. You'll see rusty filling stations where once there were livery stables. There used to be blacksmith shops, a harness shop, a saddler's, and a place for mending wagons and buggies. There are gutted-out brick stores that never have been rebuilt since night-riding days. Fifty years ago the place rang with applause for great orators whose names now are not even remembered. Even the fairgrounds where the vast gatherings took place have disappeared. The keeper of the supermarket, now the biggest little store in the place, sorrowfully remembers a better day. "But tobacco-eating and snuff-dipping have just about passed out," he says. Guthrie has laid itself down to sleep without actually dying.

Then there are Pembroke and Gracie, two busy burgs of the old tobacco age. Pembroke used to have two tobacco factories, two banks, seven big merchandise emporiums, a wagon factory, two blacksmith shops, a saddler and harness maker, a score of handsome homes and a population of a thousand. There were tobacco laborers here and Negroes; but there were also many old, entrenched families of the tobacco rich. I stood across the corner from the L & N depot, now locked and bolted, in the shadow of a gutted two-story brick building, and tried to imagine some fairer time when Pembroke was a typical small but prosperous market center. There would be the evenings when the village quartet tuned to true pitch by good bourbon, sang "She was bred in Old Kentucky" in the silvery moonlight under the window of that mansion yonder across the way, now kind of seedy. You thought of romance, of some swain wedding her. Her father had a fine carriage and horses and she rode a prancing steed of her own. But when times got hard in tobacco, maybe the poor boy took to the bottle, and she rode high no more. But the girl was there and her numbers were legion. The companion I picked for this romantic journey into the past said she was one of them. At least she was middle class. She married into the to-bacco rich, and found her peasant blood not too happy a transfusion. Class distinctions were sharp, and there were four well defined ones; aristocrat, middle class, poor white, and Negro.

As for the village of Gracie, on the Illinois Central, its history is soon told. The Night Riders burnt its stores, tobacco factory, depot and other business places to the ground in two massive raids; and now you can pass the spot hardly knowing. There are four houses, a small store with a gas pump, and a handlettered sign, "Good Gulf 29.9c."

You ask, "Are all the towns ghost towns?" By no means. But ghosts often walk their streets. Clarksville, Tennessee, and Hopkinsville, Kentucky, are still world marts in dark-fired leaf. There is still wealth in tobacco. Parts of these towns go on wearing the quaint garb of their old affluent days. But the virus of modern times has established pockets in their throats, and you'll see more ramblers now than old-fashioned mansions. Russellville seems to have done a little better in preserving its pristine grandeur. The traveler with a taste for antiquity can leisurely trace its quaint streets and your hostess will point out this or that noble old pile where the flower and chivalry, properly dry-cleaned of tobacco tars and sweat, danced all night to waltzes, and gay blades drew their belles off into the discreet gloom of magnolias and recited, with slightly alcoholic breath, Byron, Keats, Shelley. The landmark of landmarks in this haunted town is an old building on a corner now withdrawn from the turmoil of the city. It was once the Planters Bank, and was held up by Jesse James and his boys. In the new bank downtown there is a mural lit night and day by floodlights, showing the imperishable Jesse putting a slug through the belly of the cashier and taking from his buddy Frank the swag handed out by the shivering assistant cashier. Hooded companions, holding champing horses, lurk in the background shadows for a fast get-away. One wonders if the Night Riders didn't get more than a hint here when they began their war on the "Hillbillies" and the American Tobacco Company.

Chapter Two

The Romance of Toil, Sweat and Tears

MEN — OLD MEN AND MEN NOT TOO OLD — WILL TELL you of the toil, sweat and tears of tobacco growing. You'll find them in lawyers' and doctors' offices, in teachers' chairs and especially in the editorial chairs of county papers, where men remember valiantly and record articulately. Occasionally their memoirs will be embalmed for posterity in vanity-published volumes, or done into even more crude books in the back office of the printer's. With eyes far out of focus, they will speak gloatingly of getting up long before dawn, eating a breakfast of fat hogmeat, cornbread and sorghum molasses (with wheaten biscuits and butter Sunday mornings) and black coffee solid and stout enough to float an iron wedge. They'd stagger from the smoked lamplight out into the icy dawn, gear up the mules to the wagon, gather the farm implements, and fall to work while the dim sun broke through the line of frozen trees. After they have warmed to their own eloquence, they'll tell you of the backbreaking work of field and woods, toiling on till nooning, when they'd return to the house for a dinner

22

of boiled cabbage with hogshead, turnip greens, fried ham and middling meat, cornbread and buttermilk, some more black coffee with long sweetening, a brief rest, and then back to work. Then the long toilsome afternoons, more killing work, till night drove them back to ungear and feed the mules and to milk the cows by lamplight, and to supper far into the darkness. Men knew nothing of "night life" in that rugged society. The old man of the place wound the clock, put the cats out, kicked the hounds away from in front of the fire, and all hands hit the hay. Folks worked hard in those times, ate hard, and slept hard, and there was no juvenile delinquency.

The cycle lasted from Monday morning till Saturday noon. After that the family, save the wife and daughters, knocked off. The boys went to town, maybe to meet a girl or maybe just to get drunk. The girls got ready for Sunday preaching. The Sabbath was dedicated to going to the house of the Lord and listening to honest hellfire-brimstone preaching. In that forthright time every sinner got a good roasting for his waywardness. Sunday afternoon our young man of long britches might have a date with a neighbor girl, going for a horseback ride or walk through the woods; and after supper a "set-around" in the girl's front room, as often as not with the family present or just barely out of sight. Despite these handicaps a good deal of fornicating managed to get accomplished, and wood's colts between tobacco crops now and then trotted out. Sometimes there would be a shotgun wedding, but as often as not the boy skipped the country and left the poor girl to her ruin. She would become the prey of every tomcatting youth for miles around. The issue of these offbeat relationships were also ruined for life. A girl who didn't own even a mule could not escape far to start life anew, and the bastard just grew up with the rest of the family, to be cuffed around and made to do the dirty work, and, if a girl, to become a little country whore. Sometimes "ruined" girls would live with their sisters, and be concubines of the men of the house. I knew one old tobacco farmer who had two families like this, his wife living in the main house and his concubine living in a tenant house. The children still call each other cousin.

There was never any long period of rest from making the crop. If tobacco growing was a man-and-mule production, it also was a year's end to year's end task. Before spring opened, the men and boys went into the woodland to cut oak and hickory for firing the barns in the fall. Piles of this fuel would rise from pawpaw stakes, to be ready to haul to the barns by late summer. Once crop time opened, there was no chance for getting out wood. There were also the great maws of the home fireplaces to be fed, and these insatiable monsters swallowed cords of wood without even seeming to warm the loosely constructed houses. Doors stayed open winter and summer. Every house had a big family, and there were yearling boys who learned to work at the beck and call of the head of the house. If now and then one smarter or meaner than the others left home by night to escape, he was prayed for, and in time was as apt as not to become the community doctor or preacher, or county editor who wrote a book about the glories of his young years back on the tobacco farm. The ones who ran away are the most nostalgic about the old years.

In early spring, before the buds began to swell, the task force of the farm went up the southern slope of some hill, cleared a long rectangular space, heaped logs and limbs and chunks on it, and set fire to burn the tobacco beds.

There was nearly always a nice spell of open weather in late January or early February, with clear cold nights and open days, and this was the time of the burning. All up and down the farmsteads the fires would glow by night. One motive was to get potash in the soil from the wood ashes. Another was to rid the ground to the depth of ten or twelve inches of unwanted weed seeds and insects. A good way to ruin a farmer's tobacco plant bed was for weeds and grass to spring up, a way the Night Riders later used with vindictive delight. Long logs were rolled alongside the burnt area, the ground was worked into a snuff-like softness, and the seed mixed with ashes was broadcast. The whole was covered with canvas to protect the young plants from the hot sun and occasional late frost.

After that began the job of putting the tobacco ground into shape. Tobacco does best in strong new soil, though it will thrive in any fertile land. Farmers always took in some new ground, as large as possible. This was the roughest job of the season. The land not only had to be cleared, but all the stumps and roots grubbed out. The stumps were burnt; the roots were torn up with bulltongue plows. The ground then got at least two thorough breakings, several harrowings, and was rolled with a log to compact it. In the old land the preparation was less arduous but not less thorough. Rows were laid out by check, three feet each way, so that later cultivations could be complete. Then came the wait for the "season." The margin of time for setting was fairly narrow. There should be a warm rain, prolonged enough to soften the ground. The farmer studied the skies anxiously, for not only must he have a good rain but he must have it stop in time. Since he had no control of either end, he usually fretted and worried and kicked the hounds and cussed his wife and prayed to the Lord. Later he could get his sins straightened out at some Sunday meeting when the preacher called upon men to testify and accept Christ as their personal saviour. There were those who scoffed at this type of religion, but they did not grow tobacco.

Suddenly the skies cleared, the crows hollered up in the woods, and the ground was just muddy enough to receive the plants. Every man jack and woman and child on the place, including the sharecroppers, black and white, were haled into the tobacco ground for setting. The girls pulled off their shoes and bunched up their skirts and carried the baskets of fragile plants ahead of the setters, dropping a plant to the hill. The setter followed with a sharp stick, punching a hole, and putting in the plant. Where the work was done on an assembly-line basis, the hole puncher was followed by another yearling boy who pressed the wet earth around the plants. A wave of these human locusts could swoop down on ten, twenty or thirty acres of land and have the tobacco set by sundown. Then all hands returned to the house, bone weary, and lay about on the floor groaning. It would take three days for the setters to get the kinks out of their spines from the stooping, and you used to see men bent like half moons who never walked upright again. Everywhere on barns and fence posts and store walls you could read the signs, "Sloan's Liniment for Aching Backs."

In the bland and sunny days the plants grew amain, and hoehands and cultivators fought the grass and weeds. If there happened to be too much rain, the whole family moved in to pull grass by hand. But usually the seasons were reasonable, and after a few weeks the dark green leaves grew broad and eventually knit between the rows. When it wasn't grass and weeds the farmer was fighting, it

was insects and worms. Back in the heyday of tobacco
growing, poisons were not generally used to control pests,
and another session of hand toil set in, with the younger
children having the advantage; for all they had to do was
lift the heavy leaves and look under for the egg clusters and
fat worms. They'd remove them and drop the garbage into
cans of coal oil. Men crushed the worms between thumb
and finger with sadistic joy, and the stain so ground into
the skin that never again did it regain flesh tint. Children
had the happy habit of just biting the heads off the worms
and dropping the substance on the ground. Their mouths
would become stained, and when they laughed gleefully at
the horror of the watching tenderfoot, they spat ham gravy.

This job of worming and suckering went straight through
the growing season. No one ever seemed to wonder where
the eggs of the worms came from. If it flew, when; if it
crawled, from where? Agricultural experts in the tobacco-
state universities finally unearthed these facts, but they were
not practical tobacco farmers, but Ph.D.'s wearing ironed
pants. Out where the hickory shirts and overalls reigned, the
juices lasted on and no amount of lye soap and battling ever
eradicated the stain.

But the farmer's toil and anxiety did not slacken. There
were hail storms that wrecked his year's labors in fifteen
minutes. There were storms that ripped the leaves and be-
dirted the entire crop. When the crop went on to ripening,
there was another uncertain season to wait for. The margin
of time might be narrow and a few days could spell the
difference between prime leaf and second quality, and 2c
to 3c a pound in price. Thus the farmer might go right
up to harvest with everything in his favor, and come to
grief at the last minute. It would mean the difference between making a fair return for his work, and losing money.

It was actually hard to figure how a tobacco farmer could lose money when he never really had any. What he lost was his toil and sweat and that of his work force. But there comes a day when the skies are ash blue, and the sun just hot enough for quick wilt, and down into the tobacco the cutters move like an army with swords. Most of the cutting tools were made of old grass scythes attached to wood handles. The cutter made a long slash at just the right angle into the base of the stalk, and he could ease it gently on the ground across the rows. They looked like dead bodies brought out of a battlefield lying so. Another crew came and stabbed the plants on sticks for toting to a rack where they were laid out to cure down till evening. If rain threatened the racks were trundled to the barns. After a few days of curing the tobacco was barned.

"Barning" a crop was a job for stout men and true. Some barns had sheds for air curing. But the main barn was a lofty square room, about twice as tall as the dwelling house to get full benefit of wood smoke, and tightly chinked to prevent loss of it. Far up in the dim dusky roof space the first bunches were hung to the topmost timbers. From there the bunches were worked down till the place was packed. It took four men to heft the tobacco into place — a floor man, who handed it to the men above standing on runners, who gave it to the man over him, who finally hung the bundle in place. The sticks might weigh from fifteen to thirty pounds, and it was all hand-over-head muscle labor. The partially dried plants would still be oozing half congealed sap ("tar") and this drip often got into the eyes of the workers, and unavoidably got on their skin and clothes. It was gooey and gummy and stinging. Up and up, tons and tons of tobacco; and four to eight days were required to get the two or three or four barns filled.

Fires then would be started, and here came another hazard, in many ways the greatest of all, as firing progressed. The fires had to be kept up day and night, never ceasing, for if they went out the curing had to be started all over again. As the moisture dried from the leaves, they would become brittle and flammable. Just let one small spark get in the dried tobacco and a barn could go up in flames while the farmer looked on sadly and saw his year's work go up with it. In my travels up and down the country roads, I have seen barns actually burning, or just burnt and the debris still smoldering. Thus the smoke man had to know his business, and he had to be forever vigilant. Dark-fired tobacco justified the work and risks, however, for curing gave an added body and flavor to the leaf which in turn brought much better prices.

And it was a season of festivity too, despite the back-breaking work. Usually the barns were fired in late afternoon, and the oldest and most dependable of the boys had the assignment of keeping the fires going through the first night and ensuing nights. Nights at this season of the year are apt to be clear and frosty, and hazy and sweet with harvest. Our hero's mom would fetch him a feed of hot biscuits and a pot of coffee to tide him along, and maybe the family came and looked on and the old man examined the crop and gave his final word of caution. Then they left and our future editor or doctor or dentist would build a fire outside at dusk, and light up his homemade cheroot, and sit with his back against a tree, meditatiing on what-ever suggested itself to his mind. A lot of dreams were dreamed then, according to the records. A novelist here, a poet there — and this tobacco region had its share of those who have come to national fame — will have a scene or a rime speaking of how ambition first sprang in his heart while he kept vigil over the curing fires. He could read the stars and the stars told him he had the makings of something more than a tobacco clod. What kind of mental processes the clods had is not on record. But the poet saw the campfires all up and down the Kentucky hillsides in the starlight, where fellows like himself kept watch; and the novelists have scenes where their sweethearts came stealing to them and lay under the blanket on the hard ground. Our hero would indulge happily or unhappily in sin, and so the hours would be speeded.

One last killing job — stripping. It's a task reserved for rainy fall and winter days, since it can be performed indoors. The sticks of tobacco are brought from the barn and the strippers tear the leaf apart from the stalks and stems, twisting them into hanks, prime leaves in one pile, lugs in another, trash in a third. The long stems and stalks are sold to be ground into snuff or made into insecticides.

On a day when the mists were heavy, the stripped leaves would be loaded in wagons and four mules would pull the load through the mud to the nearest market town. All roads in those days were dirt, and winter mud all but isolated the tobacco peasants. This traffic had to be during a wet season, so the tobacco would not shatter. At the factory it would be prized — graded — and packed in hogsheads, with a sample to identify grade and grower. This would usually be just before Christmas.

It was a gala time. Farmers got their cash, settled store bills, paid off the bank and doctor, bought a goodly supply of bourbon, and made ready for the holidays. Wives who had raised a small patch of their own bought a new dress and shoes and spent the rest of the money for the children. Usually it was for clothes. Calico, gingham, flannel — such goods went into homemade dresses and

underwear. Not many storebought clothes went on the
backs of the females. If the price of tobacco held up well,
an average family of six or seven people could hope to
clear perhaps four hundred dollars. Every one got a little
something around Christmas — a shot gun for the boys,
new shoes all around, a ribbon or two for the girls' frocks,
some grocery-mixture candy, oranges — this was the only

A typical tenant tobacco planting.

time of the year anybody ate oranges. I remember how
we used to save the peel to dry and eat on into the new
year. The kids would swallow the seeds, hoping an orange
tree would grow out of the top of their heads. There was

at least one big dinner of fresh beef to break the monotony of pork through the rest of the year, and there would be a big chicken dinner Christmas day, or perhaps turkey if the woman of the place could manage to raise a few turkeys after the inroads of disease and chicken snakes and skunks and weasels.

So this tranquil poverty lasted on, and few men thought it would ever change. There were good years and bad years, and some fluctuation in the price of tobacco, but mostly prime leaf stayed around 7c or 8c a pound, year after year. There was an insatiable demand for it. Everybody — man, woman and child — used it in some form: snuff for the women and girls, chewing and smoking for the men and boys. Western Kentucky and Tennessee dark-fired tobacco went to the four corners of the world. Hard as the life was, it had certain compensations; there was always something for liquor, and the shrill sawing of the applewood fiddle could be heard nights in the houses and cabins, and every man — poor white, Negro, pot-gutted farmer — had the Gospel preached to him.

But the tranquil poverty did change, becoming abject poverty, and this eventually led to bloody uprising.

Chapter Three

The Soulless Tobacco Trust

WE LOVE OUR LEGENDS. WE ANGRILY REVERE OUR great monsters of wealth. Back about the tobacco-heyday period of our social history we read the awed words of some financial writer in *Leslie's Weekly*: "America has many merchant princes and captains of industry, but only three industrial kings: John D. Rockefeller in Oil, Andrew Carnegie in Steel, and James B. Duke in Tobacco."

The tale goes that Washington Duke, the father of James — or "Buck" as the neighbors knew him — went to war with the Confederates much against his will. He left behind two sons and a daughter to be cared for by kinfolk, and he sold his little farm down near Durham, North Carolina, to a neighbor on credit. It could be that the neighbor secretly hoped old man Wash would get a Yankee bullet in him and never come back, in which case he wouldn't have to pay for the farm; but in any event he didn't pay for it, and Wash came home, and had a bad time ousting the neighbor. He wound up renting his own farm back on shares and paying tobacco rent for land he him-

self owned. The Yankees under Sherman had overrun all
this section of North Carolina, and they ran off all the
ablebodied farm stock, cattle, horses and mules, and they
stole all the loose tobacco within reach. The Yanks liked
the bright yellow leaf very much. Just why they overlooked
a parcel belonging to the Duke farm is not recorded. But
there it was. And Washington Duke also picked up two
blind mules the Yanks had turned out to grass, and a broken
down wagon. He and the boys fixed the wagon up and they
hitched the mules to it, beat the tobacco into dust on the
floor of the barn, sacked it, and fared forth peddling tobacco and trading and trafficking in flour and meat and
other human needments. They journeyed toward the southern part of North Carolina and disposed of the tobacco
profitably, and returned home to find that some Yankee
from up in Ohio or Indiana or elsewhere had written down
asking if he could buy a ration of that good smoking
tobacco he had picked up around Durham. James was
the trader of the tribe without a doubt, and the Yank's
discriminating taste was pleasured by some of what became Duke's Mixture smoking tobacco. Presently a lively
trade was developed in this manner. Instead of James and
his brother beating out the tobacco with flails in the barn,
a factory about twice the size of the barn was built and
Negro boys were employed to lash out the tobacco. A more
professional looking pack was fixed up, and the Dukes
were on their way to become tobacco manufacturers, and
James was on his way to becoming "king."

He had a chance to go to school in one of the private
and well taught academies growing up in the South. He
quit at approximately the middle of his sophomore year,
and no college for him. "That's all right for preachers and
lawyers," he said. "But what use would an education be

to me?" He went home and told his daddy he wanted a share in the growing tobacco business. The old man didn't give it to James on the spot, but he eventually did, after James went barnstorming with covered wagons of natural leaf up and down the land. However, the future king did not disdain a practical business education. He left Durham and went to the Eastman Business College at Poughkeepsie, N. Y., where he studied bookkeeping and business methods and had a glimpse of New York and the possibilities in that busy mart. He studied day and night, denied himself any kind of pleasure and recreation, tore on ahead of his class, and finished the course in less time than any other student. His teachers were not surprised when, a few years later, the Carolina farm boy became one of the barons of industry. James did the right thing by one of his teachers and hired him as head bookkeeper of the American Tobacco Company when it was organized.

But we are getting ahead of our legend. After Buck made his mark keeping books and buying and selling, he returned to his father's factory and became a drummer. Dealers in a dozen states knew young Duke well and liked him. Most drummers spent money freely. Not Buck. He called on customers all day and by night traveled on freight trains to save the cost of a bed in a hotel. And after a while, he turned a real trick. Our hero shaded his eyes against the rising sun and concluded there was a glowing noon and afternoon in the cigarette business. All this, mind you, while he was still not quite voting age. Blackwell's Bull Durham had the market by the tail with a downhill pull, and Duke's Mixture, while selling well, just didn't compete. The Civil War had stimulated the smoking of cigarettes tremendously. The bright tobacco of North Carolina was a natural for cigarettes. So Wash-

ington Duke and his boys changed over in Durham and
employed girls and women to roll the "coffin nails." A
day's output per skilled hand was 2000 to 2500 a day.
But James Bonsack, a young Virginian, invented an er-
ratic machine that would crank out a hundred thousand
a day. It had a lot of bugs in it, but James Duke installed
a battery of the machines in the Duke factory and himself
babied the contrivances. James got most of the bugs out
and cut the cost of manufacturing cigarettes to less than
half of the former 80c a thousand. It soon developed that
the problem of cigarettes was not in making but selling
them. The Dukes began a heavy advertising campaign and
got the jump on all the other cigarette boys. James probably got his idea from the classic portrait of a huge bull
on barn roofs all over the land, and the brick walls of
stores. That was Blackwell's idea, but he let his deal go
down when he followed the Dukes into the cigarette field.

The Dukes were making money. Their brand, however,
did not dominate the market. The older firms, like Kinney
Brothers, Goodwin & Co., W. S. Kimball & Co., and Allen
& Ginter, up around New York, did that. James Duke was
only twenty-seven years old when he concluded to do up
his spare shirt in a parcel and beard the smoke monster
in its den. He took off for New York, with $100,000 cap-
ital. He found a place with low rents on the East Side,
near the Bowery, and established his factory. His brands
were "Cameo," "Cross Cut," and "Duke's Best." Here
again our hero showed an insatiable appetite for work and
frugality. He was first on the job and last to leave the
plant. He took a cheap room and walked to and from
work. He dated no girls. He saw no New York shows.
Smoke was his middle name and toil was his maiden name,
and legs shows and girlies had no place in his plans. This

surefire formula for getting rich paid off, as might be expected in legendary America, and by skipping some of the sordid details we come finally to the master stroke, by which a man becomes an industrial king. Get rid of competition. Establish a monopoly.

It took some doing to get all his rivals lined up, but the tobacco war was by way of ruining all five cigarette companies. They cut each other's throats right and left, pouring out advertising money like water, paying bonuses to dealers, giving premiums to consumers for boxtops and wrappers and using high pressure sales methods. In one year Duke spent $800,000 for advertising and the net profit of his firm was less than half that sum. When the rival companies couldn't kill Duke off, they tried to buy him out. Duke kept fighting closer in, and finally sensed the time was ripe to present his scheme — the American Tobacco Company. The company was chartered in New Jersey on January 31, 1890, and was composed of Allen & Ginter, Richmond; the Kinney Tobacco Company of New York and Virginia; W. S. Kimball & Co., Rochester; Goodwin & Co., New York; and W. Duke Sons & Co., New York and Durham.

And now our Algeresque hero with a cigarette in one hand and a sack of Duke's mixture in the other really hit his stride. The capital stock was twenty-five million dollars, consisting of ten million 8 percent noncumulative preferred, and fifteen million common stock. Par value of the preferred was $100, and of the common $50. James Duke took seven-and-a-half million. Allen & Ginter took the same. Kinney got five million, and the other five was split between the two other firms. James Duke was president of the new consolidation.

While all this frenzied financial wizardry went on in Wall Street, back down in the hinter-provinces of Kentucky and

Tennessee, the peasantry toiled, sweat and fornicated in the erosions of the hills and hollers. The women wore calico and drawers made of flour sacks, and the men moved languidly in the summer suns plucking big green worms off the weed in overalls and hickory. About this time the dark-fired tobacco prices dropped a little — perhaps a half cent a pound the first year. The fluctuation was embarrassing but normal. None of the tobacco growers paid much attention when James Duke turned his attention next to bringing the cigar manufacturers into his combine, and then the manufacturers of snuff and plug tobacco. When this was accomplished in the later nineties, dark-fired tobacco dropped to 6c, then to 5c, and finally to 4c. There was talk that prices would go still further down, and they actually did get as low as 3-2-1 — 3c for prime, 2c for lugs, and 1c for trash. The product was sold in England, Russia and Germany and Italy for upward of $1.50 a pound. It was no figure of speech that the tobacco grower faced ruin. The rich man was growing richer and the poor man was starving to death.

During this while, the methods of marketing the leaf changed almost completely. Once upon a time the farmer carried his tobacco to the factory, unloaded, had it prized, and when the loose leaf auctions came, his leaf would be put up for sale. The looseleaf floor was a barnlike building where the sample were displayed for the buyers to examine and bid on. Here was heard the same chant of the tobacco auctioneer made familiar to you by radio commercials. The buyers might be local speculators who bought in leaf for later resale, or they might be agents of the snuff and cigar companies in Louisville and St. Louis. Certainly there would be men representing the Italian Regie, the Russian state monopoly, and the English and German companies. Competition might be keen for special crops. A farmer with

just the right sort of tobacco might well command a premium over the prevailing market. On sales days these auction rooms were the center of a town's interest.

In Martin, Tennessee, where I live, two such factories
still stand and both are in use as lumber barns. One is a
low, flat building looking like an old-fashioned livery stable.
The other is a three-story brick structure which in its day
accommodated thousands of tons of tobacco. This little
college town was never a true tobacco center, like Murray
and Mayfield and Hopkinsville. But it was the representative of thousands of modest markets where farmers went,
leaving home at dawn with their tobacco, unloading and
perhaps selling that day and getting home through the rain
and mud for a late supper. Older citizens are still fond of
recalling how, back then, every street in the town was lined
up end to end with waiting tobacco wagons, tarpaulins and
old quilts protecting the load against rain, with the Negro
drivers patiently waiting their turns. I can myself recall the
roistering youth that sold their tobacco, went to the nearest
saloon and got drunk as owls, and fell into cutting and
shooting scrapes and drove out of town at midnight empty-
ing their six-guns, lashing their teams, cursing; while I lay
on my floor pallet in terror, never knowing when a bullet
would shatter the door or window. There was always a fine
population of whores to absorb the loose money the crap
shooters and liquor men had overlooked.

The Trust changed all that. Tobacco was no longer hauled to the factories and auctioned in open competition.
James Duke's chief aim was to do away with competition
in all its forms. To that end he had associated with him the
most important companies of that day in the manufacture
and marketing of all types of tobacco products. But he also
cut out competition in buying the raw material. No one

now can say for sure whether Duke originated the plan of offering the farmer a given price for his leaf on a take-it-or-leave-it basis. Certainly it came down the pecking order from some cock in authority, and if not Duke, certainly Duke could have put his finger on the man. Now the buyers visited the farmer's barn, looked his crop over, and named a price. One year it was 5c, the next 4c, the next 3c, or 3-2-1. If a grower declined the offer, no other buyer would be along to purchase. Some farmers tried to sell in the towns. They were coldly refused. The Black Patch was organized into purchasing districts, the Italians having one region, the English another, the American Tobacco Company another. Before long, the farmers were howling, "The Trust is robbing us."

Buying leaf tobacco cheaper was not in his mind, James Duke said. In fact, he argued the prices the farmers received averaged more than before, since the American Tobacco Company eliminated the speculator, which meant more money for the farmer. On another occasion he remarked, "The farmer has got to have a good price for his tobacco, or he won't grow it. We are just as much interested in the farmer as we are in the consumer."

The words sound strange, considering that it was axiomatic that the farmer would go on growing tobacco even when he starved. The system apparently was founded on that fact.

How dire then was the poverty of the tobacco farmer? Was he, as he contended, actually losing money?

We have noted that he had little or no money to lose, and this complicates the answer. The grower figured it cost him $42 to grow an acre of tobacco for which he received $28. His loss was $14 an acre by these calculations. That seems a small sum today. But even so small a piece of cash as $14 could mean a decent wage for himself and his work force, and the foreclosure of the mortgage on his land.

The following figures were prepared by men who knew what they were talking about. It is based on four acres to the tiller, and a land value of $25 an acre. Every farmer borrowed money to make his tobacco crop.

Interest and deterioration at 20%	$20.00
Labor preparing and sowing seed beds	6.00
Canvas to cover beds	4.00
Land-breaking with plow and team, 2 days	6.00
Discing with 3 mules, 2 days	6.00
Checking with plow and mule, 1 day	3.00
Fertilizer	6.00
Hilling, 1 man, 4 days	4.00
Setting	6.00
5 cultivations, man and mule	12.00
Hoeing and topping, 8 days	8.00
Suckering, 32 days	32.00
Cutting and housing at harvest, 8 days	12.00
Cutting and hauling wood	12.00
Stripping	10.00
Hauling to market, 1 man, 1 day with team	3.00
Interest on investment in teams and equipment	18.00
Total	$168.00
Dividing by 4, cost per acre	$ 42.00

The average yield per acre was 700 pounds of tobacco, or 2800 pounds for the four acres. Thus it was necessary to get 6c a pound to cover cost of production and allow a man $1 a day for his work and $2 for his mule team. With the Trust paying an average of 2c a pound for tobacco, a farmer received nothing for his work and the toil of his wife

and children. There was just enough to pay for fertilizer
and canvas, and a little something for the store bills. How
the farmers kept on producing during the six or seven years
of gradually declining prices has never been explained except on the basis of the Trust's assumption that such men
would starve to death rather than abandon their own tobacco patches. In truth, many small farmers from 1900 to
1906 lost their farms, unable to pay on the mortgages and
pay off interest and keep up a family. Merchants who advanced money to the croppers and banks that helped the
big growers went broke. Up and down the Black Patch
there was true poverty. It struck the grower and the money-
ed town man equally. Perhaps the town man suffered more
than the cropper. As long as the farmer had his land — and
even when a bank foreclosed and he lost ownership, he
could stay on as a tenant — he could grow corn, raise
hogs, have a garden, milk cows, keep chickens, and so produce, during a good part of the year, what his table demanded. He could still grow tobacco, working his children
from dawn till dark. Profitless or no, tobacco growing was
all he knew. If there was any cash to be had at all, it was
what he might be paid for his leaf.

The works of fictions that have been written about life
back on the farm in those days were usually sentimental
creations. They are for the most part sorry enough treatises
on the hardships of tobacco farming. Yet they do portray
with reasonable truth the situation as it generally existed,
and a grim enough composite tale it is. The kids went to
school at a plank school house two or three months each
winter when work was slack. The schoolhouse had cracks
in the floors and chinks in the walls and was indifferently
well heated by a single big-bellied stove, fed by cord wood
toted in by the older boys. I happen to know about this

part, for I taught in just such schools during those years. The teacher could usually read and write, and every so often he could cipher to the rule of Three, which was regarded as an awesome achievement in book learning. If he owned a small library of, say, 30 or 40 books, he was looked upon as a wizard. I remember how my pupils used to stare at my small case of books and ask in hushed voices, "Have you *really* read all those books?" Many teachers preached on the side, picking up something from the forlorn little plank churches. And they, too, grew tobacco along with their neighbors. Theology was the straight hellfire-and-brimstone brand. Women who taught school now and then married the community's well-to-do widower, who might have one or two children in school, and thus they stepped from one reasonably thankless job into another. In winter you traveled from place to place on mule back, for the roads were knee deep in mud. You could walk short distances, following the used turfy pathways above the roadcuts. There was a lot of rain and snow and cold, and everybody got sick. Children sniffled all winter. Doors of houses were never shut. The good died young, people said. Certainly the mortality rate among the young was high. You could visit old graveyards back in the eroded wastelands and to this good day see how the infant population was decimated. And always there was the work, the men feeding the mules and looking after the stock; the women bogging through the barnyard mud and manure to milk, to feed up in case the man of the house got down on his back with the misery. Half the news of any neighborhood was about sickness. Doctors came to visit much more often than they were paid.

The modern student of status-seeking could pretty well establish the norm of the tobacco grower. Aside from the big landed men, he would find in a loose statistical survey that this fellow owned an average of 25 acres of land, though actual owners probably had farms of 50 to 60 acres, with the renter owning none; he had one and a half mules; he had nine-tenths of a wife, for tobacco growing and children were hard on women and this was a culture where the male survived and the female died; he had five and a half children and six hound dogs. He owned a shotgun and rifle and all his sons had guns and pistols. He belonged to the Christian Church, the Holiness Church or the Church of God, though Baptists and Methodists were numerous among them. He believed the Bible literally from "kiver to kiver," and if he ever heard of the theory of evolution he shouted that it was a device of Satan to lead men to hell. He still owned the suit he married in and in most cases he could make it meet around his lank middle. He believed it was a sin to swear, though he usually did. He was positive the place of a woman was in the home, and he questioned the value of education for girls, though he sent his daughters to school. "You're only educating another man's wife." That proved true. His daughters had a habit of running away around the age of fifteen, trying their luck, starry-eyed, in the holy bonds of matrimony. His characteristic epitaph, when he died, was: "He was a kind husband and indulgent father." But he had a way of trying to lick his sons till they got big enough to threaten to leave him, and then he treated them like men, for he needed their labor. He helped his daughters toward matrimony by flogging them regardless of how old they were. Their misbehavior was usually that of straying away from the homeward path from church on Sunday nights. His favorite medicines, by which he lived and died, were Peruna, for all human ailments — 65 percent grain alcohol and various percentages of this and that herb; Dr. Pearce's Golden Medical Discovery, for coughs,

colds, consumption and grippe; Grove's Tasteless Chill
Tonic, sure-shot for malaria; Thedford's Black Draught for
constipation and sour stomach; Sloan's Liniment, for aches
and pains; and for his ailing old woman, Wine of Cardui
and Lydia E. Pinkham's. At Christmas he would go on a
big bender and one of his neighbors would fetch him home
from town about midnight.

A tough, knotheaded people they were, and I remember
them out of my boyhood as neither quite human nor wholly
animal.

The tobacco growers were not stretching the truth when
they declared James Duke's American Tobacco Company
was ruining them. And I've often wondered what Duke and
his financial wizards thought of these unwashed dirt farmers in Tennessee and Kentucky, and the South generally,
while they ran their gold gloatingly through their fingers.
Or did they give any thought to them? Far removed up
there in New York, figuring in terms of hundreds of millions
of dollars, what did 3-2-1 a pound mean to them?

I remember visiting Duke University during World War
II. It had begun as the little Methodist college of Trinity.
Now there were the elaborate buildings, in Gothic architecture. I stood staring at the chapel spire against the pale
blue North Carolina sky. Toward the close of his life, perhaps buying surcease from his conscience, James Duke
had put more than forty million dollars in buildings and
endowment. Some carping critic in *The Nation* had his
opinion of all this elaborate business of stuffing education
down the throats of Tar Heels.

Mr. Duke in his naive way believed that he could build a great
university as he would build a factory — by going out and buying the brick and stone, the machinery and tools, and the work-

men to operate them. He forgot that he was dealing with the most elusive commodity in the world. He could no more create ideas in the wholesale fashion than he could later create a market for them. Thus he started to build his university at the wrong end. . . . He assumed that it was want of money — and of money he knew he had plenty. If North Carolina had no great university, it might have been that she had no desire for one.

But she got one, and I remembered that James Duke had told his daddy that he wanted no part of a college education.

I tiptoed with awe into the crypt where the Dukes are buried. Effigies of them in fine Italian marble, sculptured by the finest artists, lie peacefully on the granite or marble tombs, their eyes closed, their hands folded on their breasts. James Duke is there, and his father, Washington Duke. They wear a serene if not a holy look. I stood in the light of the stained glass and thought of half-starved children biting the heads of tobacco worms and the juice squirting.

Chapter Four

Tobacco Worm Bites Trust

ON SATURDAY, SEPTEMBER 24, 1904, FIVE THOUSAND TO-
bacco growers foregathered at the fairgrounds in Guthrie,
Kentucky, to formulate means of fighting the Trust. This
was the same Guthrie that today is a ghost town. But that
year the small town was one of the markets of the dark-
fired tobacco region. Because of its central location it became the capital of the resistance movement. There were
all manner of men, from the wealthy planter, to the moder-
ately well-to-do farmer, down through the renter, cropper,
and Negro. The object of the meeting was to form an association that could control the sale of tobacco to the American Tobacco Company and its associated companies. These
were the Imperial Tobacco Company, that handled the crop
in England, and the Italian Regie, that controlled the monopoly in Italy, France, Spain and other countries. The Regie
syndicate sought to avoid the stigma of being part of the
Trust by maintaining an aloofness from the American Tobacco Company, but the Kentucky and Tennessee farmers
were not fooled. There was every evidence of a secret un-

derstanding, such as the Regie not intruding on the territory
of the other companies, and paying the same prices for the
corresponding grades of tobacco.

A. D. Stanley wrote the charter for the Association, a
fairly dry document containing seven articles stating the
purposes and intentions of the tobacco growers. Charles H.
Fort was elected president, Charles E. Baker vice-president,
Frank Walton secretary-treasurer, and Felix G. Ewing general manager.

In many ways Felix Ewing was the wheel horse of the
outfit. He had conceived the plan as early as 1893, when
the Trust began depressing prices. His former home was
Nashville, Tennessee, where he gained considerable man-
agerial experience in two factories he established to manufacture carriages and plows. They were fairly modest enterprises but they did make him considerable money, and he
became something of a financial figure around Nashville.
In 1903 he sold out and moved up to Robertson County,
bordering Kentucky, to become a full-time tobacco planter.
His plantation consisted of 3000 acres of rolling tobacco
land, an impressive white mansion situated a mile off the
public road between Adams and Cedar Hill, two villages
some 25 miles from Clarksville. There it was said he lived
in princely style. There was no finer home anywhere in
western Kentucky and Tennessee, and it compared with
famous estates in the bourbon-swigging Blue Grass. It was
a seat of elegant and gracious living, with great barns and
driveways and fine trees and spacious views, the best tradition of the Old South. Men who loved their phrases — editors of newspapers and orators with a bagful of grandiose
adjectives — said he had all the elements necessary to con-
stitute a man: matchless courage, sincere truthfulness, ster-
ling integrity, patience as gentle as a mother's love. More-

over he was educated, brainy and rich. Warm hospitality,
embracing a well stocked cellar of choice wines and liquors,
was dispensed at Glenraven. The very name of the place
makes one think vaguely of Scott, Jane Austen, and Tennyson. Someone started a move to celebrate this godlike man
with a monument. "Well may the planters," he orated, "out
of admiration for this modest gentleman, build a monument
on the triangle formed by the railroad at Guthrie, of the
purest white marble, with his features accurately chiseled,
that the generations yet to live in this country may have a
correct likeness of the man who has led the greatest civil
revolution of any age for the people of the Dark Tobacco
District of Kentucky and Tennessee."

It was a day of hero worship, and the tobacco growers
sorely needed a hero. Mr. Ewing rejected this eulogisic
scheme, saying, "I have no desire to be worshiped." Visiting
Guthrie, one misses that monument today, and it is easy to
wish the plan had been put through to add a bit of light to
the gloom of this forgotten community. But if they had no
marble monument of the man, they could give him grand
names: Mr. Ewing came to be called "The Moses of the
Black Patch, who had led the children of toil out of the
wilderness." It was a slightly premature assumption, and
perhaps it would be more accurate to call him simply "King
of the Black Patch."

When one sifts through the adjectives to the real men,
there appears a person of considerable education, stature
and devotion to the cause of the tobacco grower. He labored
valiantly for decent prices and it does not detract from the
man that he had a personal investment in tobacco growing.
His health was not robust, and he carried the double burden of his own plantation and the Association.

Charles Fort was a less redoubtable personage. As a tobacco planter he was prominent in the locality, having been president of the Clarksville Tobacco Growers Association. He was a Justice of the Peace. Charles Barker lived at Pembroke, the other ghost town, though a thriving tobacco town in that day. Walton lived in Guthrie.

These men had met previous to September 24 to do the paper work, and all the growers had to do was meet and vote on the constitution and elect officers. Guthrie was chosen as general headquarters and Clarksville was selected for the Association's salesrooms. Hopkinsville might have seemed a more logical place, but Clarksville had river connections — the Cumberland — and railroad facilities, and was the largest tobacco town in the eastern district. Moreover, it was nearer Mr. Fort's and Mr. Ewing's homes.

The five thousand growers returned home believing they had entered an association that would control the situation and raise the prices of tobacco from the current average of 3c to the 8c they set as the price for prime leaf. No doubt great numbers had the notion, easily come by in the minds of simple farm folk, that fine rhetoric and mouth-filling "whereases" would solve their woes, as, a generation before, the freed Negro slave in the South was easily persuaded he would be given forty acres and a mule, with every day Sunday and two chickens in the pot. The leaders themselves had no such illusions. They were at pains to impress on the farmers that success depended on a great many factors, all difficult of achievement. They set 70 percent of all the growers as a minimum number to control. And above all, members must be faithful. It seemed easy to be faithful when there was a glow of hope on the horizon, but they would have to cling together even when hope faded. One wonders why tobacco growers were not chilled by the cold facts Ewing and Fort made no effort to gloss over. No member could be paid for his crop till all the tobacco was sold. The Association had no contract for sales. It might be possible to advance money after a while to members of the pool to meet loans and payments on mortgages and running expenses, but currently the Association had no funds to assure this. They did not even have any cash to defray the expenses of the paper organization. The officers were serving without pay, and the office in Guthrie was supplied free of rent.

There were reasons for the more intelligent and influential of the growers to join the Association in spite of these handicaps, for men of vision could see that the scheme was feasible, if audacious. In some ways the Association was fashioned after the American Tobacco Company. There was not, of course, the enormous prestige of Wall Street and James Duke behind it. But men like Ewing and Fort, were curiously undismayed by his power and prestige. The leaders of the movement were men of integrity, and the situation was desperate.

There were troubled questions in the minds of thinking men. Could the farmers be persuaded to put up the solid front necessary for victory? No one knew better than these practical fellows the percentage of recalcitrants in any cooperative farm venture. You could count on a wavering percentage that would sway as the wind blew. Some would be loyal to the end, though no one could guess how many or how few. And there were always those that would rather die than cooperate with their fellows against a common enemy, even as powerful and ruthless as the Trust. What could be done with these? The answer was never arrived at by open discussion. But thoughful men had misgivings on their way home. Force, coercion, must have been in their minds.

The faithful began an energetic campaign to enroll their neighbors. It was here that the men were quickly separated from the boys. Numbers joined promptly. Some balked, doubting that the scheme would work. Others objected that they would be turning their tobacco over to visionaries with plenty of schemes and fine words but no money. Others simply refused to have anything to do with the Association.

Meetings were held in the little plank schoolhouses and austere churches to plead, cajole, pray the reluctant growers to present a solid front to the Trust. The local chairmen opened such meetings with prayer and closed them with the benediction. Cases are on record where the chairmen, after the manner of the old-time camp meetings, would get the doubters down on their knees and pray God to show them the light. Real inducements were offered by men of substance, such as a larger share in the tobacco crop, advances of rations through the growing season, cash without interest to meet loans and mortgages. Gradually the 70 percent was passed, and some districts reported up to 95 percent of the tobacco growers signed up with the Association. Each member signed a contract making the Association his agent for whatever tobacco he produced.

One of the wisest things the leaders of the Association did was to make use of what today is the crop-acreage allotment plan. A grower with fifty acres of land was requested to limit his tobacco crop by five acres. After that he was asked to cut acreage two and a half acres to each additional fifty acres. This was not part of the pledge signed by a grower, but obviously it was a means of cutting production and raising prices. A careful record was made of all growers who joined, and a blacklist was prepared of those who refused. The term "Hillbilly" was applied to men who refused to come into the Association. The word became an epithet.

A Hillbilly, typically, was a wormy fellow who lived on the back roads in the rolling eroded lands, though many men of substance also declined to sign up. Two psychological factors seemed to operate to prevent growers from joining. One was a combination of ignorance and stubbornness and a traditional taste for independence. The other was unquestionable cunning. While it was apparent that a common battle front would in time reduce the American Tobacco Company to compliance with the demands of the Association, it was also apparent that keeping tobacco off the market in large quantities would bring about high prices for those free to sell. Some small percentage of men were happy to profit by the sacrifices of their neighbors. Herein would be the seeds of bitterness and hate between man and man when grimmer methods than persuasion would come into use.

But at that time eloquence was the great ammunition employed against the Tobacco Trust. Joel Fort and John M. Foster were men who followed up every rally hurling invective at the Trust and painting glowing pictures of the fair day when the top rail should be the bottom rail and the bottom rail should be the top rail and every tobacco slave should drop his chains and stand forth stout and free. Colonel Joel Fort, brother of the president of the Association, established himself as the "Tennessee Warhorse of the Black Patch," when men were in sore need of warhorses and stalwart heroes. He was the man who said he was going to bring suit for damages against the American Tobacco Company, and with grim enough humor he added, "Every time I make a speech the American Tobacco Company decreases the price they offer me for my tobacco by one cent a pound, so that eventually, if I keep on talking, I'm going to have to pay the Trust a dollar a pound to take the tobacco off my hands." And there was no doubt the Trust was using such methods to silence a man who swayed the wavering growers.

Meanwhile tobacco was growing in the hot steam loamlands of a thousand flats and valleys, and men and women and children bent to pluck the fat worms from the broadleaf. A crop was coming on, and more than oratory and noisy rallies were in order. The leaders arranged for pledged tobacco to be stored at leased warehouses or warehouses hastily built with funds raised by selling stock in the local associations; and enough money was obtained so that from 25 percent to 50 percent of the value of the tobacco could be advanced to the grower. (All this has a strangely familiar ring today with government loans to wheat, corn and cotton farmers.) One of the first such Association warehouses was at the village of Cobb, in Caldwell County, Kentucky, in 1905. The name of Dr. David A. Amoss was associated with the enterprise, and we shall hear much of this man as the lines of battle are joined between the tobacco growers and the Trust. He was a country doctor living in a modest white house in the village, and though he was not himself a tobacco grower, he was intimate with the problems of the farmers, and deeply in sympathy with their struggle to secure decent prices for their produce. Nor was his interest in the success of the venture due to the fact that he collected his fees only when the farmers had money, though no doubt the worthy doctor had this stake in the business. But men still live who remember him saying he was a Christian gentleman, and here and there can be unearthed a native who speaks proudly of having been delivered from his mother's womb by Dr. Amoss. But Dr. Amoss was more than just a beloved country sawbones, as

we shall presently see. Men of lesser stature have been embalmed in bronze and stand in public parks.

But after the dust of oratory and the technical nomen-
clature of contracts and techniques of marketing had been
settled, the main business remained: to sell the tobacco. No
buyers came to the factories. The hot autumn sun shone
down on the tin roofs of these sprawling shacks, raising a
mist of tobacco fragrances, but the buyers of the hated
Trust stayed away. Not one showed up. Felix Ewing and all
the other wheelhorses of the revolution realized that something must be done. Ewing went to New York, paying his
own expenses, in hope of finding purchasers among the
various "independents."

While in New York he found confirmation of what had
been obvious to him and other leaders all along. Trust
agents and indepentent buyers admitted to him, "It would
never do to let the tobacco planter know his strength, for
if we do it will cost us millions of dollars." If in the beginning these fellows did not take the Association seriously,
having seen such farmers groups fail before, they realized
well enough that if the tobacco growers stuck together,
they had the underhold. Tobacco they must have, not only
for the Trust, but to hold their own jobs. Many of them had
been in tobacco all their lives — as agents of the tobacco
companies, as buyers on their own, speculators, warehouse-
men, and even as farmers. Ewing went back without a sale,
but holding the torch higher than ever. If *all* the growers
can be brought into the organization, they could control
the situation.

The Trust was impressed if not frightened. They thought
enough of the Association to start their propoganda mill to
grinding, saying in effect, "Association tobacco won't sell,
and even if it does, it will sell for less than we've been pay-

ing. You haven't any backing, you won't be able to get an advance on it, and without money the banks will foreclose on your mortgages and merchants will sue you for your accounts." Besides, they went on, "We don't need your tobacco. We've been expecting this, and we've got enough surplus to last us a year." In a year's time the planters would be begging the Trust to buy their tobacco at any price.

The editor of the Clarksville *Leaf Chronicle* furiously denied this. He dipped into his vitrolic ink of statistics and hurled figures right back into the teeth of these infamous propagandists. The tobacco companies, he said, always kept a year's supply in reserve. Foreign markets required 200,-000,000 pounds of dark, rich, heavy tobacco of Kentucky and Tennessee. The Tobacco Trust had contracted to deliver this tobacco. Morever, the countries themselves were heavily involved in the movement of tobacco. They collected an average tax of $1.29 a pound. Italy imported more than 27 million pounds, and collected a revenue of more than 40 million dollars. England imported almost 97 million pounds with a revenue of more than 60 million dollars. There were France and Spain and Austria and Russia, and they chewed Star Navy and spat ham gravy in fabulous tonnage. And apart from the commercial aspects of this business, there were the appetites of the customers, who might reasonably riot if they did not get their ration of long green. One telling point the editor made: the foreign governments made more money out of tobacco than did the growers in Tennessee and Kentucky.

If the farmers of the Black Patch stood together under Felix Ewing and slugged it out with the Trust, they could bring the American Tobacco Company to its knees. But if they broke and failed, they were lost for all time.

It is hard to believe that James Duke did not know what

was going on. He, and the American Tobacco Company, had brought into the Trust the major manufacturers of plug tobacco, snuff, and cigars, who were the major users of dark-fired tobacco. If Duke himself was more interested in manipulations on Wall Street than in the prices of raw tobacco down in Kentucky and Tennessee — as he well might have been — certainly men under him, and no doubt with his orders, were concerned with breaking the Association. Their methods were ruthless and simple. If the tobacco farmer, hog-tied by his allegiance to the Association, asked 8c a pound for his leaf, the Trust would offer those who had not affiliated with the Association 10c or 12c per pound. In November and December, 1904, the American Tobacco Company ordered its buyers and agents into action, and riding far and near over the counties they offered a minimum of 8c for average leaf, and up to 12c for the best grades. They took in key farmers who had not pledged their tobacco to the Association and instructed them to buy from their neighbors "at any price," the Trust agreeing to take the tobacco off their hands.

A case in point is a farmer I know in Kentucky who lives some ten miles from Hopkinsville, who, far from being a Hillbilly, actually owned two farms of 400 acres each in some of the best tobacco land in the world. Not only did he refuse to pool his tobacco, but he bought for the American Tobacco Company, and though he almost got himself killed for his "perfidy," he steadfastly refused to join up with his neighbors.

There were just enough of these men to strike fear into the hearts of the rest of the tobacco growers. There were too many men who had debts and mortgages hanging over their heads for ready cash not to make its appeal. It was bitter irony to the Association members that their own sacrifices resulted in the Hillbillies getting twice as much for their crop as the market was paying. Meanwhile, Ewing's efforts to find a market for the accumulated tobacco failed. Then in May, 1905, there came a break. He sold six thousand hogsheads to George Reussens in New York, who shipped to France through the port of Bremen, and began thus to move the whole 1904 crop in the hands of the Association, 24,700 hogsheads, at an average price of six and two-thirds cents a pound. Though this was less than the price of 8c set by the Association, it was nearly twice the average price paid by the Trust for the past three years. Men spoke of this as a victory over the Trust. And so it was. Barely.

Chapter Five

Rally Round the Flag, Boys

IT WAS AN ERA OF "EATING" TOBACCO, DIPPING SNUFF, smoking long green, cussing great blasphemous oaths, county fairs, political barbecues, and Ringling Brothers & Barnum & Bailey's circus, John Robinson's, Wallace's, Forepaugh & Sells Brothers, and toil and sweat. Next to a lynching, a barbecue was what fetched in the populace. On September 23, 1905, the Association, whose tail was longer that its head — The Dark-fired Tobacco District Planters' Protective Association of Kentucky and Tennessee — held its second conclave at the old stand of Guthrie, Kentucky. To the original 22 counties in the two states six new ones had been added, and the membership now stood at 7000.

Eighteen thousand people attended this second gathering. They were not only tobacco farmers and their families; doctors, lawyers, merchants, large and small, who had a stake in the success of the Association lent their presence and sympathy. They gnawed barbecued ribs and listened hopefully to the fiery words of "King" Ewing, Joel Fort and Dr. David Amoss. Mr. Ewing stood forth on the high plat-

59

form in the fair grounds and figuratively beat his chest. The man's face poured sweat in the September heat, and he must have felt profoundly moved as he said:

"The Association is before the world on its merits. It invites investigation. It is the champion that dares to stand against the Trust's efforts to reduce the tobacco grower to menial servitude. It appeals to you to save yourself from ruin, and if all work together it surely can be done. Obstacles have been daily thrown in our way. First, to prevent our organization. Next, to belittle our efforts by ridicule. And then to prevent the sale of tobacco. Now we are ahead. The tobacco world expects us to win, and that we must do so upon an honest, conservative basis should be one thought in the mind of every honest tobacco planter."

One cannot help but note that Felix Ewing used the word *honest* twice in the same sentence. He had reason to put emphasis on honesty. Already, deep-down passions had been aroused. Hates were stirring. Men who had lived on adjoining farms for years now were hostile to each other, one pooling his tobacco with the Association and often doing without the necessities of life; the other, a "Hillbilly," succumbing to the blandishments of the Trust, selling his tobacco at a price well above the normal market figure, and living in the lap of luxury.

Still, the meeting this year was a shot in the arm to the uncertain growers, and they became feverish with hope that success was just around the corner. Drives were made to bring in the hold-outs. Joel Fort bulled his oratory up and down the dark land, at schoolhouses and churches and crossroads stores, and Dr. Amoss paused between deliveries of babies to harangue the recalcitrants. It was Dr. Amoss who fell upon the idea of the boycott. He said,

"Those business and professional men who fail to encourage the tobacco growers in their struggle for better
prices are not worthy of their patronage."

The words were like a torch to a dry sedgegrass field.
Association members stopped trading with merchants who
were indifferent or hostile to the growers, and lawyers,
doctors, schoolteachers and ministers were quickly sorted
out and put in their places. The rural regions were full
of little-room schoolhouses. They could be found every
four or five miles. Thus there would be hundreds of them
in a county. Though no loyalty oath was exacted of them,
teachers not on the side of the Association found themselves without schools. No preachers as yet had been
tarred and feathered and ridden out of the country on a
rail, but that was probably because the few who might be
hostile to the gathering storm kept their eyes fixed on
biblical texts. A merchant who talked too much found
his store empty on Saturdays.

Newspapers almost unanimously stood behind the Association. The Cadiz (Ky.) *Record,* next to the Clarksville (Tenn.) *Leaf Chronicle,* was one of the most influential voices of these, due no doubt to the energy and
violent partisanship of Henry Lawrence, the editor, who
could sling as mean a stick of handset type as the next
man. "Abuse — greed — robbery — enslavement — death
grapple —" he tossed the biting phrases off prodigally, and
his editorials were printed far and wide by editors who
were not so handy with the language. Inevitably this kind
of invective was silently building up hate between the Association members and the Hillbillies. Either you were a
child of God or an imp of Satan. To save your immortal
soul you had but to place your tobacco in the pool.

But we are here dealing with the curious psychology

of the primitive man. The more the Hillbilly was cursed, the more stubborn he became. Sometimes he had to go underground with his cussedness, but he kept on selling his tobacco to the hated Trust for 10c to 12c while his neighbor wallowed in poverty. When the heat began to be applied to the Hillbilly, he simply stiffened and refused to associate. Robert Penn Warren has one such in his novel *The Night Rider* say, "You can kill me, but you can't make me join." In the end the Night Riders hung him, and the man, poor, gnarled, wormy, never did yield. These simple men must surely have seen that their long-run interests lay with the Association. What satisfaction they derived from stubborn pig-headedness none ever made clear, for they were not articulate souls.

In any case, the Trust agents had a lean year. However assiduously they cultivated the Hillbillies, they could not buy the amounts or types of tobacco needed. Thus the companies began to dig into their reserves. The buyers in 1905 went onto the highways and byways and bought tobacco still in the fields, or October leaf that had just been harvested and not cured. They paid prices of 8c, 10c and 12c. The temptation was too much for some Association members and they broke their contracts and sold to the Trust. The Association brought suit against these people in the court of Judge J. W. Stout, at Springfield, Tenn., and lost. According to Judge Stout the Association was merely the agent of the grower who had a right to revoke the agency at will.

Up in Kentucky the Association fared better in the courts, and refractory members who moonlighted their tobacco were brought to taw. The result was what was known as the Crecelius Tobacco Law, named after C. F. Crecelius from Pendleton county, which prohibited a grower from selling tobacco he had pledged to the Association, making him liable to a fine up to $250.00. Two things began to happen. The Trust was slowly forced to buy from the Association, and the Association was forced to sell in order to sustain itself. Again the Hillbillies made profits from the buyers paying a premium for unpledged tobacco. There was no question but that the Trust was out to break the growers' union. A buyer by the name of Ferigo, representing the Italian Regie, visited Hopkinsville and Clarksville to buy ten thousand hogsheads of prime leaf. The Association warehouses offered him the tobacco for nine and a half cents a pound. He offered only eight cents, though the price in Italy was 12c. Felix Ewing refused to sell at such a price and got in touch with the Italian government direct. Ferigo moved swiftly to buy tobacco from the independent growers at 10c and 12c per pound. Rumor had it that the Italian Regie spent a half million dollars fighting the Association in 1905. Despite their efforts, Ewing was able to sell 6000 hogsheads, direct to the Italian government at 9c. But a wave of bitterness was sweeping the Black Patch as a result of this economic throat-cutting.

In 1906, hoping to consolidate their positions, the Virgina Dark Tobacco Association joined the Kentucky and Tennessee group, rewrote their charter, and began taking three-year pledges from the growers. In Kentucky and Tennessee the Association members grew to 12,000, and, on the whole, the second year was somewhat better than the first, though still far from what could be called success. The Association managed to raise the price level only about a half cent a pound from the previous year, and even some of that increase might be attributed to a

short crop. Meanwhile the Trust unceasingly spread dis-
content by paying decent prices to the non-conformists.

Still in all, the growers' union was battling valiantly,
and the Association began its third year with the largest
and grandest meeting it had ever held, at Guthrie on a
Saturday, September 22, 1906. Never was there another
such day in this little Kentuckian tobacco mart. Twenty-
five thousand folk foregathered that hot September day on
the narrow streets and dusty fairgrounds to listen to orators
with grandiose phrases and glowing promises of a brave
new day, to drink sodapop, lemonade, eat icecream and
hamburgers, and smoke cigarettes manufactured by the
American Tobacco Company, "Duke's Best." They
smoked cigars manufactured by the same hated company,
and chewed Star Navy manufactured by the plug-tobacco
division of the American Tobacco Company. If anybody
remarked on the irony of this, there is nothing written
in the record to that effect. Special trains brought the
bigwigs from Nashville, Hopkinsville and Clarksville, All
night trains rumbled and rattled from the remote provinces
of Fulton, Murray, Paris, Mayfield, Martin, Princeton,
and the nearer, walled cities of Springfield, Madisonville,
and Russelville. "They came on foot, on mules, on blooded
horses, and behind prancing teams that sparkled in oiled
harness and polished trappings." The average small tobacco grower hitched up his two-mule wagon and filled the
bed with chairs and family, and, getting a start long before day, rumbled dustily into Guthrie and hitched at the
big parking lot adjoining the fairgrounds. Not all were
tobacco farmers. Many were sympathizers, and some were
enemies. No account was ever offered of the hangers-on
who came to gnaw great hunks of barbecue, or merely
to court, or fornicate — for the country whores were out

in force, as those of us who recollect such rallies can testify. The gathering combined all the features of a huge circus, a Negro-lynching, a political convention, and a grim business enterprise.

The populace dearly loved its parades. This one was so big it required an hour and ten minutes to pass any given point. It assembled downtown at the railway station, and Colonel John B. Allen, chief marshal, headed it. He rode a noble stallion, in due and ancient form, and with him were Mrs. Felix Ewing, herself a notable rider after the hounds as well as at horseshows throughout the blue grass; and Charles Fort, Mrs. Polk Prince, George Snadon, Mrs. N. E. Greene, E. T. Bondurant, and Miss Martha Townsend. Men still remember the gloss on the rumps of their fine steeds in that glowing sunshine. They recollect the grace and charm of the ladies in their habits, the plumes in their hats, the classic style of their horsemanship. Next to his tobacco and bourbon, the Southerner admired his females, and it was fitting that the shapely wife of their leader should stand forth second to none in this demonstration against the hated beast of the Tobacco Trust. Then came carriages and buggies and surreys, with their silken tassels shimmering; and then, in a hastily assembled and motley mob, came the footmen — the farmers from all sections of the Black Patch. The cavalcade was divided into ten sections, and there were ten brass bands from ten tobacco towns, raising a hideous racket while the dust choked their noses. A thousand Negroes, many in Masonic uniforms, fetched up the rear, immediately behind a string of floats, the most impressive of which was the Black Patch boat, with effigies of C. H. Fort as captain, and Felix Ewing as pilot. Unfortunately, Mr. Ewing was ill that day, and was obliged to view the parade from the window of his hotel room.

The music would naturally be Dixie and My Old Kentucky Home, and there would be a banner, done by the dedicated fingers of Mrs. Ewing herself, showing a rich tobacco leaf against a white silk background.

Nothing would have been right if the happy darkies didn't have a chance to clown. Rufus Andrews of Hopkinsville, a six-foot strapping factory hand in the tobacco auction rooms there, toted the banner for the colored population:

DOWN WITH THE TRUST OR WE NIGGERS BUST

They played banjos and danced and shouted and sang, and oozed great drops of sweat.

But all this was nothing to what they marched to out at the fairgrounds. In the hot September noon this motley collection of hungry thousands pressed around five tables each 250 feet long, upon which were twenty thousand wood platters loaded with rations for two, and the business of gulping this tonnage of food got under way. Five hundred and seventeen cattle, hogs and sheep had been barbecued by an all-night staff of colored cooks, supervised by the best barbecuer in the country. There were five thousand pounds of bread, and pickles out of nine barrels. Barrels of icewater and lemonade were arranged for easy drinking out of long-handled gourd dippers. An hour later nothing remained of food or beverage, save picked bones of beef and pork and mutton, and empty bottles of sodapop. Dogs ran hither and yon, and the weary repaired to rest rooms consisting of a tent for the ladies and a plank barricade for the men. In that slum-

brous hour when packed bellies rassled with their diges-
tive jobs, men lazed under the trees, or hunkered in knots,
and spoke in monosyllables, waiting for the afternoon's
deluge of oratory. The women waited around the wagons
or other vehicles, or spread old quilts on the ground for
themselves and the babies. There was a certain indefinable
atmosphere of tension. Already men, later known as
Night Riders, had been abroad in the Black Patch, sometimes neighbor against neighbor, resulting in the burning
of tobacco barns of Hillbillies, and ruining of crops in the
fields. A Trust buyer by the name of Jefferson Bane
from Paris, Tenn., had been held up along a lonely road
in his buggy and warned that if he came into a certain
community he would be killed. Ominous notes and
threats had been received up and down the land. A house
had been fired while the family was at church one Sunday morning; and while it might have been a simple
accident, rumor had it that angry men had put the torch.
But of greater significance even than these actual events
was the feeling that more than oratory, more than organization, more than banners and fine ladies riding at the
head of a fine parade, must be used if the plans of the
Association were to prevail. But in that lazy, well-fed
group none of this was put into actual words.

Then the speaking began, led off by Bob Taylor of
Tennessee, an impressive figure of a man in white linen
suit and white mustache, with the homespun humor and
idiom the common man in overalls understood well enough
to elect him governor of Tennessee. Men stood lounging
and laughing at the great man's engaging sallies of wit and
wisdom. Joel Fort followed Bob Taylor, then President
Charles Fort, and others great and small, mostly small.
Their names linger on in old newspaper files — A. O.

Stanley, Ollie James, John Rhea, John Gaines, Will
Fowler, George Snadon. At last Mrs. Ewing was presented, representing her ailing husband, and she was ac-
corded a roaring ovation. She officially presented the
silken banner to the Association. "Tell them," she said,
"to do nothing in the name of this asssociation that would
stain that white banner." So Mr. A. O. Stanley of Henderson, Ky., gallantly assured her that nothing would be
done by the Association by night or day "to bring a
blush to the cheek of her who made it." Everybody
cheered loud and long, publicly disclaiming any part in
the wave of lawlessness already breaking across the Black
Patch. How many Hillbillies took part in this demonstration is not of record. One guesses there were many.
Some of them were undoubtedly talked into joining the
Association. Many more were merely confirmed in their
stubborness. Greater numbers had fared too well at the
hands of the Trust to be moved by this show of unity
and brotherhood. But men were present who had already
decided on a course of action to control tobacco prices
and force the American Tobacco Company to terms.

One man was heard to say, "If the Trust wants to renew
the fight, let it come. We are not going to ask any quarter, and we are not going to give much. They have got
to march through a slaughter house into an open grave,
or we will do it. Which shall it be?"

This determined declaration was the word of one
Shanks Anderson, of Keysburg, Ky. It was widely published in the newspapers of the tobacco counties.

That late afternoon the meeting broke up and the
mass of folk dispersed along the country roads leading
to Guthrie, or loaded in the ancient blackened coaches
of the special trains for the hinterlands. The wagons

creaked through the hot dusk of that September day, and galloping youths on mules and fast saddle horses, well fortified with whiskey, tore along, passing the wagons and their more sedate seniors, going on to discharge their pistols along the lonely roads. These hotheads would be part of the army of hoodlums that was soon to ride the black banners of the Night Riders.

Chapter Six

The Lash and the Torch

DESPITE ALL THIS VAST DEMONSTRATION OF UNANIMITY and strength, good men and true in the Association had their misgivings. In spite of the pledge they had publicly made to the attractive wife of their noble leader, these men knew in their hearts that they had contrived only a holding operation, and that the monster Trust might well crush their feeble resistance movement this autumn when the tobacco crop came on to the market by pouring out its hoard of gold on the greedy or needy individual tobacco grower. After the hurrahs had died away and the dust of many thousand feet had settled, even Felix Ewing had his bad dreams. The great gathering of this field of folk meant little in actual show of power. It was at a season when work was slack, and rural people had leisure to attend every public function that made a big noise. Camp meetings, protracted meetings, political rallies — they were all the same. The farmer loaded his family in the two-mule wagon and took off to absorb the speechifying. Add a gorge of barbecue and lemonade and you had him in the palm of

your hand. But a Hillbilly could gnaw as big a bone of barbecue as an Association partisan, and men who swore by
Felix Ewing saw poor whites by the hundreds gourmandiz-
ing the refreshments. That night on the way back to their
thousand farms, a lot of men must have had prayerful com-
munion with themselves, and decided that, if worse came to
worse, they would sully that white flag with a right good
will.

The Guthrie meeting was in the latter part of September.
In early October, thirty-two men gathered at Stainback
schoolhouse to organize what went by the innocuous name
of Possum Hunters. Felix Ewing was not among them,
but since the meeting took place only a thoroughbred
horse's heat from his farm, it can readily be surmised
that he knew about it and had perhaps secretly given it
his blessing. He surely knew the thirty-two men involved,
as they knew him. The document that emerged from this
gathering bears all the earmarks of having been scrawled
out in the classic rhetoric of Mr. Ewing's goosequill pen;
if not by his, then by that some other equally gifted author
of resolutions. That such a paper could have been composed in one evening at a country schoolhouse by a bunch
of tobacco farmers is nonsense. Someone had obviously
come with the paper in his pocket. At any rate, they heard
it read by lantern light and subscribed to it heartily.

After the preamble, the stereotypic phrases of hate began
to flow: the Trust had multiplied and grown rich and arrogant . . . nefarious violaters of the law . . . a menace
. . . arbitrary destroyers of the law of supply and demand
. . . infamous, greedy . . . impoverishing and enslaving
the tobacco grower . . . patriotic citizens have become
angered and enraged, and justly so. . . . And thus the
group of farmers proclaimed to the world that the Trust

was a law-breaker. Then they branded the acts of the Trust as illegal and criminal, and added a most significant statement:

"We further proclaim to the world that any farmer or other persons who aid the Trust in any way by selling to it their tobacco at a high price is an accomplice of the Trust and is in good morals as guilty as the Trust."

They paid their respects then to the man who hired out to the Trust, branding him as a criminal and not worthy the respect of decent citizens.

Though the adoption of these resolutions and plans to act were actually the beginning of night riding, these men probably had no real plans for open violence. A roster of them shows a group of Baptists and Methodists and perhaps a few members of the Church of Christ, and nothing in their commonplace English names suggests lawlessness. They were J. C. Crawford, J. M. McNelly, J. M. Highsmith, Jim and Ben Smith, Frank Brown, T. J. Sampson, Lije Morgan, Bob Holloway, H. E. Montgomery, M. F. Gullet, L. W. Smith, J. G. Bailey, E. B. Stainback, T. B. Brown, W. C. Riley, G. H. Smith, J. C. Harland, D. R. Fletcher, W. S. Cobb, Sam Ayers, C. Riley, A. L. Briggs, G. W. H. Farmer, W. B. Dye, R. L. and J. B. Harrison, A. C. Smith, W. I. Rust, George Smith, J. L. Fletcher, and A. S. Briggs.

It was ordained that committees of not less than five members, nor more than two thousand, visit the farmers outside the pool, and "counsel and instruct" them as to their future course in dealing with the Trust. They protested against the use of violence. But any backland farmer seeing as many as two thousand men on horseback, even with their faces showing, would no doubt be impressed. There were plenty of men alive who had seen action in the Civil War, and there was more than a hint here of military power.

Yet when the Stainback fellows began their crusade, they did nothing more drastic than distribute handbills up and down the countryside at night, under cover of darkness because, as Mr. Ewing himself said in the *Nashville American,* by day they were hardworking tobacco farmers. The crop had been cut and barned, and now was drying over the wood smokes. Soon the buyers would be abroad, and it would be well to put the fear of God into the recalcitrants. In November the Association officials met in Guthrie at the official offices above the Racket Store, and officially disclaimed any indiscretion or violence. That would remain the official position. But the meetings spread, outgrowing Robertson county, overflowing into adjoining Kentucky and more Tennessee counties, and in a matter of a couple of weeks the movement had spread like wildfire into virtually every hamlet in the Black Patch. Bands of men riding barefaced by night visited independents and warned them. They contacted agents and buyers of the American Tobacco Company and told them not to be found buying tobacco from the barns.

But buyers did buy, and Hillbillies did sell, and by the tenth of December, at 2 A.M., the tobacco factory of James Chestnut, an Italian Regie agent, was burned to the ground in Trenton, Kentucky, along with 3000 pounds of bootleg tobacco that had been delivered the afternoon before by some determined independent. Trenton was a little town some ten miles north of Guthrie. The next night, fifty men, armed and masked, held up the night passenger train between Guthrie and Elkton, another little tobacco burg due north from Guthrie, and searched the cars for

buyers from the American Snuff Company, who were said
to be on the train. In the best tradition of Jesse James
and his bully boys they flagged the train on a lonely stretch
of road with a red lantern and stuck their pistols in the
ribs of the engineer, fireman and conductor, and system-
atically explored the cars. They found no buyers. Two
reasons were advanced for this failure: At the last minute
the snuff men did not board the train; or if they did,
while the stick-up was getting going, they jumped from the
offside of the coaches and took to the bushes. Forty of
the vigilantes returned to their horses, but ten of them,
wanting to enjoy a free train ride through a December
night, rode on to Elkton.

Or these ten fellows may have had other ideas. Two
nights later the tobacco factory of Mrs. M. B. Penick of
Elkton, in use by the agents of the American Snuff Company, was blown up about two in the morning with
dynamite. Oddly enough, most of the 30,000 pounds of
tobacco was salvaged, but the building was practically
demolished, as well as several nearby houses and three
railroad coaches.

On the eighteenth of December, forty masked men visited
the Italian Regie buyer, J. W. Scott, and warned him if
he bought any more tobacco they were going to work on
him, and suggested that perhaps he had better leave the
country. He moved — from the village of Olmstead to the
larger town of Russellville.

Though these activities were isolated in time and distance, they began to reveal a pattern of well planned terrorism. By the end of December, urged on by a protest
direct from the Italian government, Governor J. C. W.
Beckman wrote a sharp letter of protest to Felix Ewing,
asking him to use his influence in stopping these atrocities.

Without accusing Mr. Ewing of having a hand in the business, Governor Beckham implied that he had the power to end them. Mr. Ewing wrote back that the Association was composed of the "flower of manhood of both states," and assured him they would bring no stigma upon either Tennessee or Kentucky. There was no evidence that this was the work of Association members, and even so it seemed to him it was the business of the Governor to uphold the struggle of the farmers against the greed of the Trust.

It is notable that these first activities were directed against the snuff interests and the Italian government. It would have been an opportunity of a lifetime for a statesman in the governor's chair at Frankfort to visit among the people who had elected him and try to get at the bottom of the trouble.

The only other notable event of this year was a speech by A. O. Stanley before the growers at Springfield, Tenn., a few miles from Felix Ewing's place, pleading for them to stop "night-riding." He coined the name that soon became that of the protest movement.

A smoldering peace lay upon the land into the following year. Threats and violence had not kept the Hillbillies from selling their tobacco. In April plant beds showed graywhite on a thousand Black Patch hillsides against the spring sun. Here was a strategic area for the work of the Night Riders. In eight counties plant beds were scraped, killing the young plants that the scalawags expected to set for a new crop. In September and October the practice of burning the barns of non-Association growers came into use. In November there was a series of dynamitings of tobacco factories in Eddyville and Fredonia, Kentucky. The Rice Brothers' factory in Fredonia was saturated with coal oil and put to the torch

so stealthily that the biggest fire ever seen in that little
town was roaring before the town knew what had happened.
Here and there were whippings and beatings. Warning
notes were tacked to the gateposts of the non-conformists.
During this time a great deal of secret business went on,
in two-score counties, in a thousand communities, where
schoolhouses and churches were the clandestine command
posts of men dedicated to large-scale organizing.

Already in 1906 the secret order was established, and
a ritual patterned after those of the Masons and Odd Fellows, and no doubt the Ku Klux Klan, were mouthed in
due and ancient form by leaders who at last were sick and
tired of trying by reason and persuasion to establish a solid
front among the growers. The first lodges had been established in January, February and March, in the counties of
Todd, Logan, Robertson, Montgomery, Christian, Caldwell,
Lyon and Trigg. Soon ten more counties in Kentucky and
Tennessee were added. Meetings, both open and clandestine, were held in schoolhouses — the best-preferred spot
— or in churches, barns, tobacco factories that now were
empty, or sometimes in a secret spot in the deep woods.
This country was still deeply wooded, and no retreat was
more in keeping with the lodges than some well beaten
clearing among the big oaks and hickories and poplars.
Boys hunting rabbits would find these localities with their
thousand beaten horse and mule tracks and wonder with
awe what fell business went on there.

The members were not only tobacco farmers but professional men, merchants and bankers. If the farmers did
not make a living, the doctors and lawyers collected no
fees, and there were no taxes to pay the meager salary
of the schoolteachers. By the same token, a merchant who
could not collect the bill the farmer owed him for ad-

vances through the year, or the banker who carried the mortgage, found themselves in bad straits. Generally the men in high places, like preachers and the big bankers and store owners, played their game underground. But their sympathy, even beyond their pocketbooks. was for the neighbors and customers whom they had known all their lives.

The avowed purpose of the Night Rider organization was to compel non-Association people, by whip and firebrand, to join up. To that end they were prepared to destroy their tobacco beds, burn their crops and barns, and flog and terrorize them out of the country. Theirs was a "blood oath." Violent death and an unmarked grave lay in store for any who violated that oath, or betrayed the clan secrets to outsiders. Neighbor-witnesses and Almighty God looked down upon the initiation. The reluctant members driven into the fold probably mouthed all those solemn words with a shiver of apprehension. Down deep in their secret hearts they may have been scheming to get out of the outfit as soon as they could, but they respected the grimness of the bonds that held them in.

There was a military atmosphere about the lodges. There was a general and lieutenant commander, and colonels and captains, and lesser petty officers. The rank and file were privates. No uniforms — members wore ordinary clothing. But when the raids became more numerous, masks of black and flowing robes were worn, draped over man and horse, for men were sooner recognized at a distance by their mounts than by their features. A system of passwords and handclasps and signs and tokens were established, by which a member might be known by night as well as by day. When moving out on a raid, these men rode heavily armed, and since they were usually skilled

woodsmen and hunters, they knew the trigger end from
the holes where the lead came out of their shotguns, rifles
and revolvers. They rode saddle horses and mules, and on
a big raid some rode in buggies to bring back any who
might be wounded in the bloody business. Back of all this
organization and military precision lay the tightest civilian
protest movement known in this country since the Civil
War. The many men who remembered that War accepted
military discipline as essential to the success of their enterprise.

How much work went into developing this intricate
underground network no one ever really knew. Once
started, it grew swiftly enough. Men around the crossroads
stores talked quietly and plotted grimly. They met in the
towns on Saturdays and mule-trading Mondays and in-
variably groups would collect and mutter ominously. Sometimes only a significant look would convey the bitterness
and accumulated anger of a dozen quiet men. The typical
tobacco farmer was not a very articulate soul. He whit-
tled a piece of cedar, spit tobacco juice, pulled his old
beat-up felt hat down over his rusty face, and said a lot
with sun-narrowed eyes. A lowdowner might pass such
a group on the public square of Cadiz, seat of Trigg
county in the heart of the Black Patch, and hate was con-
veyed in the slow glower with which they followed his
quick steps around the corner and out of sight. Men were
marked like this, and a time would come when they sub-
mitted their raw backs to the lash, or stood away and saw
their tobacco barns go up in smoke and flames above a
silhouetted array of masked horsemen.

The man who was the big wheel in this movement,
and brought it to a workable degree of military per-
fection, was not himself a veteran of any rememberable

war, neither the War between the States nor the Spanish-American War, now only a matter of a few years past. He was in actual fact a kindly country doctor by the name of David Alfred Amoss.

Dr. Amoss lived in the village of Cobb, Kentucky, in a modest white wood dwelling set down in a spinney of oaks. His land ran back into the country and became an estate of pasturage and cornlands and garden, and he was fond of horses and rode somewhat after the hounds in the neighborhood fox hunts. He had a nice family, and a particularly attractive daughter, whose name, oddly enough, was Harvey. Among Harvey's earliest recollections of the homeplace were the summer nights when she went to sleep to the sound of the horses dragging their trace chains after leaving the farm equipment on the other side of the farm, and the Negroes singing to the rhythm, or later in the evening, singing with the banjo in the moonlight. She remembered the guests that came from Hopkinsville and Clarksville to the hunts — the excitement, the horns, the smell of horses, the distant fires on the hillsides where the hunters paused while the hounds cried far away under the stars. Withal it was the life of a widely beloved rural doctor, prosperous enough but never rich, and high in the esteem of his neighbors.

Dr. Amoss came from a family of distinguished doctors. His father, Dr. E. N. Amoss, was active in practice up into his 70's. His sons and grandsons became doctors and Ph.D.'s, and at least one, Harold Lindsey Amoss, was in *Who's Who in America.*

Cobb today is a half-forgotten village 20 miles north of Cadiz, which in turn is 20 miles west of Hopkinsville. In 1906, when the tobacco wars were rising to fever heat, Amoss was 49 years old. He was a rugged, stocky person, and he went through life with the military bearing he acquired at the military academy of Colonel James O. Ferrell in Hopkinsville, where he worked himself up to drill master at the academy. His schooling was in Wallonia Institute, which today is Trigg County High School. He was known as "brilliant" in all his studies. He took his degree in medicine at the Homeopathic Hospital College in Cleveland, Ohio, in 1880. Five years later he married and settled down. "He worshiped my mother," Harvey said. "She was a brilliant woman. A strict disciplinarian. My father was lenient and amiable. Through all the troubles she was loyal to my father."

Dr. Amoss was so proficient in military practices that one finds it easy to imagine that, if he had been born early enough to see the Civil War, he might very well have had his statue in bronze standing in some court square for distinguished service, and perhaps have become a General by more than the courtesy of a Night-Rider underground. He not only rode up and down delivering babies, sawing bones and haranguing the yokels to organize and arm, but he worked out a complicated strategy to conduct a rebellion and took these raw troops in a score of lodges, and even in the streets of Cadiz, and drilled and instructed them in obedience, and become their commander-in-chief.

In formulating techniques of underground warfare he had, of course, the Ku Klux rituals as guide, and something from the Masonic brotherhood as further example. It is possible he may have been a member of the KKK at one time. But in 1902, when he returned to Cobb to resume his practice after educating his children in Paducah, he became immediately sympathetic with the plight of the tobacco growers and shared in the pinch that followed the drop in leaf prices. He became an active member of the Protective Association, speaking often during those four years to meetings in Hopkinsville, Russellville, Murray and Clarksville.

He enjoyed making speeches and now and then preached and conducted prayer meetings in his home-town Christian Church. One imagines that he may once have debated in his mind whether to join the ministry. If no preacher could officiate at the funeral of a patient, Dr. Amoss would pinch hit and deliver an oration described as "fine." Likely a doctor learns much of a man who dies filled with his pills and potions, and Dr. Amoss showed his kind soul on such occasions. Moreover, when a good Association member died, Dr. Amoss might be some while collecting his fee. Thus we have the image of a man who measured up to the best that was the old-time country doctor.

In person he was five feet six inches, weighed around 160 pounds, with a rather large head set on firm square shoulders. His coloring was florid, his eyes blue, and his chin was that of a man of "iron will and undaunted courage." His shock of hair was dense and dark, and now and then he allowed his beard to grow out, though usually he settled for a handle-bar mustache which permitted his iron-willed chin to show. He was neat of dress, and, oddly enough in a tobacco world, he used the weed only in form of an after-dinner cigar. He also enjoyed a good poker game. Men still remember his solid dark-garbed figure as he strode from his buggy up to a farmhouse porch and went in to console the ailing.

He appears first in the printed history of the tobacco wars on September 8, 1906, in a news report of the tobacco rally in Princeton, a small town north of Cobb and Cadiz, when a thousand farmers formed a parade and

moved up and down the streets in Masonic-Ku-Klux formation, lead by Dr. Amoss and "others." At the time, he
was vice-chairman of the Caldwell County Association,
but already his genius for military strategy was showing
in the precision with which the footmen, the horsemen,
and those driving buggies, moved around the small burg
and returned to the lodge without a false move. We do
not know if he had a hand in the great Guthrie parade,
though it is likely. He was a close personal friend of
Felix Ewing and the other bigwigs in the Association.

The "others" in the parade were Guy S. Dunning;
W. H. Malone, a colonel, living on a Caldwell farm
near Nabb Schoolhouse where so many of the great secret
meetings took place; John W. Hollowell, chairman of the
Caldwell branch of the Association, who lived near Otter
Pond; Sam Cash, a blowsy bronzed fellow who was sheriff
of the adjoining Lion county, and present here to ride
in the big parade. The fact that a duly elected officer
might show himself in this company was evidence of the
high repute of the still unofficially named Night Riders.

Guy Dunning was lieutenant commander and second
under Dr. Amoss. In 1906 he was 33 years old, a stout
churl, a six-footer, well proportioned, athletic, a natural
when it came to leadership. He was a college man —
graduate of Center College, Danville, Kentucky. He combined the rustic qualities of a dirt farmer with the quiet
dignity of an educated man. His belly was flat, his back
straight, and his clean-shaven face sunburnt from his out-
riding in his tobacco farmlands. He had one of the
best farms in the Wallonia neighborhood, a thousand
acres with a dozen tenant families. He also farmed his
mother's 1500 acres. He had been a tobacco grader, and
was immediately elected prizer for the Association ware-

houses. He was Dr. Amoss's neighbor and the two were close friends. Both had the same ideas about how the Association could command the bulk of the tobacco crop and its marketing, and he was a perfect foil for the 50-year old Doctor. As general inspector of Association tobacco he travelled a great deal and had contact with growers, officials, other inspectors, and was another active speaker before the lodges. As the secret forces began gathering for formidable demonstrations of power, he carried messages and other information from Amoss to distant lodges. All this communication was oral. For a written word to have come into the hands of a hostile critic of the "Inner Circle" and "Silent Brigade" would have betrayed the entire underground. He too lacked only the Civil War to have had his name chiseled on many a granite monument.

I can find but little of his private life. He had a wife and family and his home was not the least pretentious, in spite of the fact he was a big-time tobacco farmer. First and last he must have been prosperous, but he appears to have remained a modest fellow, as did Dr. Amoss.

Chapter Seven

Flash, Firebrand: Clash, Battle Axe!

MEN, SOME MEN, SOUGHT TO DELUDE THEMSELVES WITH the idea that the Association was succeeding. But in their realistic moments they knew this was not true, or at best only partially true. Earnest men still clung to the hope that persuasion and reason would bring the growers into the organization essentially 100 percent strong. But the weaker of the farmers succumbed to the Trust and the stronger of them were sorely tempted. It was not all contrariness on the part of the little man that kept him from joining up with his stouter brothers. He had to have money. The Trust stood there with a wide grin and many greenbacks. Both Dr. Amoss and Felix Ewing knew that force was going to be the only persuasion the wavering, weak and greedy would recognize.

These two men really shaped the destiny of the tobacco association. Dr. Amoss wielded his influence in the underground. Mr. Ewing stood as the stately, above-reproach leader of a perfectly respectable and legal union. They were not supposed to have any official communication. Actually

there seems small doubt that they kept in close touch
through the events of that year and the complications and
troubles to follow during the next two or three years.

Amoss understood the tobacco siutation in all its aspects.
He believed the night-riding movement was morally right,
and Ewing believed the Association was both legally and
morally sound. They believed legal procedures were so
slow that they would be ruined before redress could be
had in the courts. They had had a sample of what could
happen when the tobacco farmers resorted to law. Already
as far back as 1902 A. O. Stanley, member of the House
of Representatives from Kentucky, had introduced a bill
that was designed to give relief to the tobacco farmers,
H.R. 9870, and H.R. 10857, in the second session of
the Fifty-Eighth Congress, December 7, 1903. One of
the bills passed. But when it reached the Senate it was
pigeonholed through the lobbying efforts of the so-called
Independent Tobacco Manufacturers' Association of the
United States, consisting of some dozen manufacturing companies such as the United States Tobacco Company, Rich-
mond, Virginia; Strater Brothers, Louisville, Ky., and the
Brown & Williamson Tobacco Company, Winston-Salem,
N. C. Behind these smaller fry was undoubtedly the power
and prestige of the American Tobacco Company. Meanwhile the other bills were introduced — H.R. 3574, by
O. S. Trimble; H.R. 11889, by a Mr. Flood; and H.R.
14617, by a Mr. Gibson. They came to the same in-
conclusive end.

To be sure there was the Sherman Anti-Trust Law, and
President Roosevelt's buster boys were peering slantwise at
the American Tobacco Company. But far down in the remote provinces of Tennessee and Kentucky men's guts were
growling, and neighbors were cursing each other, many

were fixing to ride by night and see if something couldn't be done now. In the end they hoped the law would be on their side. Right now they had to take the law into their own hands.

Dr. Amoss said to these men, "To burn the factories and warehouses of the trust and its agents who have robbed you of the fruits of your labors, is taking no more from them than they have from you. The law has enabled them to rob you, and you have had no recourse. To burn, or otherwise destroy, the property of growers, and to whip them, and other persons, who refuse to co-operate with you in winning your fight against the Trust is no more than they deserve. There is no reason why a few persons should continue to make the masses suffer when their co-operation would not only *not* be to their detriment but would increase the earnings and thus improve the conditions of all equally."

So men met at the lodges by night, drilled, accepted discipline, learned how to communicate under battle conditions, and Dr. Amoss worked out his procedures.

The Night Riders gave due notice of their intentions. A "Proclamation" was sent out to most of the county papers in the Black Patch area and was widely published. Someone with the gift of proclamation composed the opus, and dipped his goosequill freely in the current cliches: ". . . appealed and petitioned the tobacco captains of finance for relief, but have been spurned with contempt from the feet of the financial thrones of the country." The rich "feasting and banqueting as in the days of the French Revolution," a few "small depredations" had taken place, but their own movement was in no wise a mob, but a "band of cool, deliberate and honorable men." And then he went on to insist that "no trust had any legal or moral right to rob the people of their rewards," nor did the Trust have the right to recruit

what amounted to local Quislings to ruin and impoverish
their neighbors, friends and kinsmen.

And we hereby call upon all members of the Protective Association to neither buy anything from, nor sell anything to, any
person who does not come boldly out for the association. All
that we ask is that bankers and merchants take a stand with us,
and we will win with hands down in ten months, for we are in
this cause to win or die, so all people take due and timely notice and govern themselves accordingly.

So it was spoken by the "unkown and silent power."

Who wrote this nobody now knows. It might have been
Dr. Amoss or Guy Dunning, the college graduate; or both
of them, by a lantern in an old soiled schoolhouse with a
pencil and scratch tablet.

Meanwhile Trust buyers worked the backlands and Hillbillies sold their leaf, for this was autumn and the crop was
coming on to the market. Men recall that the fall was open
and nights clear and cool, and through October and November there had been no snow and not much rain. Along
the winding earth roads the two-mule and four-mule wagons
clanked and rumbled, driven by idle youths who dreamed
of liquor and women, or older men hunched grimly over
the wagon tongue, meditating upon just how formidable
were the threats of the Night Riders. Princeton, the market
in the Otter Pond, Fredonia, and Nabb localities, was a typical little Kentucky county town, seat of Caldwell County,
with such landmarks as a gray brick courthouse in the center of square and town; the police station across the street
in the northeast block; the Illinois Central Railroad, going
to Paduch in one direction and Louisville in the other; the
depot; and the fairgrounds at the south edge of town. There
were three populated streets, Seminary and Jefferson, run-

ning north and south; and Main Street, east and west. By no means the least of the landmarks were two large tobacco factories, the J. G. Orr factory north on Seminary, and the Stegar & Dollar factory, on south Seminary, just across from the I. C. depot.

And of course some thousand people who lived off two things — the business of the county town, and the trade of the tobacco people. Tobacco was the money crop. A little corn, some wheat, a few hogs perhaps. The townsfolk were rural, and even the county judge kept his milk cows, saddle horses and pigs at his place at the edge of town. The most successful doctor in the place lived where town left off and farmlands began, and he had a "farm," with the usual complement of milk cows, saddle and buggy horses, fattening shoats and a large family, mostly of females. It was a placid, easy-going place, good enough to live in if you were born and raised there, or got into business in tobacco and located there. It would become a community divided against itself, for while its instincts were rooted in the land, its current interests belonged to the urban culture, such as it was.

During the Friday before December 1, more people than ordinary were stirring in town. There was a good deal of desultory coming and going of men in overalls and boots, riding horseback. They hitched at the lot across from the courthouse, or down at the fairgrounds, or back of the line of stores on Main Street. Afterward a hardware merchant remembered selling ten sticks of dynamite to a farmer he didn't know very well; and down at the dirty general stores clerks filled five-gallon cans of kerosene. The two saloons did a good business, too. Saturday would be a big day in grog; Friday was nearly as good. Yet talk was low, and the atmosphere could have been described as tense and ominous if anybody had been alert enough to study it. Down at the factories loiterers took note of the incoming tobacco and who hauled it to Orr and Stegar & Dollar. All three of these tobacco merchants were buying for the American Tobacco Company and American Snuff Company, as well as the Italian Regie — all part of the Trust.

Then there was the business of that series of letters back in the early fall to two companies insuring the tobacco barns in Princeton — the New York Underwriters Agency and the Pheonix Insurance Company, which the local people by now seemed to have let drift from their minds. The letters were in pencil and unsigned and had been mailed in Princeton. They read:

We are determined to put John Orr, of Princeton, out of the tobacco business. The scoundrel has bought and put up tobacco for the Tobacco Trust long enough, and Stegar & Dollar or any other buyer in Caldwell county or the town of Princeton, Kentucky, who buys from the trust will be treated the same way. We do not want to damage parties who are not concerned in buying. This is to notify you to cancel insurance immediately.

The punctuation of this document alone would indicate a writer of education. It was a day when not many men knew where to place their commas.

The companies promptly cancelled their policies, sending Orr, Stegar & Dollar copies of the warning. J. G. Orr decided he was not going to be bluffed or intimidated, and soon thereafter published an open letter in the Princeton *Twice-a-Week Leader* inviting growers wanting a ready market that he was at the same old stand. "I will be at the old stand where I have been twenty years and am prepared to pay you fine prices for good, ripe well-cured tobacco." And then he hit the Association in its tenderest spot: "And you don't have to wait a year for your money. It is ready for you when you deliver a load." As an inducement, he offered a premium of $20 in gold for the grower who brought in the best load of leaf. Not a grand reward by any means, but to a poor white who had no more than $40 to show for a year's work, it was sufficient. So the wagons of tobacco clanked into town, and the Association spies noted the growers, and prepared their next move.

An examination of the activities that took place in Princeton a little past midnight on December 1 indicates a remarkable genius for planning and executing a major raid on a town. That such a move, involving an estimated 250 men — and probably more, counting reserves outside the town that never came into the actual work — could be maintained with absolute secrecy over a period of weeks, long enough to mature the plan in every detail, is even more remarkable. Hundreds of families were involved with the Night Riders, and no inkling of the plans must seep to women and children, lest an inadvertant word reach a hostile neighbor who was selling his tobacco to the Trust agents. Otherwise warning could have gone swiftly out and Princeton citizens, who that night had lain down on their feather beds in perfect confidence that all was well with this best of all worlds, would have got out their shooting irons or taken to the old Indian forts. The first they knew of the doing were shadows of masked men, on foot, hurrying along the plank sidewalks, or along the brick walks in front of the Main Street stores. They moved in squads, each squad with an assigned station and duty. The next contingent were squads of horsemen, the hooves of their beasts deadened with gunny sacks. They made almost no sound in the gravel-earth streets.

A heavy task force from along the Cadiz road fell upon the police station and swiftly disarmed the two drowsy small-town cops there. At almost the same instant other squads of footmen were taking over the local telephone office. One cut wires leading out of town, so no calls could go out. A cordon was thrown around the courthouse, the telegraph office was isolated, and the city water supply cut off so the fire department could not function. All this happened so swiftly that few of the townsfolk were awakened. Not until the Night Riders began shooting salvos of their rifles and pistols did the populace realize things were happening and fell out of their beds and made for the windows and doors. Lights were flashed on, oil lamps were lighted, and just as fast the attackers shot out the windows where the lights showed. The town came alive in a murmur and mutter of questions, muffled cries of women and children, and amazed oaths of men.

Curious people who ventured outdoors were poked in the ribs with revolvers and told, "Get back!" Anyone caught loose on the streets was arrested and corralled in doorways under guard. The best points of vantage were upstairs windows with no light showing, and many a window was cautiously raised and dim shapes of folk peered forth and whispered fearfully. "It's the Night Riders! The Night Riders are here!" It was a windless night with many stars, and the thudding of horsemen going out to the Illinois Central depot and freight yards made many a local heart thump against the ribs. If they ran to the telephone to ask Central what was goin on, they would be answered in a gruff voice, "The Night Riders are here." The switch engines were manned, and a rear guard was stationed along the Eddyville, Fredonia and Dawson Springs roads, by which many of the mounted riders came into town, so that these roads should be open for retreat. Then the main work of the night, the focus of all this activity, got going.

The J. G. Orr factory on North Jefferson was surrounded; D. H. Gardner the night watchman, was held prisoner in a coal shed; and men with cans of kerosene followed on the heels of other men who broke the doors down with axes and entered the wide, low dark regions of the warehouse. Great piles of loose leaf were everywhere, and the rank, close fragrance of the tobacco was a familiar smell to the efficient arsonists. They poured coal oil freely here and there, placed sticks of dynamite with fuses attached under the piles, and, backing away, a man struck a match and everybody retreated. The flames built up swiftly, and burst from the doors and windows when the glass exploded. The howling inferno cooked down to the dynamite and thundrous explosions tore the building to splinters and spread the fire wildly.

The Orr factory was one of the largest stemming and rehandling plants in the world, and Orr bought for the Imperial Tobacco Company. More than 200,000 pounds of tobacco was stored there, awaiting cars for shipment; and some of these cars were even now on the siding, awaiting only loading on the morrow to move to Louisville. One of two of these empties caught fire from flying brands after the explosions, and a line of houses next to the railroad tracks, mostly Negro shacks, were next ignited.

Then the brandsmen rode four blocks south to the Stegar & Dollar factory, and applied the torch with the same methodical precision. Once again the flames mounted to the December skies, and the little town shook with detonations of dynamite. This factory, operated by J. A. Stegar and J. G. Dollar, was allied with Gallaher Limited. Gallaher was not associated with the Trust, but he fought the Association with the same fury, and many a man must have watched with supreme relish as something like $50,000 worth of leaf went up in smoke and flame, without a penny of covering insurance. The Trust and the so-called independent would carry the loss of more than $100,000 alone, for the practice was for the tobacco companies to advance the cash to their agents, like Orr and Stegar & Dollar, since these operators did not have sufficient capital to finance the buying. The cropper, of course, got paid for his tobacco. He at least had that satisfaction. It ground the souls of the Night Riders, who wanted to get at the Hillbillies also, but in any case they did their best to paralyze the Trust.

When certain that everything had worked out to their satisfaction, the Riders, mounted and on foot, assembled at the court house. The signal for dispersing was three blasts on a ram's horn, supposedly blown by Dr. Amoss. While the fires burned lurid against the sky, the Night Riders quickly dispersed back the ways they had come. Horsemen moved out north of town over Hogan's Hill to their points of origin — east to Dawson Springs; northeast to Fredonia; west to Eddyville, interestingly enough the location of the state penitentiary. The main bodies had come in by way of the Cadiz road. The footmen had left their horses at the fairgrounds. Two hundred rode out of town singing, "The Fire Shines Bright in My Old Kentucky Home." They had come in about 12:30, and were leaving now about 1:30. The townsfolk, now free, emerged into the streets and picked the remaining meat of excitement from the bones of terror. The tobacco factories were piles of incandescent tobacco and timbers long soaked with the tars of the leaf. The publicity-minded folk, notably the publisher of the local paper and the telegraph dispatcher, who served as correspondent of the city papers, rushed to the Western Union office at the depot, while the local volunteer fire department worked to keep the fires from spreading to the white sections of town next to the railroad tracks. Boys and dogs and curious men jammed the streets. They were filled with a confusion of emotions. The wild excitement that attends a big fire — and this was the biggest Princeton had ever had — anger and indignation at the outrage of a bunch of "furriners" coming in and burning them out; a certain reluctant admiration for men who dared take the law into their hands and do something about their grievances. No doubt there was an increasing body of sympathy for the growers who were fighting the Trust. But mainly it was the heart-pounding satisfaction that attends any public spectacle.

There was one last defiant explosion of dynamite at the Stegar & Dollar factory. Riders going out of town heard it, and one heard it with more than passing relief. This man had acted as part of the dynamite gang, and had carried the sticks in his handbag. What was even more horrible, the handbag had his name embossed on it in gold letters. He could not remember for sure if he had it when he came out. The deafening blast informed him that all the evidence was destroyed.

One cannot help wondering if this man were not Dr. Amoss. Who but a doctor toted a leather bag with his name on it done in goldleaf?

Chapter Eight

The Fires Grow Dim on My Old Tennessee Home

WE HEARD A. O. STANLEY WHILE SITTING WITH OUR BACK to an oaktree at the fair grounds of Guthrie, Kentucky, that sweltering day in September, 1904, stuffed to the gills with peppered barbecue, brushing away the flies while we mopped the grease off our faces with alder leaves. The man stood up there on the platform amidst the banners and bigwigs, lank and clean shaven, sweating at every pore, his collar wilted, his tie awry, lashing the hot air and fulminating in his high-pitched angry politician's rhetoric at the Tobacco Trust. Stanley had drafted the constitution of the Association, "to protect," he said, the members and growers "from illegal combination in restraint of trade." He named names, was perhaps the first to shout savagely that back of it all was James Duke. Then we heard him again and again, at Hopkinsville, at Russellville, at Nabb's Schoolhouse, at Murray and Fulton and Mayfield — a score of rallies up and down this dark land. His clarion voice rang across the Black Patch.

95

Once he stated, "We have introduced bills in successive congresses to remove the tax off the leaf, but so many times the Trust, by secret and nefarious machinations pigeon-holed and throttled the measures in the Senate. Unable to secure relief from the Federal government and having experienced the remorseless rapacity of the Trust [we have] determined, as a last resort, to protect [ourselves]."

Hard words, podner, and he didn't smile when he said them. But A. O. Stanley was a dedicated representative of his tobacco-patch voters down in the Henderson District of Kentucky. Nor was he alone in his legal battle. Ollie M. James, Marion, Ky., and John W. Gaines, Nashville, Tenn., were no less devoted to the war. These three members of the House of Representatives, working with others, made valiant efforts to get something done for the plight of the tobacco growers down in the forgotten provinces of Tennessee and Kentucky. As early as 1903 Stanley was belaboring the American Tobacco Company and the Imperial Tobacco Company, England, accusing them of conspiring to oppress and rob the farmers, averring that unless the Trust was checked by Federal law, the growers stood to be reduced to commercial servitude.

A list of dead bills makes morbid reading, but let's at it bravely, so as to understand that kerosene and dynamite were not the only weapons in use. In the fifty-eighth Congress, second session, March 31 to April 18, 1904, Volume 38, part 4, serial No. 214, page 5008, those who love their statistics may read: "The bill was ordered engrossed and read a third time, and accordingly it was read a third time and passed." Motion to reconsider the bill laid on the table. April 18, 1904, page 4999, H.R. 14896 referred to Senate Committee on Finance, where it died. In the Fifty-ninth Congress, first session, March 4, 1905 to June 30, 1906, a corresponding bill was read a third time and passed, but again died in the Senate Committee. To go on reciting subsequent efforts to get a tobacco bill through the Senate would be to compound the dullness. But the three musketeers Stanley, James and Gaines kept laboring for relief.

Meanwhile petitions from the Tobacco Boards of Trade of Hopkinsville and the Eastern District of Kentucky were forwarded to Washington, and aroused enough interest in the Ways and Means Committee of the House to lead to an invitation for interested parties to appear and discuss the tobacco situation. There was no doubt the news of the raid on Princeton was having an effect. Charles H. Fort, C. P. Warfield of Tennessee, and C. E. Barker and R. E. Cooper of Kentucky, hurried to Washington to testify in favor of the tax easement. Stanley had figures to show the tax repeal would not materially affect the national income, but would help to relieve the burden of the growers. He openly demanded an investigation of the Tobacco Trust under the anti-trust laws.

In the course of the injuiry R. E. Cooper testified, "I've been in the tobacco business 17 years. Around Hopkinsville alone we used to see as many as fifty buyers. Then the American Tobacco Company moved in and sent only one. He offered 3 to 4 cents instead of the 8 and 9 we used to get. The American Tobacco Company has undersold the free market in Bremen, Germany, and froze it up. I've lost heavily in these dealings." He shouted, "Help us fight the American Tobacco Company!"

Cooper's talk was backed up by dealers and buyers from Hopkinsville, Clarksville and Springfield, Tennessee, and other market towns. The story was the same. Poverty and misery among the growers, black and white, merchants and bankers on the verge of bankruptcy.

One main said, "We used to get around 7 cents and 8 cents for our leaf. In 30 years I have never seen prices as low as 4 cents. We're ruined."

The Trust officials did not take this lying down. They retorted, "Low prices are due to the low quality of recent crops. The leaf has deteriorated from the time it's barned. We're handling tobacco at a loss, as it is. We were not treated right on the open market. We've been forced to go directly to the farmer's barn."

"It's all lies!" shouted a farmer. "I know tobacco from A-to-Izzard, and the quality of the leaf is as good as it has ever been in my knowing. Tobacco doesn't deteriorate once barned, it improves. The whole game is to redistrict the tobacco country to prevent competition and make James Duke and his henchmen more wealth."

It was a common tale how a farmer with two barns, one on each side of the road, might sell the buyer one barn and say, "Now step over and look at my other barn." And the buyer would shake his head. "Nope, not in my territory."

A buyer snorted, "Hell fire, it's a damn lie!"

But maybe it wasn't, really. The tobacco boys produced A. O. Dority, of Pembroke, Kentucky, who testified, "I'm a buyer for the American Tobacco Company, and I was given just such instructions and my territory defined."

There was a lot of shouting and cursing and fist-shaking, but in the end the meeting seemed not to bear any fruit. Stanley went back to the hinterlands determined as a last resort to encourage the tobacco growers to protect themselves.

If this proved anything, it was that the Kentucky and Tennessee tobacco farmers were not a bunch of lawless hoodlums, intent on raiding tobacco markets and burning tobacco factories; and calling men out and laying the lash on their raw backs. At least in the beginning they had no pleasure in the business. But war toughens men's hides and hearts and brings out the savage in them and the determination to win at any cost. Men were saying after the Princeton raid that this was War.

An ominous quiet followed the raid. The wreckage of the Stegar & Dollar factory, and the Orr factory, was viewed by all the excited citizenry, shivering in the December dawn and waiting for any stray sticks of dynamite to explode and blow the curious to mincemeat; and when this did not happen, and the last blaze of the burning shacks had been extinguished, the night watchman freed from the shack to yell, "I know some them goddamn sons-a-bitches! I can name 'em!" the folk went back to bed to sleep late and then rise to talk all over again the big doings.

The story going out on the wires to the four winds created another kind of excitement in the New York offices of the American Tobacco Company, and the Regie and Imperial in London, Rome, Berlin and a dozen other countries. "Down with this lawlessness!" was a rising cry. Tobacco had always been a hazardous enough risk, first in the curing barns, then in the flammable factories, and now under the torch of lawless men riding hooded by night bearing cans of kerosene and sticks of dynamite. Worse yet they moved in secrecy so deep that nobody knew when or where they would strike next, and they moved with military precision. The insurance companies heard the news with horror. The New York Underwriters and the Pheonix fellows remembered the letter notifying them to cancel John Orr's and Stegar & Dollar's policies, and they had accordingly done so. They carried hundreds of other policies in the troubled counties of Caldwell, Christian, Trigg and Lyon; and other companies carried hundreds of other policies, and this

Night Rider raid fell upon them like a bomb. All the companies began cancelling policies right and left. No matter that Orr and Stegar & Dollar brought suit against the four companies they were insured with. They won in the Caldwell Circuit Court but lost in the Kentucky Court of Appeals, and thus the tobacco factories lost the whole of their $100,000 valuation. There was a riot clause in the contracts, and the raid was defined as a riot.

This was a fringe benefit of Night Riding the leaders hadn't figured on, but they were to find it cut two ways, for insurance companies cancelled policies on most of the Association's 31 warehouses in operation at the time. At first the Riders and Association men were aghast. Well, they argued, why not start an insurance company of our own? Wasn't that the way insurance companies got started anyway? Someone else had a happier idea. "Why not just we go to the insurance people and guarantee them against loss? Good and well we are not going to burn our own tobacco." The companies restored most of the policies on Association tobacco when assured they were safe against Night Riding raids.

The Trust did not fare so well.

John Orr's face was still red when he remembered his open letter back in August in the local paper offering a prize of $20 in gold for the best load of tobacco delivered to him this season.

A week after the fire Association officials met in Princeton to do something about the hubbub of the raid. They met in an empty jury room at the court house and the chairman read a telegram from Felix Ewing. "In the name of fairness and justice to our cause, keep down lawlessness." The resolvers went into immediate action, deploring the calamity, denying any hand in the business, and offering the reso-

lution, "Be it resolved by this meeting of tobacco growers
that we condemn all lawlessness, riot, and destruction of
property." Every man present took the pen and signed.
Probably all of them had taken part in the raid. Dr. Amoss
must have enjoyed a secret chuckle when he signed his name
in a big bold handwrite. He was fond of his ironic jokes.

When the state fire marshall came to the battered little
burg to carry on his investigation, he sat in the courtroom
like a judge and sent his deputies into the highway and byways and haled in an assortment of innocent citizens, guilty
Association members, county and city officials and factory
workers at the burnt warehouses. Only one lead developed.
A frightened Association fellow of the name of Price Morse,
after considerable brain-washing, implicated Dr. Amoss. He
was present at a district meeting at a country school house
where Dr. Amoss said, "I want all those who will pledge
themselves to take up arms and shed blood for the Association to stand." Those who wanted to retain their blood got
up and went out. Price followed. The Oath was administered, and that was all Price could testify. But witnesses did
name William Winters and John T. Jackson as having been
members of the raiding party. One was a farmer, the other
a railroad section foreman. D. H. Gardner, the night watchman who'd been locked in the coal shed, named Winters as
one of his captors, recognizing the man's voice and size.
But later when Winters and Jackson were tried, it was
proven that Winters was not the man, though it came out
that the guard was an Association member from Wallonia.

Little was left to investigate, and the hearing ended. Excitement subsided during the winter. But Night Riding did
not subside. There was a series of systematic persecutions
of non-members to drive them into the tobacco pool or ruin
them or drive them out of the country. The underground

was definitely following Dr. Amoss' leadership and A. O. Stanley's insistence that they must take the law in their own hands if the law itself should prove inadequate.

Chapter Nine

Hell Raising in the Hills and Hollers

IF YOU FLATTEN YOUR THUMB ON A ROAD MAP OF TEN-
nessee and Kentucky, at the junction of the counties of
Trigg, Lyon, Caldwell and a part of Christian, you will get
burnt in the hot-coal bed of the Night Rider movement. It's
a monstrosity, the half-secret, half-open underground. The
monster's head, mouth, and sharp tooth was down in sunny
Tennessee on the front gallery of Felix Ewing's Glenraven
where the "king" sips mint julips, dreaming up fine phrases
and empassioned denials of any part in lawlessness. But the
brain of the critter goes to far off Washington where you
run into A. O. Stanley. Dr. Amoss and Guy Dunning are
the gold fillings in the poison tooth. The cannon fodder —
the riffraff — who bind themselves with the blood oath administered by the two midnight leaders are scattered hither
and yon in the back hills, in the eroded farms, or as croppers
in the wide rich plains of this good earth of Kentucky. The
Hillbillies are where you find them.

The three strongest lodges were in Wallonia, in Trigg
County, and Nabb Schoolhouse in Caldwell County, and

Cedar Grove Schoolhouse in Lyon County. Guy Dunning was leader in the first, Dr. Amoss in the second, and Sherriff Cash in the third.

Membership fluctuated in these lodges as the movement rose and fell, from an average of 200 up, at times of great activity, to twice that. When the Trust was reaching deep in its money bags to tempt the frail and needy and greedy, members had a habit of staying home and minding the baby. When the Association made a killing, these wavering sons of the soil sneaked back into the fold, hoping nobody had missed them.

How much the Night-Rider oath held the faithful true it is impossible at this late day to say. One can picture Dr. Amoss, in his chesty voice, and Guy Dunning, in his crisp authoritative manner, administering the oath and making it as dire and binding as possible. There is a haunting echo of Ku Klux, Masonry, Odd Fellowship and Anglo-Saxon legal jargon in this pledge. There are several version to select from, but the following seems to be pretty much the one used:

I, Blankety-Blank, in the presence of Almighty God and these witnesses do hereby and hereon solemnly swear and that I will forever conceal and never reveal the secrets, signs, passwords, neither by voice nor hand; that I promise to communicate only with fellows after due trial and those justly entitled to same; I swear that I will obey all orders and summons coming from my lodge, either by day or night, unless prevented by sickness of myself or some member of my family. I promise and swear that I will not use the cloak of this secret order to vent my revenge on enemy or neighbor, but will at all times conduct my actions in conformity with the well-being of the whole. To all this I swear upon the penalty of death, my body cast to the fishes in the sea or burnt to ashes and ashes cast to the four winds, so help me God.

It was well enough understood that an unmarked grave awaited any who broke the oath, revealing the names of members, the secrets, the plans; and most of all in any trials coming up testifying against the Riders, or even the Association. The administrators of the oath were grim enough in the ritual to make members believe they meant business — and they did.

Years ago an old ex-Night Rider gave me a vivid picture of his initiation. He hadn't wanted to join up.

I didn't want to mess up with them bastards. But things was getting hot on all sides. One of them Trust rascals come to my barn and opened his hand and showed me gold dollars. My old woman was fixing to have a fresh baby. Dr. Amoss would have a hand in the business. Hell, I couldn't make Dr. Amoss wait for his fee while I bedded up with that Trust skunk. Then I could see where if the Association got the underhold in time it would work out for the good of all us poor farmers as well as the rich. So one night when the lodge was meeting I snuck off from my old woman and the kids, saying I thought I'd look for a stray calf, and went down to the Cumberland River where the meeting was. They'd put enough heat to me, God knows. They were separating the men from the boys, and I didn't much want to find myself a boy, with a new baby coming, and my plant bed right there to be scraped. Even Doc Amoss when he come to see my old woman pointed that out. Well, here I was at a sycamore tree at the edge of the big timber. The night was overcast and the air was close. A feller in a mask jumped out of the shadders at me. "Halt!" says he, and boy I halted. "Sam Hill." That was me. [Not his real name.] "Is this of your own free will and accord?" "More or less," I says and he says, "Yes or no." "No," says I; then I changed it. "Yes." "Give the pass word." "I don't know no pass word." "Come with me, I got the word for you." So I went down in the deep woods with him and I reckon he found the most tangled part of the woods to carry me through. I never seen so many vines and tangles, and I'd hunted these woods since I was a shaver. Then we come up on a mess of masked men away down in the jungles and all I could see was their eyes in the masks by the light of a little fire in the clearing. So they went through all the hocus-pocus again, and the password proved to be "Sinking Fork." While they had my neck chained down to a stump I heerd a clap of thunder far off beyant the river. and I smelled a storm coming on. They ast me a last time, "Is this of your own free will and accord," and this time I didn't stammer. I think it was Guy Dunning that ast me, "You understand the obligations you incur?" I said I did. They were more than I liked, but this was no time to back out. As sure as the world they'd of called on me in a night or two and hollered me out and my old woman would have heard strange noises down back of the barn. So on my knees I repeated after Doc Amoss (I soon recognized his voice) ". . . in the presence of Almighty God and these witnesses . . .," and I mumbled and got through with the oath. Then they lifted me up and taken off their masks and I knowed about half of 'em, and I was a Night Rider. Then the rain busted loose and it poured like an hour, and wet that hull mess of Night Riders to the hide, and you never heerd such another clapping of thunder and the lightning played so it was like day and you could've read by it. Well . . .

There were some score present at this lodge. But twelve would have constituted a lodge. When they met at a schoolhouse later, there were fifty. Sam Hill knew mules and horses and his official job became that of the hostler, who stayed with the beasts in a raid and helped hold them in readiness for the retreat. He toted a gun and was ordered if he saw any slinking shadows about a meeting to demand who comes there and shoot if the correct return was not made to his hail. He was a "private" and he never rose above that rank, though he might eventually have become a "lieutenant." He attended the drills at Nabb Schoolhouse and Wallonia, and began to enjoy the maneuvers under the brisk commands of Dr. Amoss or Guy Dunning. He had joined up in time to handle the horses at the fairgrounds in the Princeton raid. His wife at first raised hell; but after the baby came and Dr. Amoss was so good to her she made Sam a mask out of one of her old dark petticoats. He held bridles so earnestly that he was fiinally provided with a shotgun as well as his daddy's Civil War Confederate pistol. He liked the starry nights, wintry crisps, or springlike and fragrant. When he planted his own bed on a hillside, he had the warm pleasure of knowing that all his neighbors and friends were sworn to fight with him against any enemy that tried any tricks.

Then came the order to assemble at Nabb Schoolhouse with thirty-five other riders. Their mission was whipping one Noble Robinson. This was on May 27, 1907. At first dark the schoolyard was alive with riders. The colonel of the outfit that night was Sam G. Cash, sheriff of Lyon County, living in Eddyville. After counting noses and identifying every man present, assigning them their numbers while still unmasked, Cash led the way into the big road and they were off. They were riding to whip Robinson and destroy his plant bed. The thought gave Sam no pleasure. Worse yet, he had been assigned to cut the switches when they came to Otter Pond, 20 miles away. It was the policy of the Inner Circle to recruit squads from afar, for two reasons: It made a barn burning or whipping or bed scraping somewhat impersonal, and kept a neighbor from informing the victim out of kindness.

The squad rode at ease, talking little, and only once did Sam hear someone laugh. He smelled the fragrance of good tobacco, and occasionally the rider ahead of him would spit and Sam would catch the scattered spittle in his face. They stopped once at Locust Hill church grounds, lolling about and resting a spell, and Sam held the nags. They'd brought coffee in jugs and Sam drank black coffee from a gourd dipper after a score of others had drunk from the same gourd. Some men had brought whisky. Sam did not accept a snort. They then put on their masks and started away again, double file, silent shadows in the deepening spring night. Along narrow roads they passed hulking tobacco barns and dark dwellings. Only once where maybe they were sitting up with a sick person did he see a light. About one in the morning they reached Robinson's nondescript house. It was a plank-and-log dwelling of two big rooms and a dogtrot, and an L in the back for kitchen and dining room. In back were a barn, sheds, woodpile and privy.

The growling and snarling dogs, lunging at them against the paling fence, had long since warned Robinson and his old woman that Riders were abroad.

Cash raised his hand. "Fire!" The thirty-six men emptied their revolvers, with a few firing shot guns. Sam had always wanted to shoot through somebody's dogtrot and this night he had that satisfaction. The hounds took to their heels, yelping in terror. After the hideous fusillade had died away Cash disguised his voice and called, "Hay-oo in there, Nab Robinson! Come out of there!" He cursed and fired his gun. In the following silence no light showed, there was not even a sound. "Nab Robinson, are you coming out or do we drag you out?" Sam by instinct became aware of some stirring inside. There was another long wait. Then, "What — what you all want?"

"We want you, Robinson, by God!"

"I — I can't come out, my old woman's sick."

"Hell, we don't care if your old woman's dead, you come out of there!"

"I — I —" quavered the voice. "Wait till I get my pants —"

"Goddamn your pants, you come on or else!"

The shapeless figure in a baggy nightgown came along the creaking hall floor. Robinson was plainly terrified of the visitation. He had been warned too many times. Now he shambled to the warped steps, Cash urging him on by shooting just over Robinson's head. Inside the house Robinson's wife was weeping and praying. Clinging to the walls for support as long as he could Robinson came down the steps into the yard. He stumbled on to the gate. Even in the gloom his face looked ashen and his hands shook as he grasped the gate for support. What puzzled Sam was why this man, and others marked like him, simply did not put aside their pride, their greed, whatever it was that held them back, and pool their tobacco and take pot luck with their neighbors and fraternity brothers. But Robinson had made his brags around Otter Pond. "Be goddam if I let e'er man tell me what I can or can't do with my terbacker." Now here were many men saying he was not a free man and might have a harder choice if he didn't listen to other men.

"Get your hoe — got a hoe?"

"I ain't got no hoe here."

"Where's your hoe at, down at the barn? Come along. We got to have us a hoe."

They covered the shaking farmer with their guns and went out to the big lot gate and to the barn. From the hoes hanging to the shed wall Robinson took one down. "Now your plant bed. Where's your plant bed at?" Robinson gave a sound between a groan and a sob. The masked men urged him along, Cash taking the lead up the pasture calf trail to the hillside bed. Cash called Sam's number, "Number 211, cut them sassafras switches." Sam cut the ugly switches with his barlow, his heart sinking. He couldn't even whip his children, let alone this moaning, sobbing man. But he had sworn to obey all commands of his superiors. Robinson dropped the hoe once. A masked Rider kicked him and he nearly toppled over into his plants when he recovered it. A ready hand tore the canvas free. The Riders surrounded the bed, Robinson in the middle of it. He began the ironic job of scraping his own plant bed, muttering a gibberish of prayer. "Lord forgive 'em they know not what they do." "Like hell we don't know what we do!" some one said. Once when Robinson faltered Cash said, "Number 211, lay on your switches." Robinson resumed scraping before Sam could fumble at the sassafras.

Noble Robinson would make no tobacco crop this year. He'd do no more dickering with the Trust buyers for 8c and 9c while his neighbors in the Association were offered 4c. He wouldn't starve, if he planted his tobacco land in food crops and bred a couple more sows for hogmeat and helped his old woman grow a big garden. No neighbor would sell him plants; even the merchants might not give him credit. He'd have a year to brood on his revenge, and he likely was vowing it this minute; "Goddamn their souls, I'll kill 'em! I know these sons-a-bitches. I'll lay low and shoot some of 'em." His old mother-hubbard gown flopped open behind as he cut the last of his plants. He blew his nose and Sam realized the man was crying. His posterior hung out, a curiously ugly thing in the starlight. When the job was finished Cash signalled.

"All right, men, let's ride."

Number 211 dropped his switches with a deep sigh of relief. A wash of air cooled his hot face. The horsemen mounted and soon were galloping away. Here and there, miles down the road, groups began separating, making for home where the roads forked. Sam was back home about three-thirty. His mule got back faster than it had gone, a characteristic of homing brutes. Sam gave the beast some corn and then went to the horse pond, where he pulled off his clothes and plunged into the chill water. His body felt the sharp needles of chill but somehow his soul was purged. Yet to his dying moment he would remember Nab Robinson's arse, misshappen and obscene, as his old gown flopped open when he scraped his last scrape.

Chapter Ten

Techniques of Terror

THERE IS NO QUESTION IN MY MIND THAT DURING ALL the previous months of 1907 there had been secret meetings between Dr. Amoss and Felix Ewing, and in the office of the Association in Guthrie these men met, along with Guy Dunning, Charles and Joel Fort, and perhaps a handful of trusted faithful, to formulate strategy, to develop techniques of terror. All these men were openly active in making talks before lodges, some established, some in the process of being established. The two Forts travelled over the Black Patch importuning individuals to join the Association. Guy Dunning in his travels to the thirty-two Association warehouses prizing the 1906 crop, took occasion to lend his voice and influence. Dr. Amoss made the fullest use of his professional contacts, even to the most humble like Sam Hill. Felix Ewing rigidly maintained his aloof purity but administered the business of selling Association tobacco as efficiently probably as it could have been done by any man. When A. O. Stanley came down into the tobacco country to mend his political fences, he was available for speeches, and he did not hesitate to work with Joel and Charles Fort.

It added up to a formidable talent. But a lot of dirty work had to be done, as well as the lily-white-hands jobs. Not only must the recalcitrant hold-outs be brought in, but an intricate network of silent, secret membership must be developed. There was first the law — judges, lawyers, county officials, sheriffs, magistrates, constables. Next were the bankers and merchants, and lesser business men. There were the professional men — doctors, dentists, even the horse doctors. Not the least in this pecking order were the editors of the county and city papers. Once the courts were controlled by the Silent Brigade, there could be no effective prosecution of Night Riders. Merchants and bankers would refuse credit to men who did not join the organization. Editors would seek to control public opinion.

On paper it looked like an airtight arrangement. The flaws were that many men in the catagories declined to join; some merely remained aloof while others were hostile; and there were always the agents of the American Tobacco Company to support the timid or buy off the hostile. And there would presently rise the hue and cry of law-and-order people, sincere enough but asking nothing better than let us have peace. There were the top-rail entrenched, who never lend themselves to revolutions that impair their own authority; and the great middle class who hunger and thirst for the status quo. The city press was almost unanimous against this lawlessness, led by the redoubtable Henry Waterson of the Louisville *Courier-Journal*. There were judges like Judge A. J. G. Wells, of Murray, who would have no part in these illegal activities, and who took every oppotrunity to fight both Night Riding and the Association, on the hypothesis they were one and the same. And finally there would be the state authorities — Governor J. C. W. Beckham and his police authority and troops.

If the leaders of the Night Riding movement had not believed their cause just, and the provocation unendurable, they would never have organized into such a widespread resistance movement. So they had fallen to work on the spectacular phase of their activities, raiding the tobacco towns and burning the Trust warehouses. Princeton was the first of these, and Hopkinsville was scheduled to be second, some time in the January after the Princeton affair. But the time was not propitious; Hopkinsville was openly hostile, and the Night Riders were not sufficiently organized for such ambitious demonstration of power. But the speech makers were busy, and Colonel Joel Fort, our well known wheelhorse of organizers, had composed an oration about goats that never failed to rock his crowds with shouts and laughter and bursts of applause. Hillbilly suggests goats, and Fort made the best use of the ridicule and analogy between the butt-heads and men who refused to join the Association. If there were Hillbillies present they ground their teeth and perhaps escaped or even went so far as to join. It was the business of the plant-bed scrapers and floggers to fetch in those who could not be swayed by threat or ridicule or pesuasion.

Noble Robinson was not the first of these victims. He was merely the most picturesque. In May, 1906, a year earlier, the first important bed-scraping occurred in Christian County. L. L. Leavell and J. T. Garnett were two leading farmers living not far from Hopkinsville who declined to join the pool. One night they found young plants on nine hundred and fifty square yards of beds de-

stroyed. The outraged planters borrowed bloodhounds from
the county sheriff and put the brutes' noses on the trail
from beds to road. From the tracks it appeared that five
men had done the work about two o'clock in the morning. They had got in three buggies and driven away.
The trail was lost. Garnett undertook then to buy plants
from neighbors to set his land, already conditioned for
setting. No neighbor would sell to him. Some felt they
did not dare; others had none to spare. Garnett cursed
the Riders to high heaven. But when he found a sheet
of scratch paper on his gate post with a rough sketch of
skull and crossbones, he subsided into a dour silence.

About this time there was an intensive campaign of
threatening letters over the counties. Usually they were
rough notes tacked to gate posts. They bore such messages as "Put your crops in the Association. We are running things now. Night Riders." Everywhere over the
Black Patch there were clandestine meetings of lodges and
men shouted passionate and incendiary speeches. Night
processions of hooded Riders, masked and bearing torches,
rode through all the small towns — Cobb, Otter Pond,
Gracey, Sinking Fork, Fruit Hill, Bluff Springs — solemn
and menacing, armed to the teeth, and by their very
sinister silence, spreading terror. They made no overt
moves. The only sound was the thud of their horses
hooves and the stretch and snub of saddle leather.

Roistering youths emulated their elders and on Saturday nights might tank up on rotgut whisky and gallop
around the countryside cursing and bellowing and dis-
charging their guns. Some wore imitation masks. These
activities helped rather than hindered the terrorism.

In January the shortline privately-owned Cadiz Railroad to Hopkinsville received a warning to haul no more

tobacco to Trust warehouses. The company chose to
ignore the threat. Here and there a farmer would find a
bundle of switches at his yard gate. "If you want to save
your back and that little tobacco of yours, you must have
it in the Association by [some stated time] or you will get
hell on your back and your barn burnt." Not far from
Russellville one morning a hold-out discovered to his
horror a grave dug in the middle of his plant bed, the
tender plants all trampled, and a rough board as head-
stone with his name printed in pencil.

For the time being threats were mostly in use. They
were proving effective enough momentarily to drive in
a number of faltering Hillbillies. Around the stores and
blacksmith shops exaggerated accounts of these doings
were mouthed by the loafers to keep non-conformists uneasy or plain scared. On January 4, 1907, while still
the smell of smoke pervaded the debris of Stegar & Dollar
and John Orrs' places, a strange voice came over the
telephone to the office of Charles Mayfield Meacham,
mayor of Hopkinsville and publisher of the weekly *Kentuckian*. "The Night Riders are coming on a massive
raid!" Mayor Meacham's sparse gray hair and white mustaches bristled. "What's that again? Who're you?" But
the old wet-cell phone was dead; the caller had hung up.

Mayor Meacham sat there gasping. This was on outrage. The very idea of his fair city of eight thousand
souls — no mean city at that time —suffering the same
insult as Princeton! He tried to think what move to make
next. He knew that he was unpopular out in the hinterlands. His stand against this increasing lawlessness had
won him no friends; even in town among the merchants
that bought advertising he seemed to be losing influence.
Nevertheless Meacham was a man of resources. He owned

what had been a lucrative publishing business. He was
president of the Kentucky Press Association. He was president of the board of trustess of Bethel Woman's College. More notable than these honors, he was author
of a 700-page *History of Christian County, Kentucky,*
which weighs something like seven pounds and is a
historical *Who's Who* of that block of Kentucky land, ex-
tolling the virtues of pioneers, bankers, society leaders,
Confederate generals, merchants, natural bridges, one
chapter of Night Riding (of which he took an extremely
dim view), and more than five thousand names to command a wide circulation for his book. Parts of it are
interesting to readers who know the name of Kentucky
only on whiskey bottles. In person he was lean and
handsome, grayed and mustached after the manner of
Southern gentlemen; and there was a haunting odor about
him of burley pipe tobacco, good cigars, and fine bourbon.

After deciding this was not a trick but the warning of
a friend who dared not come into the open, he rang the
phone and called the office of Deputy Sheriff Lucian
Cravens. "The Night Riders are coming!" He gave details in an excited voice.

Then, as Childe Harold put it, "there was hurrying
to and fro, and gathering tears, and tremblings of dis-
tress," except the tears were profanity, and the "mustering
squadron and clattering car" was the local law swinging
into action. Company D was a body of local militiamen,
and to augment this arm the Sheriff hastily swore in a
roster of citizens who were ready to fare forth and shoot
Night Riders just for the fun of seeing them topple from
the saddle. Excitement was intense, for Hopkinsville
citizenry had spoken out loudly against lawlessness, and
voices had been raised in counter threats as to what they'd

do if raided. A couple of hundred men rushed hither
and yon for revolvers and rifles and shotguns, and while
a guard took over the two important tobacco factories
in town, the rest rode out the Cadiz and Princeton road
whence the warning call was supposed to have come. They
deployed a few miles out at some woods and an open field
and little schoolhouse. There they assumed a battle formation and looked to the waddling of their muskets. They held
their post all night, and soon became distressed with hunger.
They slacked their bellies with branch water and watched
the dawn come thundering up over sleepy Hopkinsville.
All at once they realized they had been sold down the
river. They dispersed, going sheepishly home to bed, not
knowing whether to laugh at being hoaxed or to vow
vengeance on the first hooded horsemen they saw.

It was not immediately apparent that the warning had
been to test the defense system of Hopkinsville, to dis-
cover whether there was force enough to neutralize an
actual raid. It was an open secret that such a raid was
in the cards. But Dr. Amoss and Guy Dunning, and the
rest of the captains and colonels were of the opinion this
was not the time for one more massive demonstration of
Night Rider power. The Association still did not have a
strong foothold in the county, for a rival organization, the
American Society of Equity, pretty much took care of the
local tobacco pool. But the Forts and other organizers
were laboring night and day to correct this situation. Scat-
terings of hold-outs were joining, for rumors of plant beds
scheduled for scraping, barns to be burnt, and men to
be flogged, were rife. The excitement of the threatened
raid had its effect.

But the scare subsided, and Charles Meacham took
his old Oliver typewriter in hand and hammered out a

blistering editorial against the underground, and the need for eternal vigilance.

On the night of May 1, 1907, came the episode of Mary Lou Hollowell.

I've examined all the evidence I can find on Mary Lou, and studied much about her, for any attractive female is apt to interest a man. Mary Lou at the time this business took place was a good looking hunk of woman. The formal portrait of her I have shows a buxom person of maybe thirty-five, well fed, pretty, intelligent, nicely dressed, and withal, a personality. You would hardly expect to find such a gracious lady stuck off on a dirt farm nine miles from Princeton, a mile from Nabb Schoolhouse. The faded snapshot I once saw of the Hollowell home was of a farmhouse typical of small tobacco planters — frame, two big rooms with dogtrot, and in back an old log structure of some kind that may have been the original house but now used for a kitchen. Bushy trees were about and the usual paling fence and awry gate, slung shut by old plow-points hung to a trace chain. There seemed an air of womanlessness here.

She was married to Robert H. Hollowell, but what the man was like I have no idea, for he left behind no incriminating portraits. They had an eleven-year old son of the name of Price.

Father and son leave one with the impression of a pair of colorless people, the man mild and probably kind; the boy somewhat frail and good in his books. I find no direct proof of this. I surmise it from what I find about Mary Lou and her doings and what took place afterward, and the blow below the belt it eventually became for the Night Riders.

We go back to the Princeton raid. Mary Lou was not

stuck back on this dirt tobacco farm at all. When Dr. Amoss's and Guy Dunning's bully boys rode into Princeton and showed Orr & Stegar the kingdoms, she was living in Princeton, a stylish city slicker, and sending Price, her son, to the first rate school there. It is presumed that the drafty Nabb place with its hard benches, pot-bellied stove, and tough master, was no place for a sensitive lad. The sour feet and manure-tipped brogans of the uncouth boys were unfit for the aesthetic nose of our young master. No matter. Mary Lou removed to the city and left Bob, her husband, out on the farm in the care of a Negro cook and housewoman.

One thing for sure, she had to make her own way in this enterprise, and the most plausible explanation I have found is she kept a small, select table in a house just off the public square, where she fed the judges, drummers, city officials, lawyers, and other important men. She was known as an excellent cook, and made a fine showing on herself of her own calories. She was attractively dressed, and the tobacco buyers and drummers paid 50c a meal gladly when the going rate at other joints was a quarter or 35c. Mary Lou served them her dimples along with her dumplings, and no riffraff were welcome. She fried chicken for no less a potentate than Augustus Willson when he came to the Black Patch to feel out public pulse on his candidacy for governor on the Republican ticket (he didn't get much encouragement), and John G. Miller, Sr., who practiced law in the courts at Princeton, never failed to food himself at her board. Both these contacts would serve Mary Lou well in the coming law scrape that nobody at this time even dreamed about.

Before she closed her house to return to the farm in April, she had taken it on herself to request the Grand

Jury sitting on some warehouse burnings to hear her. There seems no question she had eavesdropped on the low talk at her table between perhaps even Dr. Amoss and Guy Dunning, and certainly the banker, the county judge, and Walter Krone, the prosecuting attorney, who was bitterly hostile to the Night Riders, and was already under the shadow of threats on his life if he didn't stop messing with loose manure. "The more you stir manure the worse it stinks," and Krone was marked for murder. The Grand Jury almost to a man was composed of Night Riders or Association men. They heard Mary Lou with horror. Swiftly the word spread. Mary Lou had named names. By the time she got back home, Bob Hollowell had already informed the Association people he would not join. This compounded the insult. In reply the Night Riders visited his farm the night of April 18. They left not one plant standing. They'd worn gunny sacks on their feet to avoid tracks. So silently did they work, not even the dogs were disturbed.

Bob said nothing, knowing any outburst would be used against him. He had a premonition he might get a good going over, and Mary Lou, screaming to high heaven at the outrage, did not soothe savage breasts. "They ought to be made to pay! If I had my d'ruthers I'd see 'em hung!" She named three neighbor men she strongly suspected had been in the scraping party.

It was more than coincidence that on the night of November 30, 1907, the beds of these three neighbors were scraped. In looking for evidence one of the farmers picked up a little Black Draught memo book, dog-eared and soiled, with figures and the name of Steve Choate penciled in it. Steve was one of the two tenants on the Hollowell farm. He was a nondescript ratty fellow, and Ned Pettit, a Negro,

was the other. Pettit had had polio and walked with a
stubby limp. His footprints were traced to his cabin by
this infirmity. It took no Sherlock Holmes to deduce that
Mary Lou was back of all this. Choate and Pettit were
immediately arrested and the white man broke down and
confessed, saying that Mary Lou had promised him ten
dollars for the job and he had taken the Negro along for

Harry Harrison Kroll 64

Nabb Schoolhouse, Caldwell County, Kentucky, Dr. Amoss's lodge.

company. By nightfall these horrible tidings were in the ears and mouth of every sworn Night Rider in ten miles. Their indignation knew no bounds. They waited no longer than candlelight of the following evening for forty of them to gather at Nabb Schoolhouse, armed and unmasked, and determined to revenge this insult. The brotherhood would see that the three farmers had plants enough to set their land; it was the principle of the thing.

Among the squad were two other Hollowells — Bob's brother John E., and his cousin John W. Both men were active in the Association, as well as in the underground. Others were Wallace and Firm Oliver, John and Bill Turner, Joe Murphy, Spurlin and Will Murphy, Jim and Jack Chambers, Buck and Urey Lacey, Sid and Ot Smith, William Tandy, and a scattering of Riders from the adjoining counties.

They hitched their horses around the school grounds and took off down the farm lane toward Bob's on foot. When they passed the now empty Choate cabin a voice said, "Give 'em hell," and they emptied their guns in the shack. It was still early bedtime, but the restless Hollowells may not have turned in. The dogs raised a great howl at the shooting, and the family was dressed when the band arrived at the front gate. John E., the leader, making no effort to disguise this voice, shouted, "Hay-oo in there! Hello, hello!" The usual silence attended this hail. The dogs lunged and someone knocked a hound down with the butt end of his gun. When still no answer came the command was given to shoot up the place. In past such attacks the Night Riders fired in the air. This time they blasted the windows out, moving at angles to get at side-windows, and they shot the doors through and through.

The Hollowell family had taken refuge behind a barricade of furniture. Bullets sizzled about the room.

"Come out of there, Mary Lou!"

Mary Lou started toward the door. Bob implored, "No, don't, they'll kill you."

Mary Lou nevertheless went into the dogtrot, scantily clad as she was. A roar of gunfire hurled her backward, and a squirrel shot caught her in the face. Streaming blood, thinking perhaps she was killed, she screamed at the attackers, "You've shot me!" A voice cried right back at her, "Goddam, that's what we come to do!" The cordon had moved in close to the house and men stepped into the hall to grab Mary Lou. Nothing was left Bob but to appear as brave as his wife, and coming through the door he was swiftly pinioned. Price showed up, a shivering and sobbing figure. Mary Lou kept screaming, mopping the blood from her face, and probably sickened more at the thought of losing her good looks than dying, she yielded to captors that dragged her, with Bob, into the yard. When it dawned on her the men were going to horsewhip Bob, she grew faint and fell on the ground. A young man kicked her in the posterior. His name was Firm Oliver and he had been working on the place last year. A young man kicking a handsome woman on her behind! Freud might have had the answer to that. Then a woman's voice screamed out, "Ah but this is sweet revenge to me!" It was John E.'s wife, Mary Lou's sister-in-law, who was in the mob. Then Mary Lou fainted.

The boy kept begging the men not to kill his mother. "What's she done?"

"We'll kill her if she don't keep her goddam mouth shut!"

"What'd she say?" quavered Price.

"Talked to that Grand Jury, by God. It wasn't none of her damn business."

Leaving Mary Lou still in a faint, the men carried Bob down toward the barn, ordered him to strip, and stark naked they lashed him with buggy whips till he was bloody from head to foot. While this ruthless flogging went on, men kept Bob covered with their guns. The frail man, after the first agonizing blows, swallowed his whimpering and stoically accepted the punishment. When they'd worn whips to the stock they took him back to the house.

"Now get the hell out of this neighborhood and if you show your face we'll kill you."

They left him moaning on his step. Mary Lou had come out of her faint. She bawled and cursed, and stopped making feeble efforts at her face and turned to help her husband. As the Riders passed the Choate shack they once more pumped their guns into it. Dim as was the starlight, Mary Lou could click off the names of some thirty of the forty men. Her brother-in-law, the other Hollowell, the woman, the young man that kicked her, and many of the men from adjoining counties, for she knew a great many men. How she happened to know so many men does not show itself clearly in the record. Right now they had to have a doctor for Bob. Her fear was that Bob might be dying, or would die before she could get medical attention. "We'd better pack and start for Princeton," she muttered, and hastily flinging on some clothes, she went to the barn and geared up the mule team. She put some clothes in a grip and helped Bob dress, and they loaded up. They must pass through Cobb on their way to town. Probably it was a bitter pill for her to swallow that Dr. Amoss was the nearest physician and the best; she swallowed her hate and put her pride in her pocket and passing the Amoss house, she shouted the Doctor out, who got from bed to bandage up the broken man, and put a suture on Mary Lou's wound above her left eye. He may thus have saved her sight.

She then drove on to Princeton, reaching there about dawn. Soon afterward the Hollowells left Kentucky for Oklahoma, after putting the farm up for sale. The man who bought the place in was one of the Hollowell neighbors, and he carefully filled all the bullet holes in the walls, and afterwards painted the house to cover the effects of the attack.

Steve Choate and Ned Pettit were tried in the next term of Circuit Court and sentenced to the Eddyville penitentiary for a year and day each, under a new law recently passed to catch the Night Riders in their plant bed scraping. The Grand Jury sat and indicted Mary Lou for her part in the work, but by then the Hollowells were beyond reach of Kentucky law.

Chapter Eleven

All Quiet on the Night-Rider Front

THE IMMEDIATE EFFECT OF THE BOB HOLLOWELL flogging was to cause the hold-outs within radius of the Nabb Schoolhouse lodge to rush to join. Among these fringe figures was Sanford Hall, a tenant on one of the farms, who was noteworthy for being the biggest liar in the community. He was a lank sallow fellow, with a bean-stringy undernourished wife and a couple of puny children. He lived in one of the sorriest cabins around. He kept hounds and neighbors said he fed his dogs cornbread that should have gone to the mouths of his young ones. Hall was typical of those who talked as openly as they dared against the Riders and Association, but under pressure reluctantly joined the underground and became finally a member of the Silent Brigade. The more far-reaching effects were numerous plant-bed scrapings in five counties, as the news spread. The Louisville *Courier-Journal* and Memphis *Commercial Appeal* featured the outburst of lawlessness, and Henry Waterson editorialized, "How long are such outrages going to pass unpunished?"

Governor Beckham issued a statement, condemning such doings, and Felix Ewing, voice of the Association, issued a statement deploring the flogging. There was an outcry for more law to deal with Night Riding, plant-bed scraping, and whipping, but the state legislature had already taken cognizance of the movement and, as we mentioned, one of the first cases to be tried under the new law ironically snared some of the people it was supposed to protect — Mary Lou Hollowell and the guilty tenants. Under it the Grand Jury indicted Mary Lou, though she had quit the state. There was a rising wave of resentment among the city folk of Kentucky, and demands for police action.

But heavy rains had fallen, giving a perfect season for setting the tobacco plants, and the labor force went to work. At first the plants looked sickly and limp and yellow, frail as cobwebs. But the sushine made them lift their heads bravely, and soon the fields were geometrical with their beauty. Then began the war with weeds, grass and insects. Little time now for Night Riding.

But it was only a lull. Between stints working on the crop, men rode. Mostly the riders were picked squads from the Cadiz, Wallonia and Nabb lodges. It's reasonably certain that these forays were led by Guy Dunning. It's also certain that Dr. Amoss planned the movements. They were executed with the swiftness of Nathan Bedford Forrest's troopers, indicating that Dunning and Amoss, and perhaps in the dark background Felix Ewing, understudied the redoubtable cavalry genius of the Confederacy. There was the case of the Golden Pond foray. W. R. Wilson operated a prizing house there, but the past winter the Association had moved in and built a competing factory. In those times Golden Pond was a considerable gathering of homes, stores, churches, a school-

house, and these two warehouses. In the narrow valleys
of the back hills in this between-rivers, rugged land much
fine tobacco was grown. Wilson's place was filled with ten
thousand pounds of leaf, mostly prized and packed in the
monstrous hogsheads; and Wilson had been rolling these
to Rockcastle, a steamboat landing on the Cumberland
River, and shipping to Trust warehouses in Clarksville.
He also sold wagons, buggies and harness, and the sheds
of his warehouse were filled with this merchandise. Word
had been quietly sent out for Association members to get
their tobacco out of Wilson's place. One night thirty-five
picked "veterans" swooped down on Golden Pond and burnt
Wilson's place to the ground. He lost not only the tobacco
but his wagons and buggies. The Riders had come to the
river, left their horses in charge of hostlers, had broken
the locks of skiffs along the river bank and taken over the
ferry. They marched to Golden Pond, some 3 miles distant, did their work, marched back, recrossed the river,
and rode away as they had come.

It wasn't the first time Rockcastle had seen them. Back
in February 25 masked men, emulating the Boston Tea
Party, appeared and rolled six hogsheads of tobacco down
the river bluff into the stream. Johnson Hendrick ran
the place: he operated the hotel, ran a big store, owned
the saloon, was post master and justice of the peace, and
general bigwig of the shipping point. He was the one-
suspender type of individualist, and the Association agents
had worked hard to win his membership. Joel Fort had
even wheelhorsed him without results. "I'm doing all
right," he said. "Why should I mess up with you boys?
I'm a big frog in a little pond."

It was a built-in situation for a raid. On August 23,
after tobacco was laid by, the Night Riders appeared at

one o'clock in the morning and shot the place up. They yelled Hendrick out of his hotel quarters and cursed him roundly. "Shut your big mouth or take the consequences." When Hendrick still showed no inclination to pool with the Association, the squad returned November 25 and fired the store when the wind was out of the north. In a few minutes the flames spread to the hotel; then hopped to three nearby residences, caught in two livery stables, and went on to the blacksmith shop and saloon. In two hours the little town was all but gutted. Soon afterward the Riders were back, burning the buildings the first fire had not consumed. The landing never recovered from these saturation raids. Hendrick was ruined. He was no longer any kind of frog in any pond.

The news of this uncouth series of burnings went over the wires and men read in New York, Chicago, in London and Paris, and in Rome. Distance lent exaggeration, and there were cries from governments and editors. Over the Black Patch it should have been a warning to all men. But a prominent independent near Roaring Spring, Steve Moseley, refused to join the Association, again denying Joel and Charles Fort. He said coldly, "I prefer to run my own business in my own way."

Shortly dark figures made sowing motions over his plant beds; they wore towsacks over their shoes and left no tracks; Moseley did not know they had visited him till he was ready to set his tobacco, when he found the plants adulterated with weed and grass seeds and all but ruined. He managed to salvage sufficient plants to set ten of his seventy-five acres. In June the Riders were back, placing shells on his step, and cutting his telephone line. Following this threat Moseley made a gesture of joining the Association. The Night Riders were convinced of his two-facedness when he sought to buy plants. On July 23, one hundred Riders from the Cadiz, Wallonia and Roaring Spring lodges rode Indian fashion around his house and riddled it with bullets. They barely avoided killing his children and wife. Moseley was wounded twice in the face by gunfire and a near miss all but blinded his eye. One bullet went through his hand. His wife was actually blinded by a squirrel shot. Not long afterward Moseley sold his farm and moved to another place near Hopkinsville, where still the Rider movement was not well organized.

These were the spectacular affairs. But every Hillbilly found threats, warnings, and now and then a galloping squad would shoot into his house. This organized terrorism brought many members into the lodges, but the more determined hold-outs decided they would form a resistance movement of their own, and some hundred gathered in Cadiz, known already as the Night Rider capital, and formed the Farmers Independent Organization. They promised armed protection to any farmer who wished to sell independently, and legal aid to Trust buyers and speculators. The gesture did not last through the year. The Night Riders met and sent out word that any Trust buyers and so-called independents would be met in Trigg County with hemp and powder, and any farmer dealing with a representative of the American Tobacco Company or Regie or Imperial would be killed. On the age-old principle "if you can't lick 'em, join 'em," the Hillbillies came into the Association, with the understanding they could sell their 1906 crop to the Trust, as they had already bargained. The true and faithful grumbled about this concession, but the movement settled down to enjoy the tranquillity of victory.

The scene shifts from the brooding Tennessee and Kentucky tobacco lands, smothery in the summer heat as the broad leaves knit between the rows and weary men and women hope for a good crop and better prices, to the faraway and fabulous city of New York and the golden canyons of Wall Street where James Duke — we no longer think of him as Buck — sits on his heap of tobacco, gloatingly running his $200,000,000 fortune through his un-gnarled, un-worm-tarred fingers. If he puts his ear to the ground and listens he will hear marching men in the moonlight, moving to the barked commands of Dr. Amoss and Guy Dunning, and their quick step in imitation of advancing Confederates. If he reads his New York Times he'll see items of barn burnings, floggings, plant-bed scrapings, swift raids on places he'd never heard of before. We have no evidence that he ever read such news. In any case his heart was throbbing to the age-old charms of love.

Our hero seems to have grown a little weary of the triumphs of high finance. He has brought the cigarette manufacturers to their knees, subjugated the cigar makers, licked the snuff grinders, and liquidated the Star Navy pressers. Now he has time to cultivate art, culture and women. A man who has ridden freight cabooses all night to save hotel bills isn't going to spend money on just any women. He's going to select wisely and well. That is, not too wisely, not at first. His first roll of the bones was in 1904. He was forty-eight years old then. He married Lillian McCready, who had been the wife of a New York broker of the name of William D. McCready. That was the year leaf tobacco hit the bottom of 3-2-1. At that time James Duke's fortune was a paltry $100,000,000. But marriage costs money.

Something turned sour. We are not told what the trouble was, beyond the item that James named one of her former suitors as co-respondent and was granted a divorce in the New Jersey courts. It was said he provided liberally for Lillian's support, but he never saw her again.

A bachelor till he was forty-eight; married a divorced woman, divorced her in a year. It must have caused talk but I do not find it in my references.

Nothing like taking a second shot, and on July 23, 1907 — and you will recollect this was only a few weeks after Mary Lou Hollowell and her Bob and Price took off for the Wild West — James Duke married Nanaline Lee Holt Inman, widow of Walter Inman, of Atlanta, Georgia. Five years later, a daughter, Doris, was born out of this union in which Duke is said to have found his greatest happiness. He lavished his affections upon wife and daughter.

If you can feel sorry for a man as rich as Duke was, you can sense the pathos of his love-starved life up till he was fifty. And there's something odd here, too. I have been unable to find any hint of romance in all these previous years. In both his marriages, he sought wives previously married, rather than a far younger and fresher woman, as he might easily have done. And just one girlchild. One wonders.

Besides killing himself counting profits from sales of watered stocks in the American Tobacco Company and the unholy returns of a tobacco monopoly, what did James Duke do to entertain himself? I wish that I could report that he read a good book. It's not recorded in any of my references. You recall that he renounced college, having no taste for formal education. But he was fond of horses, and bought himself a pair of spanking

roadsters and a brougham. Though caring nothing for
display, he made a drag on his shipping room and
fetched out a handsome yellow Negro of the name of Alex,
fitted him in colorful livery, put a coachman's hat on Alex
with a cockade on the side and a moonstone the size
of a toadstool, and went afternoons for drives along the
avenues frequented by the fashionables. He had never
owned a home. Not even when he'd hit the jackpot with
his first million did he know anything but hotel bed-
rooms and nearby beaneries.

All that was past. He must have felt a muscular spasm
when he reached in his jeans, brought out the old sock
bank, and paid for 326 acres of land in New Jersey, the
John Veghte place. He began farming and dairying with
205 registered Guernseys. He bought fine horses, established a stable, and built a half-mile trotting course. He
finally erected Duke Farms with 2200 acres.

Like so many men who spend the bulk of their lives
making money without knowing how to spend it, he
plunged. He imported from Italy and France and England, landscape gardeners, architects, horticulturists, sculp-
tors, stone masons, stained-glass artisans; he hired armies
of workmen, with a steam shovel and donkey engine; he
built what was called a "veritable fairyland." As many
as 100,000 trees and shrubs were imported from all over
the world. There were miles of roads and arched bridges
and scores of fountains in this dreamland. Something
deep in his childhood must have hounded him, for where
he would pinch a penny over lumber bought for a Sunday
School picnic and chide the parson for chiseling on the
bill, he deluged money, making streets, grassy banks,
stone bridges and thirty-five fountains rivaling, it was
said, Fontainbleau and Versailles. He fashioned his formal

gardens after those in Italy, and one notes that he did not go down into North Carolina where he was born and raised for any of his motifs. To cap it all he had a three-times lifesize statue of William McKinley cast in bronze in Florence and installed among his statuary. He spent thousands of dollars moving McKinley here and there till a suitable spot was found to please Duke.

The original house was enlarged until it had fifty rooms. Later a mansion on the order of the lavish Vanderbilt mansion in Asheville, N.C., was erected, with greenhouses covered by 110,000 square feet of glass. Here he grew orange trees, peaches out of season, grapes, melons, nectarines. He won prizes with his orchids. He answered to a question whether he knew the cost of each item, "Ah yes. I have a complete record in my office." Here we have the remarkable spectacle of a great man carrying millions of dollars in one side of his head and thousands of plants and shrubs and flowers and fruit in the other.

One can understand how, when he got all this done, he suddenly lost interest in it all. The ornate artificiality was not in the nature of the old tobacco boy with Wash Duke in North Carolina. What was there here of James Duke, one asks? If he had made up a model tobacco farm, with an old-timey house with dogtrot and mule wagons and darkies and toilers in the burning suns, he'd have been far nearer his genius.

Then he married, and the best was none too good for his womenfolk. He built one of the finest marble palaces on Fifth Avenue in New York, employing all the architectural genius he could find, and all the art he could buy. One catches a deep breath and just stares. "The furniture, largely of Louis XV and Louis XVI design, included examples of the best periods of France. In the main hall hung notable works of art." In the mind's eye one can see James Duke pacing to and fro on the Ispahan palace rug that covered the floor, hands clasped thoughtfully behind him; or sitting on the sofa of Beauvais tapestry, near the two statues of Couston — "Girl Playing the Flute" and "La Musique" — staring at the Gothic panels and tapestries out of the French Renaissance; at the works of the Flemish and French artists — "The Hunt," "Musical Festivities," "Betrothal Scenes" — at the Chinese temple jars of the Yung Chang period, or paintings of great worth, and asking his heart, "What the hell's it all about?"

This collecting no doubt was due to the free masonry of cash exercised by a young wife. A Georgia girl wouldn't spare the purse of a man who once was a North Carolina tobacco peddler. She would globe-trot with a right good will and come home loaded with loot. New York's Four Hundred must be impressed at any cost. James Duke must have paced the floor many a night contemplating the mystery of fate that had set him down in this lap of luxury when time was that he hardly knew where the next meal of hog-meat and hominy was coming from. It was a question to engage the mind of a far greater thinker than Duke was. One can go crazy to this day trying to figure it out.

But James and Nanaline — a lovely name, by the way — really hoisted themselves out of the poor white class into the plantation quality when Duke bought the old Frederick W. Vanderbilt mansion at Newport, "Rough Point," a pile facing the sea that awes one just to stare at the picture of it. It must have been something to write home to the folks about, spending summers at this shack among the folk of wealth and fashion. If Buck didn't cease spitting tobacco

juice in the fireplace now, it wasn't because he wasn't ex-
posed to the refined habits of millionaires.

We turn for a close look at Duke through the eyes of one
of his associates in the tobacco business, of the name of
Fuller.

In form and feature Mr. Duke looks like a well bred Scot, robust, standing erect six feet two inches in height. The large
head, covered with red hair, has a broad brow, straight nose,
kindly mouth, clear eyes. A fresh healthy coloring sets off the
strong face and his British ancestry. His dress is simple . . .
his manner reasonable . . . his memory remarkable for its tena-
city and accuracy . . . self-reliant . . . cool and courageous in
action . . . modest and retiring in his manners . . . in political
association a Republican, because he believes that the econ-
omic policy of that party assures more happiness to more people
. . . While his sympathies naturally rise and fall with those of
the people among whom he was born and where he passed his
young manhood, his judgment guides his actions. . . . If there
is any chord that rings highest in his thoughts it is eagerness to
give work to those who would have work. Work for its own
ennobling and saving sake. . . . The idle rich do not interest him,
but the man with the single talent, well employed, commands
his attention and admiration.

There are pages and pages of this analysis and eulogy;
and one wonders, plowing through them, if James Duke
didn't have the bronze statue of Wiliam McKinley cast of
the wrong man. It should have been of James B. Duke.

On July 10, 1907, James C. McReynolds, special attorney of the United States Department of Justice, filed suit in
the United States Circuit Court, New York City, against the
American Tobacco Company, American Snuff Company,
American Cigar Company, the Imperial Tobacco Company,
and the British-American Tobacco Company, and some

sixty other subsidiary tobacco companies, and specifically
named James B. Duke and twenty-eight associates, charging
them with violation of the Sherman Anti-Trust Act of 1890.

Chapter Twelve

The Battle of the Governors

WHEN AUGUSTUS E. WILLSON ANNOUNCED HIS CANDIDACY
for governor on the Republican ticket, one of his early
speaking engagements was Hopkinsville, and Dr. Amoss
and Guy Dunning were in the audience when Willson repeated his battle cry, "If I am elected, I will put down lawlessness with all the power of my office." He was introduced
by Charles Meacham, and in his introduction Meacham
said, "I am for this man 100 percent." When the crowd dispersed from the court house, Dr. Amoss shook his head.
"Looks like Chuck Meacham and Willson will make strange
bed fellows." The next day Willson spoke at Murray, and
here he was introduced by Judge A. J. G. Wells, who was
a lifelong Democrat. When Willson cried his campaign slogan, "If elected, I will put down lawlessness with all the
power of my office," Judge Wells gave a resounding,
"Amen!" Augustus Willson went on to speak at Fulton,
Mayfield, and Princeton, but he skipped Cadiz and a number of smaller places where he might have been rotten-
egged. Judge Wells stumped the Black Patch for him.

"We've had a bellyful of men riding hooded by night, dispensing justice after their own diseased and distorted notion of justice. We have seen enough of the torch and blacksnake. Let us elect a fearless man who will root out these masked cowards and send them to the penitentiary, where they deserve to be." If Wells did not get many votes for Willson, he did give many a Night Rider a midnight shiver.

Henry Waterson, himself a staunch Democrat, nevertheless supported Augustus Willson's candidacy. "Let us stamp out this blight that is disgracing our fair state. Let us cease hanging our heads in shame that Kentucky has become known as the worst governed state in the Union." Charles Meacham wrote, "Let us crush this serpent of lawlessness with our heel!" Meacham fostered a new secret brotherhood known as the Law and Order League, that started out meeting clandestinely by night after the manner of the Night Riders, but came into the open when public opinion in Hopkinsville, and indeed the urban parts of Kentucky, backed them up.

Dr. Amoss, Guy Dunning, the Silent Brigade, realized that the tide was turning against them. In a manner of speaking it was the ancient feud between the city and the country. All this vocal urban prejudice gave aid and comfort to the Hillbillies and independents. Working under cover, the Trust began pouring gold into the fight. Trust buyers, with the new crop almost ready for market, were active, ready to grease the palm with gold of any farmer tied in with the Association. "When Augustus Willson gets to be governor, this Night Riding is going to be a thing of the past. The army is going to move in. You might just as well get on the bandwagon." As a leg up, they offered around 9c for prime leaf against the 7c and 8c the Association could command.

Amoss, Dunning and Ewing countered by pointing out that Augustus Willson had been for a number of years attorney for the American Tobacco Company, and he was spending lavishly in his campaign Tobacco Trust money. Willson's picture was tacked to almost every tree, fence post, and telephone pole across the country. Streamers with "Willson for Governor, Down with Night Riding," hung in most of the towns. Night Riders would often tear these down, and they took vindictive delight in shooting out Willson's face in the pictures. But there was a feeling in the underground that this was a crisis.

Down in Tennessee, where the politics of Kentucky were of no concern, the most active enemy of the Association was a neighbor to the Forts and Ewing, a man of the name of Ben Sory, of Adams, Tenn. Sory was a bully type of man, noisy and determined, and he bought tobacco for the Trust and he dared anybody to do anything about it. So bitterly did Sory fight the Association that it was said he, more than any other man, brought Night Riding about by his vindictiveness.

It was all adding up to the necessity for the Night Riders of doing something spectacular, such as pulling off the long-delayed raid on Hopkinsville, to prove they still had the upper hand.

And while they were at it, why not raid Clarksville? Clarksville was a hotbed of anti-Association sentiment. There were four large independent factories there buying for the American Tobacco Company, the Regies, and the Imperial. While Ben Sory at this time was not a manager of one of these warehouses, he had deep roots in the town, and a raid would be a sharp slap in his big mouth.

With tobacco cutting time close on hand, this would be barn-burning season, as spring was plant-bed-scraping time.

The underground had to get busy, what with Augustus Willson thundering up and down the land, editors spilling their
vitriol and numberless honest folk wanting only peace, and
a return to the good old carefree days. After all, they said,
the price of tobacco was just about what it had always been.

A rash of unaccountable fires broke out. Dr. Amoss observed the charred areas of old vacant houses in his travels;
there was hardly an empty tenant house left in the land.
Here and there a night fire would light the sky, and he
would see the following day where some occupied house
had gone up in smoke. On at least two occasions he heard
of homes that had burnt in broad, open day. One had been
fired while the family was at church. It might have been the
work of firebugs: roistering youths, returning late from
courting their girls, might answer their craving for excitement by setting a match to the dying weeds and grass of
isolated shacks which Negroes and poor whites had abandoned in their exodus from the Black Patch. But Night
Riders got credit for the work, and they had no means of
denying it. As terrorist activity it had dubious value, for
now and then good Association people woke to see their
tenant houses in flames. They cursed the Hillbillies for their
underhanded retaliation; and perhaps there was plenty of
this.

Yet long years afterward men with faded memories admired to sit around the country stores and on nail kegs at
the blacksmith shops, or the benches in the courthouse yard,
and recall that long and beautiful autumn of 1907. They
would compare tobacco crops and shake their heads in wonder. The rich tall plants reared proudly mule-high and knit
their dark leaves like a man and woman in heat. Rains had
fallen at just the right season. Pests had gone underground.
When time came for cutting, the hot dry days were jewels.

Barning was a simple task of muscle and sweat. Ah but that was one good year, I'm telling you. In retrospect men could see the hand of the Association and Night Riders in this fruitfulness.

But old men remember the sweet of the cider and not the apple cores and insect garbage at the bottom of the jug. They forgot the tension that ran under the surface of not only the harvest, but all the growing season. They forgot the rumors, the threats, the fears, the venom of the governor's face. They recalled only that the crop was short and the price was good.

For two good reasons the crop was short. One, there was a shortage of plants. Two, there was a shortage of labor. All the empty tenant shacks testifiied to the exodus of croppers. When you scraped a farmer's plant bed, you not only put him out of business that year, but the one or two or more croppers on his land. These displaced people first moved to Hopkinsville or Clarksville or some other town, in hope of finding jobs. They found instead that all the confusion and unrest of Night Riding had shut down the job market. Not much was left but that the folk try their fortunes in the fabulous lands of Texas, Oklahoma, Missouri or Arkansas. It was a time when almost everybody spoke of going to Texas or some place else. The West was still in the process of populating, and Arkansas, the closest, was advertising for migrants, the Cottonbelt Railroad offering cut-over timberlands and undeveloped bottoms for as low as $5 an acre, and years to pay. A man with a mule and wagon or a team could find public hauling, and if he had a work force, he could put them in the cotton fields, which rumor said were twice as tall as a man and made two bales to the acre. Sawmills offered wage work. No Night Riding down among the gin houses and lumber yards.

How many travelled to these promised lands nobody
ever counted. When J. Wesley Barefield was visited by
thirty-five Trigg County Riders the night of July 19, 1907,
his house fired into and the man told to get the hell gone or
take the consequences — he moved to Arkansas — it got
in the papers and people read about it. But the cropper on
the next farm who had opened his mouth too loudly decided
the time had come for him to load his household plunder
and wife and young in a wagon and take off, and hardly
anybody noticed it. "Looks like Luke Hank's shack is
empty," might be the only cognizance taken of his midnight
departure. But there were regions where it looked as if the
Black Death had been through the land. These refugees
sometimes made up long rumbling night trains out of the
tobacco patches, and at such ferries across the Mississippi
as Hickman, Ky., and Cottonwood Point, in Tennessee,
they would converge. Once over the river they would form
camps, drawing their wagons up into quadrangles like in
Indian fighting days, and buy out the little stores, or steal
the farmers bare, unless they stood guard over their crops
and hen roosts with shotguns. They sent up weird smokes to
ward off chills, panthers, and insects.

The end result of all this picturesque tragedy was a labor
shortage in the tobacco country, which was to echo as far
away as European marts, and maybe penetrated Duke's
"Wonderland" in New Jersey, or the stately halls of statuary at Rough Point in Newport. For the planters who managed to grow crops of tobacco, it spelled a good price. All
this would play into the hands of the resistance movement.
The American Tobacco Company would have to redouble
its efforts to buy Hillbilly tobacco, and strengthen the moral
fibre of the independents against the pressures of the Association and the brands and blacksnakes of the Riders.

Meanwhile, Willson's campaign was racing like wild fire across Kentucky, gathering in the peace-loving and searing Dr. Amoss and his armies. Felix Ewing heard Willson, and sent word forth to stand steadfast. A. O. Stanley came down from Washington and told the wavering to gird their loins and redouble their labors. In Washington he was still laboring indefatigably for the repeal of the 6c tax. Stanley was a man of stature which this early had not yet really begun to show. Of all the public figures of that day, he is one who seems to loom up in the proportions of a statesman. He became governor of Kentucky in 1915, after the troubles were over, and in 1919 was elected to the United States Senate. He was locking horns with Senator Nelson W. Aldrich, chairman of the Senate Finance Committee, who blocked the repeal bill as fast as the House passed it. It was said that Aldrich and James Duke had a "hot line" between New York and Washington and were, all through the tobacco troubles, in constant communication. It was alleged that Duke had Aldrich in the employ of the American Tobacco Company.

That fall tobacco prices got back finally to the 8c average that Ewing and Amoss had been struggling for. Four years of organized revolt had raised the price from less than 3c.

There were men — Willson was one of them — who insisted that Association should get out of the market and the Night Riders had better hang up their saddles, or else. Amoss and Ewing knew how false was this doctrine. It played straight into Trust hands. Let the Association and Underground ease off and prices would immediately drop.

The woods were full of governors going and coming, and J. C. W. Beckham, another Louisville man, did not want his administration to close December 10 in a blaze of burning

warehouses and charring tobacco barns. He pleaded plaintively with Ewing to haul in his Night Riders, and spoke
vaguely of sending in the militia. He offered rewards. He
was prevailed on to do nothing drastic by his Adjutant-
General Henry Lawrence, publisher of the Cadiz *Record,*
a county newspaper that had fought steadfastly for justice
in the tobacco wars. "Let these people alone," he said.
"They will work things out for themselves." If Beckham did
not understand the Black Patch, fortunately Lawrence did,
and his counsel prevailed.

It should be noted at this point that Beckham, Governor
Cox of Tennessee, Malcolm R. Patterson, who succeeded
him, and Augustus Willson were all city men. None had any
actual knowledge of farming conditions. Beckham and Willson were from Louisville. They were lawyers and politic-
ians, little known till the governorship brought them into
prominence. Louisville knew something about tobacco: it
was one of the raw leaf markets of the world. It did not
manufacture. I have been unable to learn of any important
manufacturers even through the Tobacco Institute. "We
have checked the Tobacco Division of Internal Revenue
Service, and the Tobacco Division, A. M. S. of the U. S.
Department of Agriculture where records are kept of tobacco manufactures. . . . Neither of these organizations
have any record of tobacco manufacturies operating in
Louisville during the period of 1900-1910." It is important,
for both Beckham and Willson would have been much more
sensitive to the tobacco troubles if their home city had been
deeply involved. As it was, the leaf came into warehouses,
went out on cars and steamboats, and even the laboring
force, mostly Negroes, were of no political consequence.

Willson thus was not a happy man for the governorship
to fall to, if sympathy for the growers' plight was wanted.

Ewing and Amoss and Dunning and all the Association underground made this obvious point, and they fought Willson bitterly. But if he carried the cities — and he probably would — his election was certain.

A thumbnail biography of Willson is in order. He came to Louisville in the seventies, entering a law firm with John M. Harlan, who afterward became associate justice of the U. S. Supreme Court. Now and then he stood for office on the Republican ticket and was regularly defeated. S. W. Hager was his opponent for governor, and was a weak candidate. Nothing in his background indicates a capacity for understanding the Kentucky tobacco planter. He was a Harvard graduate, M.A., and LL.D. His ancestors were new England people. His father had come down to Maysville, Kentucky, and gone into sawmilling and lumbering. There the elder Willson talked too much about slavery and because this was burley country, he had to depart for Indiana, where his doctrines found healthier soil. Later the Willsons removed to Louisville, and Augustus began his ascent to power in Republican circles. To be elected governor he would have to bring together a number of forces: the law-and-order middle class and the let-us-have-peace merchants and professional men, the preachers especially; the editors of metropolitan papers, and the strong Republican minority. The urban population cared little for the plight and poverty of farming folk; they were unduly sensitive to the "image" of Kentucky before the world and other states.

What the tobacco revolt needed was a man in authority who understood their problems. Amoss and Ewing and their followers saw no hope except the march step, torch, and persuasion.

Chapter Thirteen

Clarksville – Queen City
of the Black Patch

I REMEMBER THE TOWN WELL, OUT OF THE OLD TO-
bacco years. There were blocks of quaint old red brick
stores, the fronts down among the warehouses fly-specked
and gaudy with cheap merchandise displayed to catch the
hungry eyes of the tobacco-patch trade, the backs a catch-
all of garbage cans, snuff and tobacco spit. There were horse
stables, myriads of flies, and that curious atmosphere from
which legends are spun. Uptown the store fronts were gay
with fashions out of New York and Paris for the ladies,
though behind these emporiums the alleys were embroidered
with coalsheds, privies, tin cans, and smells. There were the
rotting foundations of tobacco factories, where a million
tons of dark-fired tobacco had come and gone, and now
were readying for the new 1907 crop. The long heat of
dusty autumn distilled the tobacco smells of generations of
men and crops.

When I'd walk the back ways, drawn by a shyness and
loneliness I did not understand then, I saw the naked behind

of this town called "Queen." In a dim shocked way I studied these contrasts of soiled nudity and clean-washed front. I was a tobacco boy changing into what I took for granted would be a tobacco man; and though the day was hot, I shivered. Out in the main arteries of buggies and wagons and carriages and milling folk, there was the rush and madness of circus day. Ringling Brothers, The Greatest Show on Earth had come to town. The entertainment-starved peasantry jammed the sidewalks and crannies and wagon parks. The men often wore celluloid collars, the mark of elegance for the rural swain of that day. Their red necks looked ghastly against the strange whiteness of the plastic. Sweat dribbled over the stiff edges of the collars, which the swain would mop with a limp handkerchief. But these young gallants determinedly retained their coats, a gesture to the social importance of the occasion. The tired old men wore suspenders, and their Sunday pants sacked up their rears with a curious outrage to my sense of aesthetics. I remember that I thought the women were more shabbily dressed than the men, even the girls with their beaus; and today a Ringling Brothers crowd fetching in the country folks would transform this. Wagons were parked back of the courthouse and in the quadrange off the square. Women sat here with quilts spread over straw, and suckled their babies with their breasts open to passing eyes and hungry flies. Heat waves blasted me in the face, and I recall one young mother modestly draping a diaper over her breasts while I looked at them.

"Here comes the parade!"

The bands broke into a howling racket and the elephant man came along shoving the crowds back on the sidewalks, and every window in every building on both sides was packed with spectators. The rumble and clatter of the

gaudy animal cages — most of them stingily closed save
for those of a cat or two and a host of monkey — the bands
high on the lumbering vehicles; the clowns, the lovely
painted creatures in waving plumes with those fixed smiles
as if they feared they might break the procelain make-up.
There was one pretty girl who looked straight down into my
eyes from an elephant and smiled; then the camels and the
giraffes and the horses and the ponies and another band —
it all soaked into my immature soul with the permanence of
tobacco stain. If you didn't have money to go into the big
tent you always had the feeling you'd seen most of what was
worth seeing.

But I'd saved a half dollar from my tobacco patch, and
when the parade had passed, I shambled to the show
grounds, pausing at a sign, "Three bottles 5c," put down a
nickel and reached for the three bottles. The woman yanked
two back and gave me the third. I drank the goo and waited
for the tent to open. I watched the sword swallower in front
of the sideshow tents and bearded lady. When at last the
main show opened I paid my quarter and went in. The cheap
seats filled so swiftly I barely had time to find one next to
a kind of pretty girl about my own age who had snuff stain
at her mouth. I pushed in close, and we just sat there till we
were shoulder and knee together. Then came the long
dreamy hours, the endless music, mostly in waltz time —
and my soul cried out in hunger for music; the pageantry,
the clowns, the entire big top was alive with what seemed
to me hundreds of pretty girls in red tights — and I a simple
boy from the sticks with my armpits just beginning to be
fertile with tender beard, and the girl by me, smells of sweat
and cheap tight brogan shoes, and manures and Hoyt's col-
ogne, and whisky and tobacco breath — well, it was a
dreamland of time and place. I never knew the girl's name,

where she lived, anything about her. I might have found out and later sent her a post card. When the show was over we parted with one last smile between us and I lost her in the crowd. Her face and smile linger on in the debris of my recollections. Then I went back out into the late afternoon sunlight, finding reality strangely unreal, and pressed through the people to the shaded avenue where Darius my father had parked the wagon. There were Victorian and Second Empire houses along this street, and we know somehow they were inhabited by foreign tobacco buyers. There were bearded Russians, looking like Tsars; Germans, looking like Bismark; the Italian fellows looking like tenors in Verdi operas; and the dapper English, dressing like the Prince of Wales. They came down to Clarksville from across the seas, until the American Tobacco Company practically abolished the breed by cutting out bidding at the warehouse floors and sending native buyers back to the barns. In the circus I'd almost thirsted to death from that awful strawberry soda and now I drank at the horse trough. With my last 5c I bought a big stick of peppermint candy. We loaded on the wagon and I crunched candy while Darius drove out of town.

I always wanted to remember the Queen City like that — filled with town smells and this haunting glamor. I remember seeing Ben Sory standing in front of the Board of Trade building, a heavy foreign-looking character, maybe forty years old, and sinister and hateful — for we knew he was opposed to Felix Ewing and hated the Fort boys and wanted to kill Dr. Amoss. He might have been Italian. He wore a purple-flowered shirt that no native would have been caught dead in; and his heavy jowls and bunchy black hair had the same Italianate character. Years since, all the edge has worn off my memories, for I've passed through Clarksville scores of times. The buyers are long done. The Victorian mansions have been razed. No more big tops, no more Darius driving the mule team through the night, chewing Star Navy and spitting ham gravy.

Now let us examine Ben Sory and his consorting with the Queen City.

He was sheriff of Robertson County, Tennessee, from 1890 till 1896. His arrogance had given him a manner of authority, and he'd been a ruthless if efficient sheriff. His home was at Adams, twenty miles northeast of Clarksville on what is now Highway 76. Today it's a sleepy little hamlet with a few fly-specked store windows boarded up. When Ben Sory was running his merchandise establishment and tobacco factory the place was thriving. He bought tobacco from the nearby farmers for the Trust combine — the American Tobacco Company, the Regie, and Imperial. From the moment of the Association's inception, he fought it, encouraging the farmers not to pool, and always having gold to pay the rebels. He defied the Association, blackguarded the head men in it, said that Felix Ewing was nothing but a crook hungering and thirsting for power, that Dr. Amoss should long ago have had his throat cut and that Guy Dunning should be shot at sunrise. He had as little use for Charles and Joel Fort. All these men were lawless and pretty soon the law would catch up with them and land the whole kit and kilter in the penitentiary. All he ever said about Mrs. Ewing was that she was a lovely woman to be wasted on an anemic sickly man like Felix Ewing.

His open feuding with Ewing, the Association, and the Night Riders had begun three years back when twenty Association members visited him about ten o'clock one night at his fishing camp two miles away on the Red River. These were Stainback men, among the first to night-ride. Tonight they were not hunting trouble. They wanted Sory to join up with the Association because of the man's prestige and influence. George Whitehead acted as spokesman. "Hey in there, Mr. Sory. Hello, hello." The rest of the men stood back in the gloom. A lantern burnt in the window. There was the smell of the catfishy river, and the small sad noises of the insects in the tall grass and cockleburrs. Sory's big frame filled the door, and his rasping voice warned, "Stay where you are! What you men want?"

Whitehead explained courteously. Then a young man, Sory's nephew, showed up in the door, waving a pistol. Ben said, "Go see who they are."

The young man came with the lantern, held the light to each face, and each man gave his name. Sory knew them all; some were his neighbors. He finally shook his head. "I don't intend to join up with you fellers. I got no use for breaking the law. I don't like Felix Ewing and I want no part in anything he's heading up. Those fellers up in Kentucky ought to be in jail. I don't want to discuss it any farther." The nephew went back in and Sory slammed the door and hooded the lantern.

But the Association men kept gnawing at the idea. They needed Sory. He would be worth a small army when it came to bringing Robertson County into the pool. Anything to shut his bitter mouth. When the Adams lodge met, J. H. Stroud, the chairman, appointed a new committee to call on Sory. Stroud lived on the same street in Adams that Ben Sory did, and their wives were on good terms, and maybe these cordial connections would win Sory. The committee moved in a body to Sory's factory, Stroud himself politely asking merely that Ben receive them and listen ten minutes. Sory seemed to think the visitation was hostile, for he shouted at Stroud to get the hell gone, and immediately

boarded up his store and factory and hired a guard composed of his farmer friends to stand by armed to the teeth.
No Association committee was going to face a lot of guns.
Ben Sory began a campaign of invective against Stroud, the
neighbors, the Association, and the Night Riders in particular. He apparently expected his next visitors would be armed
and masked men.

The Forts, Ewing, the lodges, and even Dr. Amoss toiled
in the Red River vineyard with great diligence in the following months, one by one wooing away Sory's farmers,
until all at once Sory found his tobacco suppliers dried up.
A whispering campaign boycotted his mercantile business.
In the end he had to close his store, and his tobacco warehouse stayed boarded up for good. He moved to Clarksville,
where he interested an old associate by the name of Hayes in
putting up some money. The two together canvassed the
business men of the town to raise capital, saying, "If we
don't the Association is going to move in here and then
where will the independent market be?" Their persuasion
and the veiled threats of Ewing's outfit, which still had no
funds to pay for leaf, payed off and they raised enough cash
to buy a big vacant warehouse and thus established the
Hayes-Sory Company. Clarksville started out being hostile
to the Association and Night-Rider activity up in Kentucky.
The fact that it could very well spread down into Tennessee,
maybe even cause the city to be raided, only deepened the
town's determination to remain a "free market." Sory kept
hammering at his feud, growing more bitter and vindictive
as his tobacco business once more prospered. His venom
knew no bounds when one of his spies, whom he had in-
duced to go to Kentucky and join the Silent Brigade, returned with a report that things there were seething. Hell
was being raised everywhere, and all sorts of plans were

afoot to come to Clarksville in force, burn the city to ashes, kill Sory, and murder every man, woman and child who wouldn't aid and abet the Night Riders. How much of this was mere terror talk — for the Silent Brigade had a way of screening out suspicious members and filling them with propaganda to carry back—is impossible now to prove. Ben Sory swallowed enough to be convinced that a saturation raid was planned on Clarksville and that his own life was in danger.

He began to operate under cover, and Thomas Menees, a small merchant at Cedar Hill, became one of Sory's partners in the purchase of a threshing outfit at the opening of the wheat harvest. It was on old-timey stream traction engine and lumbering separator which travelled from one farm to another threshing wheat. Menees took no chances with his machine, knowing the ill esteem Sory was held in, and he employed an armed guard nightly to watch after the day's work was done. On the night of July 16, when men and guards were sleeping under the stars in the fresh straw, forty Night Riders fell upon them, disarmed the guards, placed sticks of dynamite in the engine and separator, and blew them to smithereens.

When Sory got the call from Menees about the destruction of the thresher, he hopped the train for Cedar Hill to get the situation first hand. He ran into Colonel Joel Fort on the train. Sory gave one look at the "wheelhorse" and found an object on which to vent his wrath. He began cursing. "Fort, it's your hell-raising and inflammatory speeches that made those goddamn Riders of yours blow up my threshing machine!" In his fury he reached for the gentlemanly, spare-built organizer, hauled him out in the aisle, and began beating his ears back. Sory weighed upwards of 200 pounds. Fort weighed less than 150. The ex-sheriff

was a fighter by nature. In no time at all he had Fort in the
aisle and had broken his glasses, knocked out two teeth, and
was trying to strangle him when the conductor and flag-
man, and passengers who knew both men, leaped in and
pulled Sory off the bleeding half-blinded Fort. The rest of
the way the two hostile passengers were kept in separate
cars.

Before this savage beating there had been plenty of hostility between the factions. All the latent bitterness now
came to the surface. Fort was laid up for several days from
the beating. Felix Ewing went to see him, and said, "It was
nothing but a bully beating a good man. I'll see what can
be done about it." He evidently planned to get into communication with Dr. Amoss, who would set the proper
forces moving. Immediately Ewing could send out the word,
"Buy no more goods from Tom Menees." There was a secret report that Dr. Amoss was ready to make a raid on
Clarksville and destroy Ben Sory's factory. At once, the
Association forces began a boycott on Menees. On Saturdays after this, there were few wagons and buggies tied at
Menees' hitching rack, and his store was practically empty.
Nothing was left to him but to close. Sory helped him float
another loan to buy a new threshing outfit, but by now the
word had gone up and down Robertson County for Association people to give their threshing to other outfits. By
this time Menees was bankrupt. He auctioned his store and
returned the threshing machine to the Case Company that
had sold it, gathered his farming equipment and livestock
and family, and moved to Missouri. There were no tobacco
associations and no Night Riders in Missouri.

Although Ewing, Amoss, and the organized tobacco men
had boycotted Ben Sory and run him out of Adams, and
now had boycotted Tom Menees and sent him kiting to

Missouri, at this time they apparently did not understand fully what a potent weapon they had in the boycott. Almost any town in the Black Patch could have been brought to its knees by it. The Night Riders were feeling out the possibilities of dynamiting threshing outfits. Wheat at this time was literally the staff of life. Next to corn, men lived by wheat. There was no wasp's-nest bread in the stores, the kind where if you squeeze the loaf it squirts. Wheaten bread was hot biscuits for breakfast, mixed with buttermilk and soda, and you buttered two while they were hot. Self-rising flour was unknown. After ten biscuits, butter and sorghum molasses, a tobacco farmer would fare forth for a good morning's work, and expect not to cave in from hunger before 11:30 when the dinner bell rang and he could take out his team and go to the house. When you blasted the thresher that harvested his wheat, you cut off his food. Yet the only thresher destroyed at this time was that of John W. Langford, who lived at Port Royal and threshed for Hillbillies. He posted twenty guards around his outfit, arming them with Winchesters. The cost of this kind of police service consumed all his profits. He moved to Sumner County. The Night Riders followed, and the next season at a time of heavy rains when Langford's outfit was bogged in the mud, they fell on him and burnt it, running the traction engine into the nearby flooded creek and whipping the strawboss, Jonas Stacey.

During this time there were four tobacco warehouses in Clarksville, Sory buying for the Regie, others buying for the American Tobacco Company, still another "independent." Only one belonged to the Association. More and more pooled tobacco was being grown in Roberston County, but much of it moved to other marts — Guthrie, Bowling Green, Hopkinsville. Ben Sory decided he would liquidate Ewing's

factory. He went to the county officers and city administration and got himself appointed as official authority over all
the warehouses in Clarksville and out in the small surrounding towns. He hired guards, and started a campaign to in-
timidate the Association people, both farmers and ware-
housemen. He would arrest drivers of tobacco loads and
pretend to search them for dynamite, damaging the cargo as
much as he dared. He would hale the drivers into magis-
trate's court and even though he lost most of his cases, he
annoyed people to the verge of murder. He sent patrols out
over the country roads, ostensibly following tips of Night
Rider activity, but actually to enrage farmers in the pool.
Ewing and the Forts concluded they would close the Association factory in Clarksville and take that business to
Guthrie. In this move they were motivated almost as much
by the insulting activity of the Tobacco Board of Trade as
by Sory's work. Word went out for no more tobacco to be
wagoned into Clarksville and when the last carload of Association leaf was shipped the big lumbering place was
empty.

In effect the action was a boycott of the merchants and
tradesmen of Clarksville, and very shortly, in the height of
the tobacco season, business fell off to such an extent that
the town was filled with consternation. There was talk of
ruin, bankruptcy. It hit the Queen City right in her pocket-
book, for Ewing's outfit had brought perhaps as much as
50 percent of the trade to it. There was honest hate of lawlessness, and the constant threat of a major raid — moving
the Association factory might indicate such was in the
cards — kept people worried and sleepless. There was an
unaccountable distrust of Ewing and the Forts. But once
an artery was cut to the Queen's gold coffers, she quickly

enough made peace and invited Ewing to bring his pool back home.

But Ben Sory was in no mood for compromise, and he laid his plans to wreck the Association and unhorse the Night Riders, and above all preserve the town against a raid.

Once his partner Hayes said to him, "You can't handle those Rider rascals. They're too heavy a majority for you."

Ben Sory rejoined grimly, "Recollect what old Andy Jackson once said when somebody reminded him about the majority against him? 'One strong man makes a majority.' "

Chapter Fourteen

Tandy & Fairleigh and Latham Circus Will Be in Town

FELIX EWING, AND DR. AMOSS AND HIS BRAVES, KNEW very well that Ben Sory was making his brags that the Night Riders would never raid Clarksville. It was a dare and a challenge, but Amoss and Dunning shrugged it off. They had Hopkinsville still to discipline. The plan had been to raid Hopkinsville soon after the raid on Princeton. That scheme had fallen through. But it remained the goal of the underground. Now that Augustus Willson's campaign was in high gear, and every city and town and hamlet, save those in the Black Patch, heard the theme song "If elected I pledge to use every power of my office to put down lawlessness," it seemed to the Night-Rider hierarchy that perhaps the best, maybe the only way, to defeat Willson was to stage the long-delayed raid just before election day. Perhaps it was devious reasoning. Dr. Amoss realized the effect might be just the opposite of that. A dramatic display of lawlessness might push Willson across the precarious threshold of victory. In any case the world would be well informed that no Black Republican, seconded by the lily-white shouting Judge Wells, could bluff the righteous cause of tobacco revolt.

Small tobacco factory — the old Ryan-Hampton Manufacturing Co., Martin, Tennessee.

In the beautiful fall weather in the Black Patch, with tobacco cut and hanging in the barns, and fragrant hickory smoke drifting languidly from the curing fires in the autumn evenings, Dr. Amoss and Guy Dunning drilled the Night

Riders at the various lodges — Wallonia, Nabb, Cobb, Fredonia, Cadiz. After a day's work in tobacco harvest, these farmers still had energy enough to go through the techniques of battle. At the end of an arduous drill session they would toss themselves on the ground, temper their craving with pipe and chew and homerolled cheroot, and the young bloods would light a Lucky or a pipe of Duke's Mixture. There would be desultory talk.

"Well, will it be Augustus Willson?"

"It will, if Judge A. J. G. Wells has his d'ruthers."

"Goddamn his soul."

"It would give me pleasure to assassinate that rascal," Dr. Amoss was once heard to remark.

"I heard him speak," Dunning said. "I got so mad I walked off. I'd have butchered him then and there."

"You men had better scatter for the night," Dr. Amoss said. "We have more work ahead."

The men dispersed and Amoss lingered a few moments for private talk with Guy Dunning. "I don't like what I hear about that skunk Ben Sory down at Clarksville."

Dunning said, "I don't either." The men reflected. "Are you thinking of the same thing I am?"

"We have half a dozen fellows who would carry out the command."

"Do you want to give the word?"

Dr. Amoss studied and finally shook his head. "I might have the day after I heard how he beat up Fort. Now I'm not sure I want to bloody our names with murder. Sory's fought us tooth and nail, but we've fought him too. When we went into this one of our slogans was 'No Bloodshed.' No, let's not kill him. One little ambush would do it. But just as soon as we get Hoptown off our hands we'll see what we can do to his tobacco factory."

That would mean no open raid, but a picked squad of arsonists. No dramatics, just a prime job of burning out an enemy. The men parted and Amoss went on to his buggy. He drove at an easy trot by the road which followed land-lines and reflected with satisfaction on the progress they had made in what they now spoke of as "The Wars." Along the road there were new frame houses going up in place of the unpainted barnlike houses that stood in the yards. There were the new white outdoor toilets he had always recom-mended. "A man should learn to crap in a clean house," he had a way of saying. He passed a couple of new churches. Tobacco at last was up to the old pre-Night-Rider price of 8c average. Association leaf was commanding full market price in open competition. Ewing was moving past accumu-lations of crops. Once there was a sale for 25c, a fabulous price. A Hillbilly was almost a thing of the past. It was gratifying to think these were marks of success of Night Riding and Association organization, good sense on the part of the growers.

There were ten major Association warehouses, all busy and prosperous. Paducah, Clarksville, Hopkinsville, Rus-sellville, Princeton, Murray, Guthrie and Cadiz, in descend-ing order. Thirty-nine thousand hogsheads of tobacco had passed across these sales floors up to this time in 1907, for a total of five and a half million dollars. Banks had money; they were bulging with it. Farmers were paying off mort-gages. People had "rattle money" in their pockets. Women-folk were buying new clothes. No more could a Louisville flour manufacturer say, "Every time the wind blows down in Dixie you read XXXX flour on the women's pants." John Robinson's, Ringling Brothers, Forepaugh & Sells Brother's, Barnum & Bailey's, all were coming through the Black Patch this fall. When the circuses travelled, there was cash,

Merchants bellyached about the inroads of Sears & Roebuck. "Them sons-of-bitches skim off the cash cream and leave us the whey of store credit," they cursed. "Did you know that fellow Roebuck was a *nigger?*" Dr. Rucker at Hopkinsville had bought one of those infernal gas buggies and was chug-chugging around in his practice, though he kept horses handy just in case he had to phone home for a team to come pull him out of the mud.

This prosperity was no illusion, but it griped Amoss and his followers that revived prosperity played into the hands of Augustus Willson.

"The work of lawless men is finished. Why not unsaddle the Night Riders? Let them disband and return to decent living. Tobacco's back to its long-time price. If there is a Trust, it's licked. Elect me. A vote for me is a vote for the law-abiding and decency and peace. Or else!" he added.

"Give us peace!" the Law and Order League was crying, their lodges springing up and spreading like Jonah's gourd.

Day Riders, so-called, were adding their war cry. "Let's have an end to this Night Riding."

Up in New York, James Duke was deep in trouble with the Federal Government. Laws were being passed in both Kentucky and Tennessee. The Crecelius Law allowed heavy damages to any Association member that bootlegged his pledged tobacco to a Trust buyer.

"Now you fellows just lie low and take it easy," the restless business man argued. Many were silent members of the Night Riders and Association and now that tobacco prices were back to normal, they would like to withdraw. Just let things quiet down, now, and it would be like in the good old days.

Dr. Amoss, Ewing, the Forts, answered, "Yes, and let us ease up and the first good old days would be 3-2-1, as fast as Buck Duke can depress prices." A considerable portion of the 1905 crop and 1906 crop remained unsold. Now the 1907 crop was moving onto the market. On the surface it did look as if the worst were over. But the Night Riders must ride, and there was the Hopkinsville raid yet to be pulled off.

Dr. Amoss set the date — November 19, 1907. This would be just before election.

There were still "small depredations"—seventy-five Riders went into the Bainbridge neighborhood near Hopkinsville and told eight farmers to join the Association. They promised. There were some barn burnings here and there. A heavy canvass of the Forts brought in 229 names, leaving only two communities outside the Association. On November 8 there were twenty-four sales on the M. H. Tandy & Co. floors, prices ranging from about 6c to 11c. Some hundred buyers were bidding, mostly the American Tobacco Company's men, the Imperial, the American Snuff Company, and P. E. West & Co., one of the smaller Trust units. They were all under indictment, and this show of competition might be for propaganda purposes, or a dry run in preparation for the real thing when the Trust was ordered disbanded by the U. S. Courts. On November 13, six masked men removed a buyer for the American from a Hillbilly home and brutally beat him with a stick. "Get the hell back to Hoptown!" they told him, and beat up as he was, the man crawled into his buggy and drove from Pilot Knob to Hopkinsville at 1 A.M. through a misty chill rain mixed with sleet. The Hillbilly took off through his back fields or the floggists would have waited on him also.

But the biggest blast of excitement was in the forenoon of November 14, when without warning 150 riders descended upon the jittery town at a moment when it was so keyed-up with rumors of raid, it was obsessed and ready to scream at any strange noise under its bed. The leader of this band was H. C. Helsley, a farmer from the northeastern part of Christian County. As the men hitched their horses at the racks around the courthouse, Helsley said to the curious men who moved in to see what this was all about, "We're not Night Riders. We got no masks concealed in our hip pockets. There's not a gun on any of us. We're members of the Society of Equity, and good church members and heads of families. All we want is to have a meeting in the court room and pass some resolutions and then some visiting around the tobacco buyers. Anybody's welcome to come listen to me make a speech." At 1:00 he talked to a sizable audience, his followers and some townsfolk, and all his words were reasonable and for peace. A committee of resolutions, consisting of himself, J. T. Lile, M. H. Dukes, G. W. Barnes, G. B. Powell, T. T. Powell, and F. B. McCown, wrote up their credo, peace, justice, and fair prices, and after that the men went to all the warehouses, factories and buyers' places and presented copies, asking only that their words be read. Almost every man contacted expressed himself in agreement in principle with the purposes of the Equity. Then the Equity riders went out of town in the late afternoon, and Hopkinsville settled back. This happened just five days before the date planned for the real raid.

In the late afternoon on November 19, well before night, squads of unmasked men formed in Cadiz, Princeton, Cobb, Wallonia, Otter Pond, and Nabb and began moving toward the rendezvous at an old abandoned church in the forks of the road on what is now Highway 60 a few miles west of Gracey. Gracey at this time was a busy thriving village on the I.C. railroad, not yet having suffered the saturation raids from which it never recovered. The afternoon was bleak and gusty, with an increasingly chill wind straight off the icebergs in the north. Men riding in from Calloway, Trigg, Lyon and Caldwell Counties dismounted stiffly and went into the old church where some one had built a roaring fire in the old pregnant-bellied stove. They beat their hands and muttered, "Jesus-God it's cold as hell!" Guy Dunning was early and Dr. Amoss appeared not long afterward. By this time — close to gray dusk — the grounds were filled with horses. The distance to Hopkinsville was eleven miles. The violence and bitterness of the north wind made it seem an unpropitious time for the great raid. But Dunning dispatched men with pole climbers and pliars for Gracie. "Cut the wires!! We can't have somebody phoning in ahead." After time had been allowed for this chore — it was now dark — the order was given to move. The Riders formed and jogged along the icy road. It took some time for this military formation to file through Gracie. Then a messenger caught up with Amoss and Dunning.

"Somebody got word in ahead. Chuck Meacham and all the police force and Company D right this minute are loading their shooting irons for you fellows! Better call it off."

Dr. Amoss blew blasts on his ram's horn and the long columns halted. The fellow was a lukewarm member of the Silent Brigade. He might by lying. Guy Dunning said, "If you're lying, we're going to kill you. Who informed on us?"

The man shivered in terror. "I swear to God it's true. I don't know who called, all I know is if you go to Hoptown tonight you'll smell hot lead."

The rising gale was sufficient alibi. "All right, boys, pass the word along," Dr. Amoss said. "We don't want anybody to get killed in this business." Anyway, in this high wind, if they'd gone on in and fired the factories the conflagration would have swept the entire town, and it was better to call

it off. They would know later if they were dealing with one
of the counter spies. Dunning promised, "Bub, if you're
lying you'd better get the hell out of these parts tonight, or
your name's mud."

Like a good general, Dr. Amoss hated to turn back after
all these weeks of planning and drilling. But again like a
good general, he had the courage to call off the raid if the
Riders would have to enter Hopkinsville shooting. It came
out soon enough that the man who'd warned Dunning and
Amoss not to go was right. He himself had not called in the
information; it was a buyer for the Trust in Gracie. But in
Hopkinsville Charles Meacham, the mayor, the sheriff, Company D, Major Bassett, and some hundred citizens quickly
sworn in as deputies hustled out to guard the incoming roads
and fire into any hostile horsemen seen abroad. A spy sent
on a run picked up the information that the Night Riders
had dispersed. Thus it proved a dry run for everybody.
Rather sadly Dr. Amoss concluded his Riders likely would
never manage the great raid.

Meanwhile Augustus Willson's campaign came to a
whirlwind finish and he was elected governor of Kentucky
by 18,000 votes.

Willson would not assume the duties of his office until
December 10. Dr. Amoss and Guy Dunning — and tacitly
Felix Ewing and the Forts — staged the long-delayed raid
on the night of December 6, running into the morning of
December 7th. In the interval between the raid that failed
and December 6, the region around and in Hopkinsville had
been combed for recruits sympathetic with the Association
and the underground. Amoss made every effort to see there
were no leaks. He kept the actual date of the enterprise to
himself, sharing only with Dunning, until the last possible
moment. Then word went out swiftly for the clans to gather

at the old rendezvous at the forks of the Wallonia, Cobb and Princeton road off from the road to Cadiz. Riders gathered from the four winds. The weather was fine and warm for this time of winter. The main body consisted of lodges in Trig, Lyon, and Caldwell Counties. Dr. Amoss addressed them. "Bloodshed is not a part of our business. We depend on the surprise attack, the disarming of the law and population; we want no increased criticism of killing. Our attack is on the Trust; our job is to burn Trust warehouses and Trust tobacco." It was the spectacle they wanted; the excitement of a coordinated military movement which they could remember with pride, and their enemies recall with shudders. Neither was destroying tobacco their sole object. Otherwise they would have sent in a dozen trusted arsonists with torch and dynamite and accomplished the task without undue fuss and lost motion. They were telling the world, and Augustus Willson, that the Silent Brigade of Night Riders were still in control. Then a preacher was called upon to bless the enterprise, and the order was shouted, "March!"

The body of horsemen moved into the big road toward Gracey. They rode at ease, hoods and masks and guns ready. It was a bland night, men remembered afterward, more like April than December. Along the road the tobacco barns were smoking, the pungent odor filling the starry gloom. The past days had been like Indian Summer, and the land was sweet and warm. Little laughter or talk rose from the long columns going southward. At the junction of the roads the Riders turned east into the Hopkinsville highway. Guy Dunning rode at the head of the line. Dr. Amoss rode in a buggy about the center. More squads from Calloway and Trigg joined near Gracie. When the advance guard entered the little town, linesmen

who had been planted ahead climbed poles and cut the
telephone lines. There was always a chance some spy had
reported the movement. Law enforcement had made their
threats. "We know all your plans. We have spies posted in
every lodge. When you come we'll be ready." It may have
been talk, or it could easily have been fact. In any case here
at last the Night Riders were on the move. For nine miles
they travelled as quietly as some five hundred men and
horses could go. They reached a schoolhouse and play-
ground two miles from Hopkinsville about 11 o'clock and
turned in, bivouacing and placing nosebags on their horses
for oats and corn, so the beasts would not be hungry when
the men returned from their errand — and perhaps hastily,
with the law on their tails.

While the nags ate, the men lay about on the ground
smoking, chewing, having a drink from bottles fetched along
for Dutch courage. It was little different from a typical surprise attack during the Civil War.

Dr. Amoss and Guy Dunning were restless, and kept
watching the road. There should be spies coming out to
meet them. When men did appear, they reported, "Town's
dead as a hammer. Not a soul suspects. You need only move
in and take over."

"You're sure?"

"Absolutely."

"What about the police — any extra men sworn in?"

"We've been in town since the middle of the afternoon.
Came in on the train. Squads of fellows have been about, in
the saloons and down at the livery stables. We've been careful not to rouse suspicion. The coast is clear."

Guy Dunning then told off twenty-five men to serve as
hostlers. He gave orders. "Masks and hoods, men." They
donned their gear. "Ready?" As far as anybody could tell

this was the zero hour. "Dr. Amoss, do you have any final instructions?" Dr. Amoss repeated the orders. The battle plan had been worked out for weeks and days. "March!"

The men wore gunnysacks to deaden their footfalls, but they marched in two files with the swing of veterans. Just outside the city limits, where the Illinois Central tracks crossed the highway, they halted again, adjusting sleeve bands for identification. In that long moment of silence men remembered the dying crickets sawing in the dead weeds along the road. They could see dark houses and Negro shacks where city and country met. There was a line of section houses just ahead. The men were tense, for danger was by no means over. It was about one o'clock and the stars were dimming. Then at a low command the columns moved again, parting, one line going into town by the dirt road, the other taking to the railroad and walking the ties. One group entered town by the bridge over Little River; the other went in by way of the I.C. depot. They converged on 9th Street. Here and there they might encounter lurking figures. Low challenges identified these as men who had ridden into town earlier in the day and put up with friends or posted their horses at the livery stables, or others who had come in on the trains and mostly loitered at the saloons. Close observation would have tied these seemingly unrelated strangers into a menace. But for some reason hard now to understand, considering the vigilence and sensitiveness of Hopkinsville to night-riding, no one apparently suspected the influx of rough farmers as parcel of a night attack.

Practically on the second, the various squads reached their battle stations. The main body marched one block to Main Street and captured the Home telephone office so the girls there would not warn the police and townsfolk.

Another squad captured the Police Station near the court-house on Main. Another group fell upon the Cumberland telephone office. Still another made their way to the office of Charles Meacham's *Kentuckian*. Other points of note were the residence of Lindsey Mitchell, a notorious buyer of Trust tobacco. But the real objects were the Latham factory next to the L. & N. depot at the eastern end of 9th Street, and the Tandy & Fairleigh warehouse five blocks south on Campbell Street, next to the Association ware-house and the impressive Acme Flour Mills. A squad looked after the Armory, to prevent Company D from arming itself when the alarm sounded.

Things picked up so fast, and all at once, that it is dif-ficult to report the events in isolation. At the Police Station officers E. N. Miller, W. T. Broderick and Joe Claxton were sleepily playing checkers and smoking long green, vigilantly thinking no evil nor hearing any Night Rider. They came to with stunned grunts when masked men poured through the door and covered them with shotguns and pistols. "Stick 'em up, one move and you're dead men!" Booth Morris, the night chief, had gone home. Whether he would have avoided this outlandish and humiliating business by swift and fearless action remains a question. At that moment the telephone rang. There was a lot of shooting in the place for a few moments, bul-lets and buckshot clattering around the walls and ceiling. Miller started to answer the phone. He caught some bunching shot in the seat of his britches. A startled female voice screamed, "The Night Riders are here, help, help!" A Night Rider answered, "Hell yes, and the Night Riders are here." Her voice was cut off in the middle of a warn-ing yell.

While the Riders were rounding up the crestfallen cops,

who realized they were going to catch hell for not being more vigilant, over at the Fire Department six firemen were getting a going over. These were John Lawson, Lee Morris, Ernest Haydon, Bob Tunks, Ennis Morris and John Hines. What they were doing at the moment is not of record, but around fire stations are always well worn checker boards and packs of greasy cards. Ernie Haydon was first to hear the noise outside, and he peered out of the window to see what was out there. The glass smashed all about his head and he jerked back with an oath. Before any of the others could start up, a pack of masked figures shoved in and covered the firemen with guns. "Don't leave! We got orders to shoot every living thing, men or horses, that attempt to leave this building!" It was the good old days when fire-fighting equipment was powered by hay burners, and the engines at the moment were taking on fuel in the form of alfalfa. Thus immobilized, the fire fighters settled back, knowing when the big blazes rose they would be powerless.

This while both telephone offices were in the hands of Night Riders. It was impossible, thus, for any word to leak to local officers or nearby towns. At the Cumberland office, Squad 4 brought the two night operators, Miss Curtis and Miss Boyd, out to the curb of the sidewalk. They were in their night clothes, both girls having turned in on their cots for the night. Some uncouth Rider started to curse them. A gentlemanly Rider kicked his shin. "Shut up that cussing, you sonnabitch. Can't you see you in the presence of ladies?" That was one version of the report. Charles Meacham gave a more civilized one. "Cut out that cursing and remember you are in the presence of ladies." At the Home office something of the same drama was being enacted.

The main job was burning the two tobacco factories. The squads marched efficiently to their stations. Tandy & Fairleigh was an immense building of brick and wood and tarred paper and Fairbanks scales and sheds and platforms. The eyeballs of the revolutionaries had been itching for months to set the torch to this gathering of pine planks, knot holes, paint, tobacco tars, and litter, dreaming of the "goddamdest fire in Kentucky!" The Latham warehouse was hardly less tempting. Both were piled to the ceiling in places with Trust tobacco. There was an estimated quarter million dollars of leaf in both factories.

By this time the town was a pandemonium. On all the main streets the gunfire reminded old Confederate soldiers of some of the battles they had been in where killing Yanks was a serious business. Pistols, rifles, shot guns — they drummed a steady uproar, and bullets sang and bounced and clattered. When a frightened citizen lighted a lamp or switched on a bulb, his shadow was immediately pulverized. Windows were shattered. People rushing out to see at first hand the wild doings were instantly arrested and shoved into a corral in a dead-end street. Judging from the musketry half the population was being annihilated.

At the Latham warehouse, men broke through the doors being armed with axes for the task. Others carried cans of coal oil. Diving into the regions where tobacco lay dark in the gloom, the oilmen dashed the kerosene about. Others threw old boxes, paper, some chairs, whatnot of junk. A dozen matches were struck by matchmen. The flames began to leap up, showing the weird and savage hooded arsonists. When certain the fire was going good, they backed out into the night, standing there till the flames started bursting through the windows, and the eddying blaze and smoke rose to the stars.

They wasted no time dashing four blocks to the Tandy & Fairleigh factory. Tandy & Fairleigh bought for the Italian Regie, and men remembered how the Regie had sued after Princeton, how this "wop outfit" had labored to grind down Kentucky growers. Their hate for the foreign Regies surpassed their hate for the American Tobacco Company, if that were possible. The past days a steady movement of leaf had been coming in from the farms. They fell upon Tandy & Fairleigh with a vengeance.

A great lurid light was blowsing up from the Latham place when the night watchman of the Tandy barn looked out and saw shadows hurrying their way, and listened to the horrific gunfire downtown. The watchman's name was W. E. Shanklin, and he did not have to be told what was about to happen to his place of business. He got ready to defend his honor and his job. But before he could make show of his bravery a fusillade of bullets rattled around the walls and sheds and crashed the windows, and Shanklin dove for the basement. Cowering there, he listened to doors being shattered by lawless hoodlums, the shoving and hauling of wicked men breaking in with kerosene and dynamite, and when the flames began to crackle overhead, and gleams of light sift down to his hiding place, he realized this was no trap for even a brave man to be caught in with his britches down. When swirls of heat and smokes eddied to him, he trundled a hogshead to one of the low windows, broke it with a brick, and began the arduous task of squeezing himself through the opening. He managed to wriggle out, cutting his hands and face in the escape, and stood outside staring at the roaring inferno of Latham factory. The eddies of smoke and sparks created a weird and ugly and beautiful picture. Already inside his own domain the same thing was happening. Here at the rear of the building he could only hear the uncouth carryings on, sounding like savages staging a dawn attack. They yelled and cavorted and discharged their guns. Away off, downtown and back among the residences, there was a confusion of sounds, compounded of terror and the rise and fall of gunfire as the Night Riders shot at every window or door showing a light. It struck Shanklin that Night Riders were only bad boys grown tall. Hearts don't change much after all.

Things began to look ominous for the bad boys when firebrands started dropping down upon the rooves of the Association factory and the Acme Flour Mills. There might be some excuse for burning bootleg tobacco, but when it came to destroying Association leaf, and burning the makings of good hot breakfast biscuits, that was another horse.

As the fires caught up, some one yelled, "Go tell the 'Gineral' to turn the fire engines loose!"

Word was relayed swiftly to Dr. Amoss, who was down on Main Street overseeing the warlike details. His headquarters were near the courthouse, and in the center of the shooting and howling and clangor and din. Guy Dunning saw for the first time that their General was wounded.

"Dr. Amoss! You're bleeding!"

"It's nothing. Get word to the fire department to hurry."

"But you are wounded," Dunning insisted, pausing a moment to watch Dr. Amoss make futile dabs at a skull wound that looked like a small severed artery. It was at a spot where Amoss himself could not get at it, and nobody else knew what to do.

"Go get the call through. It's nothing but a glancing bullet."

Here came the fire engines, and the Fire Marshal on horseback grim and determined. The equipment churned past and there was a momentary pause in the commotion. By now the fires were riding high, red and lurid against the sky.

While Dr. Amoss continued to pad his bandage against the seepage of blood, a squad assigned to the Mitchell residence to pay their respects to W. L. Mitchell, the Imperial Regie buyer, stood at the sidewalk and yelled, "Come out of there, Mitch, you son of a bitch." They underscored their demand by shooting out all the front windows, front and upstairs.

A quavering female voice cried from somewhere in the house, "Please, men, please! My baby's terribly sick and my husband can't come out."

The shooting got too hot and Mitchell called, "I'm coming."

"We won't hurt you," one voice said, but another amended, "We sure as hell will!"

Mitchell stooped out through the front door, making as good a show of bravery as he could. Riders began beating him over the head with their guns. The chief of the squad protested when this brutality threatened to kill the buyer, "He's had enough, lay off." They read him a warning. "You stop buying for the Regie or the next time we won't stop 'em when they beat your head off!" The light of the fires illuminated the scene, and Mitchell was bloody from head to foot. The Riders drew together and turned to go. Mitchell lay on the sidewalk, groaning. His wife came afterward and dragged him back in the house.

Fire Chief E. H. Hester, arrested when he had at first tried to reach the fire station, had his pumping outfit going out at the Association roof and the flour mill. Negro

houses nearby were beginning to burn. They let the two
warehouses burn.

Two blocks off 9th Street from Main stood the two-
story old brick building housing the Hopkinsville *Kentuckian,* editor and publisher Charles Meacham. Meacham
had been lambasting the Night Riders with a vindictive
quill pen and an acid vocabulary. As mayor of the city
he naturally was a law abiding man. When all the shooting began, he started downtown from him home a little
way out, but when he reached the First Baptist Church
some five blocks from the center of the rioting, he glimpsed
a squad of Riders hustling out 14th to Virginia Street.
They turned right and headed for the big fire. They had
just finished polishing off his newspaper office. First they
had shot out the large plate-glass front, and then all the
windows in the second story. They'd broken through the
front door, torn the telephone off the wall, upturned the
desk, kicked papers in all directions, and generally left the
front office in shambles. Then they had charged into the
back office, thrown type all over the shop, torn the lino-
type unmentionables from hell to breakfast; squirted
ink on the walls, rolled paper out the back door and beat
the press up with axes. Now they were headed for fresh
fields to conquer, and Mayor Meacham would have been
wine and blood to their hungering. Though Meacham
did not know how his newspaper had been demolished,
he had a strong suspicion; and aware intuitively he'd get
a going over if caught on the street, he darted into the
basement of the Baptist Church through a coal chute.
From this sanctuary he could hear the rise and fall of
the riot — the wild gunfire, the shouts, the oaths, the roar
of increasing flames. The lurid light penetrated the dusty
regions where he cowered. Now and then he'd hear flying

footfalls, of men racing past the church. He knew when the fire department went into action and saved the Association warehouse and the flour mills. Gradually the mob confusion subsided, and he heard the eerie blast of a ram's horn. But not till the vandals had re-formed and quit the main section of the city did he dare crawl out and have a look at the still flaming factories against the sky.

Afterwards when the story broke that he'd taken refuge in the Baptist Church the Night Riders gleefully told the tale: Chuck Meacham, a Methodist, was the only sprinkled saint saved in a water-dunking Baptist Church.

The ram's horn had been Dr. Amoss's signal for the Riders to re-assemble at 9th and Main. He was bleeding profusely, but he stayed on directing the attack. "Chief," Guy Dunning said, "you'd better get back home and find a doctor. You'll bleed to death." There was no point in looking for medical attention in Hopkinsville. The doctors there would more likely have cut his throat. As the Riders gathered, Dunning called the rolls by numbers. The attack had lasted about an hour. The lurid fires still burned. Riders had hidden their hoods and robes and many stayed on to mill around as the crowds began gingerly to gather. They even helped keep the fires from spreading to nearby dwellings. Dunning requisitioned a horse and buggy from a Negro and helped Dr. Amoss in, for he was too weak to tackle the walk back out to the rendezvous. Directly the men were marching as they had come, singing in swelling volume, "The fires burn bright in my old Kentucky home!"

Chapter Fifteen

Never Call Retreat

AS DR. AMOSS DROVE PAST THE LINES OF MARCHING MEN, he gave a final order. "Post a strong rear guard. Don't let 'em catch you with your britches down. These Hoptown people are going to be peeved." No military advice could have been more excellent. Unfortunately the Riders were too jubilant over their victory to pay much heed to it. Amoss reached the hitching grounds, got into his own vehicle, and started away for Wallonia, where there was a young doctor who'd recently hung out his shingle. There he had the still bleeding artery closed with a suture-ligature. He muttered, "Young feller, you may just about have saved my life. I was getting worried." He was stout enough to drive on home.

Meanwhile back in Hopkinsville the outraged citizenry took stock of their wounds. There were scores of tales of hair-breadth escapes from flying bullets, crashing missiles, and falling bricks. Most of these complaints were registered by women. By their accounts half the population of Hopkinsville were killed or wounded or scared to death. A great outcry rose. "Revenge! We've got to follow the skunks! An eye for an eye, a tooth for a tooth!" But when the actual count of casualites was made, though not till the following day, only two persons were actually wounded. An L. & N. brakeman ran the switch engine with a string of boxcars awaiting loading out of reach of the fires. When Night Riders saw what he was he was up to, they shouted, "Stop it, Felts!" Felts dropped off the engine and ran. Some one shot him in the back and he fell. Badly wounded, he leaped up and took off down among the cars. Some hours after the raid he was found and loaded on the next freight train for Nashville, his home. The other casualty was a Negro living near the I.C. depot who had kept his lamp burning during the raid. "Take your goddam head out of that window and put out the light!" he was commanded. In the shooting that followed he was wounded.

Tandy & Fairleigh and the Latham factory burnt to the ground. The Acme Flour Mills were badly damaged, and there was considerable damage to the Wooldridge factory housing Association leaf. But the Night Riders who had doffed their gear and turned respectable citizens did valiant service, and losses were held to a minimum.

Mayor Meacham, after the shock of finding his newspaper plant a wreck, hurried to the Sheriff's office and the police station. Major E. B. Bassett, officer of the local militia unit at the Armory, was hastily summoned to the conference. Meacham shook with rage; the men could still hear the retiring Riders singing.

"We've got to deputize a sufficient posse to catch those scoundrels and attack them! We've got to catch and hang their leader! This is a disgrace to our city. This is lawlessness!"

"It's only three days till Governor Willson takes over," Bassett suggested.

"Three days hell! By then these skunks will have gone back to their dens!"

There seemed nothing to do but go out into the streets where the local mob now was howling and shouting, "Down with the Night Riders!" and begin collaring these fellows crying for blood and scalps. But when the law importuned them to join the pursuit, most of them drew back.

"They'll kill a man!"

"How many have they killed tonight?"

Nobody knew at the time; probably scores. Maybe hundreds. Really from all the shooting the streets should be running red with blood. After an hour of intensive recruiting a nominal posse was organized, consisting of Lieutenant J. Stanley Bassett, kinsman of the major; Sergeant Bernice B. Gooch, Sergeant Riley Butlar, and Privates John C. Lawson and W. E. Clark, of the militia; and citizens John Stites, Bob Fairleigh, Edgar Elgin, and Mayor Meacham himself. These men saddled their horses and followed Major Bassett and Deputy-Sheriff Lucian Cravens out of town along the lines of retreat. They were armed to the teeth and outraged enough to shoot.

Meanwhile the Riders leisurely and happily returned to the hitch, moving so slowly that the posse barely missed cutting them off at the railroad crossing a few blocks out of town. Not having moved promptly or posted a strong rear guard, they would have been sitting ducks to any kind of determined pursuit. Apparently no one took thought of the fact that Bassett and the police and Mayor might attack. Thus the possemen caught up and mingled freely with the still laughing and joking Riders. They were in high spirits over their "victory." "By God that'll learn

old stuck-up Hoptown a lesson!" They had sufficient
cause for elation. That more than five hundred armed
and mounted men could come a great distance and fall
upon a sleeping town in a surprise attack was not far
short of a miracle, and demonstrated two things: The
attack was carefully planned and beautifully coordinated;
that that curious monster called public opinion was behind
the movement, or somebody would have called in a warning.

Bassett and Meacham would move in and out of the
triumphant horsemen, hoping to find Dr. Amoss, who rumor
said was heading up the Rider raids. They failed to locate
the doctor, though a couple of times they asked about him.
"Ahead someplace, I reckon. Ast somebody else." It would
have been folly to attack all these hundreds of victorious
men. Bassett and his posse drew off on a side road and
waited till the last horseman had passed. Then they fell in
behind, keeping contact until the columns reached Gracie.
There the squads began splintering off. Bassett thought
they might attack the rear guard now with some chance
of demoralizing the Riders. They fell in close behind a
Cadiz group, and overtook it where a buggy was carrying two men. "Give 'em hell!" Bassett commanded and
they emptied their guns in the buggy and dim figures of
horsemen on ahead.

The roar of the fusillade in the narrow valley filled the
night with echoes. The two in the buggy proved to be
George Gray and Clancy McCool, from Blue Springs,
Trigg County. The gunfire killed young Gray and filled
the back of McCool's head with buckshot but did not
immediately kill him. The horse ran away and then all at
once the place was reeking with Night Riders. They poured
a volley back into the law. Bassett had dropped out

of the saddle to pick up McCool's bullet-riddled cap and a bloody handkerchief, and likely saved his life from buckshot and pistol bullets. He leaped back, lay low and spurred way, his possemen tearing along ahead of him. The infuriated Riders delayed long enough to look after McCool and Gray, and thus the law managed to escape. Bassett later reported heavy casualties among the Riders, and it was known for a fact that there was a secret burial back in the tobacco hills, presumably McCool.

They galloped back to Hopkinsville. By then the excitement had died down and so had the fires, and folk had gone to bed. The only life was some prowling dogs scrambling through garbage left from the raid.

The next morning the town was throbbing with revived terror and fresh rumors and indignation that the whole police force had been sleeping at the switch and had let this catastrophe befall Hopkinsville. They took comfort from hearing Dr. Amoss had been captured and was even now lodged in jail. When this proved a lie, they felt even better to hear that Dr. Amoss had been fatally wounded and had died on the way home. His companions spirited his body off to Cobb. Then men saw Dr. Amoss making his rounds that afternoon, though wearing a skull cap and saying he had a slight headache. The rig he had gone out to the hitch in was found at the river bridge just outside of town. A dollar bill was stuffed in the cracked leather seat. It would never be said of Night Riders that they were horse thieves or would not reward the faithful.

The Cadiz *Record* came out with a description of the leader of the raid:

He was tall and erect, except shoulders stooped; was a man of middle age. His short irongray whiskers were visible below the mask he wore. He gave his orders in quick emphatic tone. His step was firm, elastic, and springy. His manner was watchful, but cool and free from excitement. He wore a brownish overcoat and a black slouch hat, both old in appearance. His legs were long, wide apart and slightly bowed at the knees. He walked with a peculiar swing. He carried an army pistol with a barrel about eight inches long.

It was a mixed portrait of Dr. Amoss and Guy Dunning; but people who read it supposed it to be Dr. Amoss. They had seen him drilling men in the streets of Cadiz.

The uproar following the Hopkinsville raid not only rose to high heaven, but raced like wild fire from coast to coast, and crossed oceans to far away tobacco marts. James Duke and the American Tobacco Company were outraged beyond all conscience. Why were not the Trust warehouses properly guarded? Hadn't there been threats of raids, and just how did it happen on this particular night that these hordes of lawless tobacco growers could swoop down and destroy thousands of dollars of good American tobacco? What were the police doing to have been so trapped and "captured?" How could anywhere from five hundred to one thousand criminals make such a move in utter secrecy if someone in authority were not conniving? Duke made the greatest use of the propaganda potential: He brought about the appearance of the most absurd and outrageous news items in the New York papers. They spoke of the lawlessness of Kentucky men, the horrible destruction of private property, the placing in jeopardy of the lives of the citizens of Hopkinsville, the torture, the whippings, the barn burnings and plant-bed scrapings and the murders. He backed the Italian Regie in its suit against Hopkinsville for the losses in Latham and Tandy & Fairleigh. Duke wired Governor Beckham, whose administration had

but three more days to go; and Governor-Elect Augustus
Willson, reminding him of his campaign pledge. Only the
Acme Flour Mills had had sufficient insurance.

There were weird publishings in New York. The read-
ership of *Harper's Weekly* enjoyed the most thrilling word
pictures of any, with full page illustrations done by artists
hastily shouted from bed to make drawings and engrav-
ings of scenes looking like Western movies, showing the
heinous activities of these uncivilized hoodlums in the
heathen lands of Kentucky. These accompanied the lurid
reporting of some author a thousand miles from the scene,
who deserved a better fate than obscurity, for he combined imagination and ignorance to a remarkable degree.

The invaders, he wrote, moved upon defenseless Hopkinsville in the dead of night, and were only prevented
from murdering and pillaging by the reckless bravery of
the embattled citizens who woke in the nick of time to the
defense of their city. The citizens — doctors, preachers,
merchants, lawyers, editors — everybody — armed themselves hastily with guns, clubs, staves, stones and brick-
bats and made a barricade in the street, countering which
the Riders emptied their guns into the helpless people.
As the galloping marauders tore this way and that, the
grim defenders drove them back foot by foot till the enemy
took refuge around the court house and public square.
In a pitched battle, with bloody hand-to-hand fighting,
the citizen-defenders at last broke the back of the attack
and sent the invaders flying out of town.

The spectacle of fellow Kentuckians, perhaps neighbors, perhaps relatives, shooting at each other with deadly intent, was
painted red by the flames of the burning warehouses. Shrieks of
terror stricken women was heard above the rattle of shots; and

the cries of the wounded answered the shouts of the new recruits to the ranks of the defenders. Slowly fighting each step of
the retreat, the Night Riders were forced from the street and
alley to alley, and finally to the outskirts of the city. There two
of the raiders were seen to fall from their horses as the bullets
flew among them. The army of citizens by this time had assumed
formidable size, but in the face of its terrific fire the invaders
made a last stand, while their fallen comrades were being placed
upon their horses. Then, with a threat to repeat the outrage, the
band galloped away.

The caption to one illustration read, "All that was left
of the Tandy & Fairleigh Tobacco Factory at Hopkinsville,
Ky., after a raid of Night Riders. In the rear are the ruins
of the Acme Mills and Elevator Company, which had a
daily capacity of 1,200 hogshead of tobacco."

Governor Willson had been elected as an avowed enemy
of Night Riders. Lacking three days of inauguration, he
had to depend on Governor Beckham to activate the one
hundred members of Company D under Major Bassett.
He properly interpreted the Hopkinsville raid as a spit in
his face and an insult to the authority of his office. He
oiled his flintlock and polished his saber, promising the
moment he took office to put the full power of the police
and military on the trail of the arsonists. Beckham, meanwhile, perhaps half-heartedly, got the militia in uniform
and Bassett to patrolling the town and outlying countryside. There was a rumor that the President of the United
States was going to send national troops down into the
rebellious state; after all this was too much like old Civil
War days to be ignored. Duke and the American Tobacco
Company were shouting to high heaven for law and order
in the Black Patch. United States marshals were quickly
established in headquarters in Hopkinsville, with T. J.

Cundiff and T. B. Pedigo as deputies in charge of bloodhounds and sleuths who moved into the hinterlands as
Bible agents, horse traders, sewing machine agents and
mechanics, spectacle salesmen and medicine men, farm
hands, lightning rod agents and peddlers, smelling out
clues. Night Riders had left no trails for the hounds, and
they spotted phony detectives immediately. They caught
these imposters in the public roads, took them back in
the woods and flogged some two score of them with raw-
hide, and sent them bloody and defeated back to Hopkinsville. These fellows were loyal to law and order but not
to the extent of toting a whipping, and pretty soon headquarters was at a loss for spies.

Willson's majority of 18,000 votes he accepted as a mandate to clean up the Black Patch, and immediately upon
his inauguration he fell to work. He called up an extra
company of troops and had five more companies to stand
by. He sent out invitations to tobacco growers, to Felix
Ewing and the Forts, but not Dunning and Amoss; to
buyers, to all men he felt would further peace and uproot
this lawlessness. A meeting was called in his office in
Frankfort to discuss the entire problem. The matter grew
more complicated when the burley growers began organizing lodges and Night Riding, with a wave of barn burnings in the Blue Grass, floggings, and the destruction of
Trust warehouses. A midnight band of these lawless renegades actually rode into Frankfort and burnt a barn of a
grower selling to the Trust. The movement swept over into
North Carolina, to the very backdoor of Washington Duke
and James Duke. Lodges were formed and bands of Riders
put the torch to the stores of Duke's cigarette and Duke's
Mixture makings. Willson must have taken some thought
of this, while shipping his soldiers into Hopkinsville to

reinforce Major Bassett's local boys. All these tobacco revolutionaries could not be wrong, though Willson never publicly admitted it.

Two days after he had become Governor the citizens, buyers, bankers, and others crying for law and order met in Willson's office. They came from both the Black Patch and Blue Grass, and for the most part were the conservative men who craved only peace. Their cry was, "It's ruining the State. It is setting an 'image' of Kentucky for the rest of the world to scorn." They had one telling argument. "Tobacco prices are back to the old time average of 8c. Why must this lawlessness continue?" Willson promised, "I will track down these fellows and destroy them." He set December 20 and 21 for a conference and notified Felix Ewing, Charles Fort, George Snadon, Clarence Lebus, C. H. Barnett, and James B. Duke to be in attendance, and asked them to join in the work of restoring order. Snadon was treasurer of the Association; Lebus was president of the Burley Tobacco Society; and Barnett was president of the Equity. James Duke we have met before, and we are eager to meet him at this conclave.

Among those notably not present were Ewing, Fort and Duke.

Felix Ewing did not say so openly, but privately he gave his opinion. "We can best settle our problems in our own way." He did not elaborate, but quite patently he meant he would do his share through the Association and Dr. Amoss would serve with his Night Riders.

The conference had a stormy session. Ed C. O'Rear, chief justice of the Kentucky Court of Appeals, faced Governor Willson in the chair and said, "Your Excellency, it's a mistake, if not a crime, to send troops to

Hopkinsville to quell those men fighting the American
Tobacco Company." Willson tried to shout him down.
Instead Willson was drowned out by the burst of applause from the two hundred tobacco people present.
The Governor subsided in frustrated wrath, sensing the
undercurrent of hostility toward him when he'd been in
office only ten days.

We can't help but lament the fact that James Duke
sent as his representative Judge William M. Wallace, one
of the incandescent legal lights busy at the time de-
fending the American Tobacco Company against the Justice
Department's investigation. He brought greetings to Governor Willson and expressed Mr. Duke's hope that lawlessness would be suppressed and peace restored to troubled
Kentucky.

The rest of the oratory were speeches from Snadon in
favor of the Protective Association, Lebus on the aims of
the Burley Society, and Barnett on the purposes of the
Equity. Editors and reporters from newspapers far and
wide wrote grandiose suggestions for a central marketing
society to handle all the leaf grown in Kentucky, overlooking the obvious fact the Association, Equity and Burley
fellows had been hammering on this thought for years,
going back to 1896 when Felix Ewing first published his
scheme. Editors always have a handsome way of curing
the evils of the world with typewriters and swivel chair
rhetoric. If a central sales method could have been adopted
generally there would never have been Night Riding and
violence. After two days of dialogue the Conference got
exactly nowhere and the meeting dispersed.

Chapter Sixteen

Hot Time in the Old Town Tonight

SOLDIERS KEPT SWARMING INTO HOPKINSVILLE. THE tramp-tramp-tramp of their hobbed heels beat the cobbles and filled the old-fashioned town with military echoes. Major E. B. Bassett was commander-in-chief of this task. In the beginning his guardsmen were local boys mostly from the tobacco patches around Christian County. There might be some question of their loyalty if called upon suddenly to fire into men who were their neighbors and kin. Some of them had been hired men of the Riders, and they had pulled green worms off tobacco side by side with these people. Some of them were courting the farmers' daughters. Within a week after Governor Willson's inaugural, reinforcements in the form of a company of Louisville troops were shipped in. Mayor editor-publisher Meacham now could confidently announce, "There is now an organized suppression of Night Riding, and this city will hereafter be military headquarters." All this reassured gentle folk, who now could sleep soundly nights without fear of a second raid. But the whispering campaign about another raid went steadily on.

There was also a howl of criticism for the killing of young Gray and the almost fatal shooting of McCool. Much of this outcry was naturally from Association people. But no small porportion of it came from honest men who deplored killing, just as they opposed burning tobacco warehouses. And there were those who cried out for vengeance.

It began almost immediately to come clear that Hopkinsville had swapped the Devil for his Imp. The worst the local military had done was keep nervous citizens awake nights shooting off their guns to see if they were loaded, and sitting on back kitchen steps eating begged food from the sympathetic housewives. This mob from Louisville had no such restraint of manners. They established headquarters at the court house, set up a Gatling gun, and opened diplomatic relations with the half-dozen saloons. Then they made a spot check of all the whore houses. After that they looked up the domiciles of the town's pretty girls. When these formalities were attended to, they looked around to fight Night Riders. They made forays into the rural regions and shot squirrels and rabbits and once they shot a farmer's cow. They whooped and hollered at the most unseemly hours, and once a squad, patrolling the I.C.-depot locality, got into a wild shooting match and killed a Negro woman in a nearby cabin. Charles Meacham once said plaintively, "The city of Hopkinsville never went through such a season as in December, 1907."

The trouble with the "furriners" was naturally boredom. They'd come to Hopkinsville expecting pitched warfare with hooded killers. Instead they found the little provincial town tomblike and quiet. They were rebuffed by the town girls and in the beginning even the country girls would have no part of them. Before the burning of the two great tobacco factories the now placid city had been alive with clanking tobacco wagons, with drivers lolling on the loads awaiting sales; the streets were busy with roughly dressed farmers, and on Saturdays trade was heavy, and there was the excitement of these many crowds. Now nothing remotely resembling a Night Rider showed his mask. Tobacco commerce had all gone away, mostly to nearby Russellville, where the warehouses began to bulge. Everybody seemed to have strict orders to have nothing to do with the soldiery. Fathers said "They're out for only what they can get." Young men said, "They're a batch of smart-alecks. Riffraff from Louisville." The noble soldiers could do little but spend their money on liquor and the squads of prostitutes that almost immediately flooded into town.

The state fire marshal set up shop and undertook an investigation of the fires. To his office in the court house he summoned citizens by the scores. He sought to sift clues from the intensive questioning. The Grand Jury was in continuous session, ready to bring true bills against any men the marshal implicated. Four indictments were finally returned — H. R. Crenshaw of Roaring Spring, and George Powell, Mat Gholson and Gano Warder of Christian County, Warder being town marshal of Gracey. In the prompt trials that followed they were all acquitted by a typical Night-Rider jury. In suits against the City of Hopkinsville for damages, the city was exonerated by the same type of jury.

Dr. Amoss, Guy Dunning, and unquestionably Felix Ewing and the Forts, were well aware that once night riding was undertaken as a means of controlling the tobacco situation the law would be upon them at once, and from the beginning they had formed a network of underground to forestall this. The membership was made up of men to be dealt with in the courts and with judges and juries. There was no doubt the law had the upper hold if only it could fasten its grip. There were all manner of laws to cover the activities of the underground. Laws were still on the books designed to control Ku Klux activities. "If two or more persons band together for the purpose of intimidating or injuring any one, or to do any felonous act, they and each shall be guilty of a felony. . . ." Or "banding together and going forth for the purpose of molesting or injuring property . . . is a felony . . ." Or "if injury results to a person or property by reason of the acts above described, persons engaged in or aiding and abetting, shall be guilty of felony. . . ." Fines ranged from $100 to $500, and upon proven guilty a person or persons could be committed to the penitentiary for from one to five years. The Toll Gate Raiders' law was much the same and Kentucky had seen violence before in protest movements against Negroes after the Civil War and against paying toll on certain highways. The Night Riders had plenty of precedents for violence. Moreover both Kentucky and Tennessee, as far back as two years, had passed laws against barn burning and plant-bed destruction, with heavy-fine sentences. Both Beckham and Governor Willson had offered rewards of $500 and $1000 to any one delivering up a Night Rider, and Willson was paying a salary of $3000 a year each to a squad of private detectives.

By the time of the Hopkinsville raid, the underground was in virtual control of all petit and grand juries and sheriffs, judges and city police. They controlled most of the lawyers, including the prosecuting attorneys, with the exception of one Walter Krone of Princeton. Nor is there any evidence to indicate they didn't control the legal machinery of Hopkinsville. Charles Meacham fought the underground bitterly, and he was only lukewarm to the Association. But he paid heavily for his personal and official stand. Night Riders almost to a man cancelled their subscriptions to the *Kentuckian,* leaving few but Hillbillies to read the ads of the city merchants. The business men cancelled their advertising because there was no one to read the ads. Meacham was hit from three directions, and for a time he realized he faced ruin.

Thus the Night Riders were able to block indictments, or if the cases came to trial, to win in the courts. It was heady brew indeed that Dr. Amoss and Guy Dunning quaffed after the great raid. The only convictions under the new law against scraping plant beds were Choate and Pettit in the Hollowell case.

Under any other condition, the jails and prisons would have been filled with men serving for arson, intimidation, assault and battery, etc. The citizens refused to enforce the laws because they could not be used to right the wrongs perpetrated by the Tobacco Trust, consequently they refused to let themselves be convicted by the same laws. [The people] failed to get help legally; they took it otherwise. They showed a disinterested public that a game could be played two ways, even though one way naturally led to violence and "illegal" lawlessness.

Yet it is an axiom of law enforcement that a preponderance of police power must in the end subjugate rebellion. The South learned that lesson well in the Civil War. Probably the Russian satellites con the same lesson nightly with their prayers of deliverance. Little

Rock, Arkansas, and the University of Mississippi have
had the same bitter pill to swallow. By and large the Law
will be served, and only when revolt is widespread and
disaffection determined, as in the Eighteenth Amendment,
can law be scorned.

No one knew this better than the leaders of the underground and the leaders in the Association. Dr. Amoss and
Guy Dunning let no grass grow under their feet before
mounting their next spectacular attack. Spies noted that
tobacco rolled into the Trust warehouses in Russellville
in greatly increased volume after the two warehouses were
destroyed in Hopkinsville. How long the raid on Russellville had been in the cards we can only surmise, for the
underground never put anything in writing for the record
in the afterwhile. Certainly it was not jumped up just to
increase Governor Willson's fury and convince him all this
was a slap at his face, a spit in the eye. The time between
the raids was so brief — December 7, 1907, and January
3, 1908 — that plans were probably perfected back in the
fall of 1907, when Dr. Amoss was toying with the idea
of a grand raid on Clarksville at the time of the Hopkinsville affair. That scheme was frustrated by the notorious
Ben Sory, his armed police powers and dire threats, and
determination to shoot it out with any Riders daring to
come to his town.

The Russellville raid was a fine gesture of defiance.

We remember Russellville. It was an old-fashioned town
of some couple of thousand sleepy souls in quaint mansions along shaded streets, sweetly vegetating in the fragrance of magnolia and azalia, dozing to the charming
rhymes of Keats and Tennyson and Byron, dancing grace-
fully to Johann Strauss's waltzes, and banking their shekels
from trading and trafficking in dark-fired leaf in the bank

once robbed by Jesse James. To see a place more "Old South" than Russellville one would have had to project oneself a half-century into the future and go out to Hollywood to graze in the pastures of Technicolor.

Amoss and Dunning had no interest in the fine antiquity of the town. They were intent on that Trust tobacco piling up. Once again we are amazed at the secrecy of their planning. Two massive raids had already been staged by the Night Riders. Why Russellville did not think of itself as a possible victim and take the most elementary precautions is beyond comprehension. The night of January 3, the clans gathered at Cave Spring, a place not even marked today on a road map, but it was on what is now Highway 79. Then it was a little spring-valley locality with a schoolhouse and a couple churches and a handful of modest dwellings with tobacco fields coming up to the back doors. Some fifty Riders made up this spare task force. This was not to be a flamboyant display of defiance. It was designed as a direct stab at American Tobacco Company factories—the American Snuff Company and the Luckett-Wake warehouse. It was the psychological moment. The past few days had been rainy, so the leaf could be wagoned without shattering; the L. & N. railroad had only recently shunted into the sidings of a string of cars to freight the tobacco out. Luckett-Wake had an accumulation of some $50,000 worth of prime leaf, and American Snuff had almost twice that of low-grade snuff tobacco.

The Cave Spring road entered the town from the south. About ten o'clock in the evening the Riders headed out along the still murky road going north. A bit past one o'clock they were coming near the town limits. There in a patch of woods they dismounted and donned masks and armbands. These were all seasoned raiders; most

were responsible heads of families, intent on getting a
clean job done without loss of time or unnecessary fire-
works.

Guy Dunning was in charge, Dr. Amoss not being
present in this party. Dunning clicked off the directions
in his crisp voice.

"Look to your guns and pistols. Squad 1, yours is
the Luckett-Wake spot." That would be five blocks in
town, going north. Off to the right four blocks stood the
snuff warehouse. Luckett-Wake was in a semi-slum region
peopled by poor whites, Negroes, whorehouses, and a string
of section houses. Here were the railroad yards, the coal
yards, the trusty depot and a very considerable saw mill
and planer outfit, with lumber yards. "Squad 2, American
Snuff for you. Oilmen-dynamite boys, ready? Got your
gunnysacks over your shoes? Walk steady. No shooting
till both fires are going good. Spare the houses and windows
and above all the women — the young women, anyhow.
We want no female blood to darken our masks, remember,
boys. We love our women."

"God yes," said a voice.

He told off a rear guard. "Remember Hoptown. We
want no pursuit, no more young men shot. If we hit it
wide open, and lose not a moment, we'll catch 'em with
their pants down. I'll be around the public square with
the rear guard. Ready? March!"

The two files moved away, walking with that fine route
step, making almost no sound. The hostlers took over the
horses and Guy Dunning and his file closers fell in behind, going on to the dark public square. The squads,
lines of dark shadows, arrived at their stations. In this
zero hour not a light showed in a window. The unsus-
pecting town was dead in slumber. The men fell to their

jobs — breaking down the doors of the two factories with axes, pushing in and saturating the piles of tobacco with kerosene, and setting the clusters of dynamite, with caps, ready for the signal from the square — a single shot. The matchmen struck and lingered only long enough to make sure the flames caught. Then they backed out. Meanwhile the telephone office had been captured. The town was so small that it had no police station. The fire-fighting force was volunteer. The warning was a bell uptown, that the fire marshal ran to and rang. Chief W. R. Bruce raced half-dressed along the street to the fire tower but was "arrested" before he managed three dongs of the bell. By then the Night Riders were shooting wildly, creating an uproar that woke the citizens to the fact the town was in the clutches of a vast raid.

At the telephone office the operator was awakened, dazed by all the hooray. A hooded figure poked a gun at her, and she pulled her nightgown close. The night bell clanged. "Please," she begged, "let me answer that. It's mother and she's worried about me." Small wonder, for now the streets were alive with confused figures and the musketry was deafening.

The Rider nodded permission, speaking in a disguised voice, "Say you're in no danger."

"Mother, I am in no danger," the girl said.

By this time the lurid flames lighted the town. The Riders were gathering in the square. They kept up their shooting long enough to pin the town down, in case a policeman wanted to try any monkey business. The details of the Hopkinsville raid were well known in local folklore, and nobody tried anything. At a signal, the firing ceased. Then six shots was a signal for all Riders to form. The sharp command came.

"Divide and close!"

The men formed two lines, with the rear guard of eight at alert. They marched around the square once and then out Main Street south, the eight file-closers marching backwards with guns ready to meet any pursuit. They'd had a fair lesson at Hopkinsville. Then back to their horses, and soon they were galloping away in the night along the clayey, wintry roads.

It was the most carefully timed and effective raid of any so far made. The small groups were easily maneuvered and there was no needless destruction of property or needless terrorizing. It was not a desperate venture. The men functioned coolly and deliberately. They did not even sing their theme song as they marched out of town. Their sole business was burning thousands of dollars worth of Trust tobacco. They could see the fires a long time against the sky. Once the fire fighters fell to work they were more than two hours controlling the burning buildings that caught from the warehouses. Down along the railroad a coalyard burned, and a string of Negro hovels. Two whorehouses went up in flames, and the chippies toted water and fought flames alongside, it was whispered with belly laughs, the same gentlemen they now and then accommodated in their beds. The King and Proctor livery stable caught fire in the hayshed and went up in wild fire, though all the nags and hacks were saved. There was one casualty. A Charles Roberts, from Indiana, insisted on watching the excitement. When ordered to get in the citizens corral he turned and ran and caught a load of squirrel shot in his rump. No other blood was let.

The Cadiz *Record* carried an item about the intrepid leader of this raid.

It is considered that the man who is dominating the Night Riders is a man of rare ability with excellent military training. This is based upon the wonderful discipline in the raids on Hopkinsville and Russellville. The Riders marched in a way that could only have been the result of training. The man in command had a perfect military bearing. He is believed to be the mysterious genius who is the moving spirit of the Night Riders.

Chapter Seventeen

Worms Off the Old Tobacco Stem

IF THE HOPKINSVILLE RAID HAD INFURIATED GOVERNOR Willson, the Russellville raid close upon its heels burnt him up. "My God!" he swore, "why don't those towns guard their tobacco factories? How can great mobs of men move in and burn out a town and nobody know about it till they're shooting the place up?" He added, "I am going to break up this lawlessness if I have to call out the entire state army to do it!" He stamped up and down his splendid office, with its polished desk and wall-to-wall carpet, and shook his fist. "Just what is going on out there in that benighted country, anyhow?"

Willson might very well have gained a clearer idea of what went on in the Black Patch if he had accepted the invitation Felix Ewing and the Forts extended him to come to Hopkinsville, Russellville, Clarksville and other tobacco towns, and look over the situation for himself. But he would also have to tour the outlying tobacco farms and talk with the farmers and listen to their side of the story. He did make a tentative promise to do this. But after he caught this Rus-

202

sellville load of spittle, he was so outraged that he changed his mind. All he did was turn some of the authority over to the local judge, Judge T. P. Cook, of Hopkinsville, and have him call a special term of court in January to investigate the raids and take due process of law. And he sent in another company of militia to guard Russellville.

These soldiers were no better than those that had already turned Hopkinsville sour on the military occupation. There were the usual charges against any soldiers: arrogance, insolence, petty thievery, reckless discharge of firearms; and worst of all this continual effort of the men to seduce the local women. A man was heard once to say, "If I had my choice I be damned if I wouldn't take the Night Riders. The worst they do is burn bootleg tobacco. They leave a man's wife and daughter alone." In spite of the fact that Charles Meacham wrote an editorial in defense of the militia, complaints from the citizens grew so loud that, exasperated out of reason, Governor Willson recalled the offensive soldiery, sending in a company of mountaineers from Eastern Kentucky, where the prevailing occupation was growing corn to brew moonshine whisky. These fellows hardly knew what the tobacco wars were about. Their skill at shooting came from killing rabbits and shooting revenuers. And some had feuding experience.

Governor Willson posted $1000 reward for any information leading to the arrest and conviction of the Russellville leader, though the rewards for Hopkinsville and even Princeton remained unclaimed. Judge Cook took the bench and sought indictments. Willson appointed a noted horseman, Major Philip P. Johnson, as his Adjutant-General. Johnson was from Lexington, a Confederate veteran, but his knowledge of race horses obviously did not include Night Riding. That carpetbagger, Judge A. J. G. Wells, of

Murray, made great noises with his mouth. "We'll make night-riding as dangerous as hell fire!" And there was the usual state fire marshal, W. F. Neikirk, from Springfield, Kentucky, to poke into the ashes of the American Snuff and Luckett-Wake.

Something new in running down Night Riders was a detail of cavalrymen, under Major George W. Albrecht, who patrolled the outlying provinces, while the guardsmen kept watch at the gates of the cities. Major Albrecht was a mountain man from Middlesboro, Ky. He was a lank, not too graceful horseman, but killing Night Riders was right up his alley. He and his fellows after a supper of beans and fatback would ride out the road to Gracie, Cadiz, Wallonia and Princeton and diligently beat the brush for hooded enemies. Sometimes he and his troop would ride into Russelville. Again he might go south toward Clarksville, but not to the Queen City, which, being in Tennessee, was outside his jurisdiction. Where ever they rode there were no Night Riders.

Another agent of the persistent quest was a group of some two hundred vigilantes known as the Law and Order League to which we have already had occasion to refer. We need to pause a moment to examine this brotherhood. It was a day when mouthing great oaths promised to cement men in good as well as in lawlessness. In the beginning the Law and Order fellows were a secret fraternity, and their oath was a mixture of Night Rider, Masonic, and Ku Klux. But soon they dared come out in the open, and their numbers grew. They were authorized to bear arms, and some of them were ministers of the Gospel. As a moral force their instincts were pure. They opposed any public official who was dishonest or disloyal — a slap at judges and sheriffs and other law enforcement men who were in league with the Night

Riders. "Regardless of party affiliation," they added, and thus they were often men who had voted for Augustus Willson. There was a salt-and-peppering of Association men who were weary of this strife, and Equity men who never had been in favor of force in the tobacco wars.

Felix Ewing and Dr. Amoss came out quickly enough against the League. "Nothing but a blind for enemies of the Association." Joel Fort said, "The whole business is concocted by the Tobacco Trust and the Louisville Warehouse Combine to damage the Association."

It had the blessing of the American Tobacco Company, who had always been for law and order. James Duke was quoted as saying, "I hope it cleans out that cancer in the Black Patch." Governor Willson personally commended it. Henry Waterson wrote editorials in its behalf. With all this show of great men in its camp, the League held its first public meeting March 29, 1908 at McCauley's Theatre in Louisville. It was a sunny Sunday afternoon and Governor Willson himself was to be noticed in the audience. The central idea was to recruit widely known men, like Governor Willson, and have them stump the state making four-minute talks about the shameful tobacco situation and pointing up the need for all good men and true to come to the aid of the law-abiding. There were leaders in both the Black Patch — one was Charles Meacham — and the Blue Grass. Among those absent were Felix Ewing, the Forts, Dr. Amoss and Guy Dunning.

The meeting was presided over by no less a personage than that eminent warrior, General Simon B. Buckner. You remember Buckner from your history book. Now president of the League, he had once been governor of Kentucky. Neither of these honors compared with his standing as hero of the Battle of Fort Donelson, down in Tennessee, when

the Civil War had swung into action. General Grant moved
on to this pile of silty hills overlooking the Cumberland
River, poked his shooting iron into the ribs of the hills, and
said, "Nothing but unconditional surrender." Generals
Floyd and Pillow handed over the keys of the dirt pile to
Buckner, who surrendered the army and set U. S. Grant up
in business in a big way by promoting the unlimited consumption of cigars. Now Buckner was a citizen promoting
peace at any price, no doubt having had a bellyful of war.

Among the orators was Judge James P. Gregory, who
called the meeting to order with stirring words, "The Law
and Order League has already driven the Night Riders underground. We have isolated their leaders. We are in process of discovering their secrets, their membership, the location of their lodges. We have frightened them until they
have hidden their masks and slunk away into the darkness.
We are going to annihilate them before our work is done."

A lady in the back of the audience had risen, and waited
for Judge Gregory to pause for breath.

"Yes, lady?"

No Kentucky judge would ever keep on palavering in
the presence of a lady. He'd have sooner declined a mint
julip.

The lady heckled, "Did you do all that to the illegal
Trust?"

For a moment Judge Gregory was at a loss for a reply,
but he got a fresh grip on his speech and finished it. There
was a good deal of hubbub in the audience, which turned
out to be an invitation for the lady to go up on stage and say
what she had in mind. She gave her name as Alice Lloyd,
and her home was Maysville. She had a master's degree
from the University of Chicago, and that made her a marked woman. Ladies of culture in Kentucky had bachelor of

arts degrees, and a graduate degree automatically gave you lantern jaws, a rasping shrill voice, flat bosom and bony legs. Her age at this remove is unknown. She would, in this good day, be branded a Communist. To worsen her reputation, she wrote articles on farming and tobacco economics for a magazine called "Equity."

Dr. James O. Nall, in his book *The Tobacco Night Riders of Kentucky and Tennessee* (page 159) gives a condensed version of her speech.

People of Louisville . . . I come from the White Burley district . . . I know something about these people . . . all over the countryside [there] is a suspicion of corporations, and it is abroad in the land, and they say the state government is against us, the city press is against us, and we cannot get our cause heard. Now that is the reason you have driven that fellow in brown jeans, with his trousers [stuffed] in the top of his boots, to use brute force. . . . I do not believe I ever saw a Night Rider. I am absolutely certain I never talked to a Night Rider, but . . . a good man said to me [that] if this sort of thing keeps up, and some remedy is not brought to bear, night-riding is not yet begun. . . . I do not want to go back to central Kentucky and when they ask me, "What did they do down at the meeting? Did they take any notice of our rights?" say "No." I tell you these farmers will clench their teeth a little tighter . . . people of Louisville, you are making night riders out of good men . . . If the city pulpit, and the city press and the state administration had recognized the rights of the tobacco growers there would never have been any crime committed. . . .

The crowd looked to Governor Willson to reply. He was disarmingly suave. "We are not here to be put by anybody, not even the voice of this good woman, in the attitude of unfriendliness or distrust or any lack of affection for any part of our people." The lady here, he said, speaks as if we were coldhearted people. "She is without the faintest understanding of the situation." He could not stand still, he said, while men were shot to death in their homes, while houses were burnt and Ku Klux rode the land; he would not be fit for office. He was opposed to the Tobacco Trust. He was for the people of Kentucky against the Trust. "But all our tobacco and all our farms and all our homes are nothing if the ghost of fear rides over them." Farmers, he said, make up five-sixths of the state's population. They were the majority that elected him to office. (As a matter of fact he was incorrect in both statements.) Without taking sides in the wars, he felt that the farmers had an honest case; and their organization (the Association) was justified. "When the Tobacco Trust combines to oppress the people by wrongful acts, the Tobacco Trust should be punished, and every man in Kentucky ought to be behind it."

Then he asked a question. "If this is wholly due to the wrongful acts of the Tobacco Trust, why haven't some of you tobacco producers done something to the Trust, either in the courts or to its property or to its men?"

Men whispered among themselves, "What in the world goes on in the head of this man? Don't he read the papers?" Every pound of tobacco burnt by the Night Rider raids at Princeton, Hopkinsville, and Russellville, in the barns of the Hillbillies, belonged to the American Tobacco Company, the Italian Regie and British Imperial. It wasn't the spinster from the University of Chicago who was without the faintest understanding of the situation. Governor Willson, though speaking off the cuff, was simply two-facing himself out of an embarrassing spot. There were the usual cliches. Men had a right to refuse to join any association;

they had the right to sell in a free country; and those who would deny these right should be sent to the penitentiary.

The meeting officially rejected Alice Lloyd's contention and passed resolutions calling on Governor Willson to send the state militia into the Black Patch and Blue Grass and track down these infamous Night Riders. Not till the whole underground was stamped out should he withdraw the troops.

All at once Miss Lloyd's name was known where men gathered at the stores, blacksmith shops, schoolhouses and churches. Reporters hurried to interview her. She cried, "My goodness, didn't the Governor get mad! I was sorry, too, but I had to tell him what the people think."

Her voice, growing more and more clarion, was heard at a hundred rallies down in the Blue Grass, and men in the Black Patch importuned her to come speak at their gatherings. They had a name for the lady, as they had for Felix Ewing and John Fort. "Joan of Arc of the Tobacco Troubles." They wanted her at Hopkinsville. They had to settle for her articles, which she now was publishing far and wide in farm journals and newspapers. She refuted Governor Willson's contentions, pointing out that his heavy majorities in Louisville and Lexington, and other towns and cities, really elected him. Louisville was a manufacturing city, Lexington a horse-racing town, with the state university to give it distinction, and Henry Clay's old home.

But for this hassle that grew up, the League probably would have drifted into obscurity, without leaving the impression it was far more influential than it was. The Law and Order League was a kind of United Nations for a bloc of public opinion.

Chapter Eighteen

One Strong Man Makes a Majority

IN THIS LONG LULL, WHILE TROOPS, DETECTIVES, LAW
and Order police, and a species of public opinion kept Dr.
Amoss and Guy Dunning and the underground pinned
down, the Night Rider hierarchy looked longingly southward to Clarksville. Ben Sory remained a thorn in the sides
of the Association and Night Riders alike. The boycott had
chased Sory out of Adams. Now the Night Riders began a
campaign to terrorize him. There was a whispering campaign that the Queen City was going to be visited by a massive raid. One date or another was assigned. Sory received
threatening letters. "Ben Sory goddamn your soul we'll get
you yet." One morning he found a skull-and-crossbones
crudely drawn on the door of his factory. On another occasion, a hempen rope was tied to the doorknob. Sory got a
genuine stitch when he discovered what seemed a couple
sticks of dynamite under his step. He loudly gave out the
dare that if he caught any suspicious characters around the
Hayes-Sory factory they would get what was coming to

them. He called names. This was the work of Amoss and Felix Ewing.

He went to the county sheriff and had himself sworn in as deputy sheriff, with authority to maintain guards over all the independent warehouses in Clarksville. It was by no means within the rights of the civil authorities, but the arrogant Sory cared little at the time for legal mystifications. He had to guard his factory, and he enjoyed once again police powers to guard the other warehouses. Thus early in the year leaf was moving in fast, and the factories were jammed. It was just such a time when a massive raid would have once again brought the Night Riders into national and international repute.

He infiltrated the Night Rider lodges with spies in Robertson and Montgomery Counties, and worked into Trigg, Caldwell, and Lyon Counties in Kentucky. What he got was a confusion of reports, though there seems no doubt that a raid on the four huge Trust warehouses in Clarksville was on the agenda of the Silent Brigade.

On the night of January 22, 1908, dark figures slipped to the back door of the Hayes-Sory factory, saturated it with kerosene, placed clusters of dynamite to blast the place sky high, and some one struck a match to the oil. Before the flames had spread guards darted in and fired pointblank at the arsonists. Two men were killed and a third was wounded. All three proved to be Negroes. One of the blacks had been fired a few days previously by Sory. The rest of the arsonists, an unkown number, fled and escaped, while the guards struggled with the fire. Clarksville was thrown into a turmoil of fear. Everybody was sure this was the work of the Night Riders, and they had used the disgruntled Negroes as tools. People began looking to their shooting irons. Sory increased his guards, and the police were reinforced. Gov-

ernor Patterson down at Nashville took notice, and alerted
the state guards, though he did not at this time call the
military up. Sory redoubled his vigilance, and his fellows
began ranging farther out in the outlying territory, determined to forestall any second raid. He had blasphemed
Felix Ewing and the Association, and the Night Riders too
bitterly to let them sneak up behind him and burn him out.
And there were the thousands of dollars worth of tobacco
in the other warehouses. The city kept the street lights burning all night, and the clop-clop of mounted police filled the
dark hours.

A matter of a month passed like this when Sory got his
next scare. One night his phone rang and a voice said, "This
is Dr. Charles Crouch, at Sango, and a squad of masked
riders just passed through the village on the way to Clarksville. Someone just told me they were Woodford fellows:
I'm satisfied they're headed for a raid on your town."

Sory swore a great mouthful of profanity and called the
chief of police. "I've just heard the Night Riders are gathering!" Then he phoned the sheriff. "Night Riders are on the
way!"

Rather than galvanizing the sheriff into action, the details
seemed only to peeve him. "We've got the town saturated
with guards. We've got you and your army. What the hell
are we keeping you for?"

Sory hung up and cursed a blue streak. "If the goddamn
law won't act, I will!" He called up his trusted henchmen.
With John Gardner, Walter Hunt, Sam Moore, Henry Cook
and Joe Gerhardt, they loaded in buggies or mounted saddles, hefted their Winchesters and shotguns, and rattled out
of town on the loose gravel and bricks. The distance to
Sango was nine miles, and it was a windy chill night and
no moon. Rains had been recent and the road was muddy.

They kept watching for Night Riders but saw not a hood or mask. They came into sight of the dark little village. Sory should have got in touch with Dr. Crouch, especially since they had seen no Riders. Instead where the roads crossed outside the village they established an ambush behind the toppling fence of a deserted cabin and hid in the tall dead weeds. Cook had once been a constable, and Gerhardt was a Hillbilly farmer who had worked for Sory when he ran his factory in Adams. These two moved off along the road a short distance and got behind a barn. The time was about two in the morning. After some impatient wait they discerned dimly horsemen coming in on the Port Royal road. There were seven all told, and Sory allowed them all to pass before he rose and emptied his shot gun into the rear riders. The sudden attack threw them into wild confusion, and they spurred away. Five managed to escape unhurt, but one, a young man by the name of Vaughn Bennett, 21 years old, was instantly killed. His horse was killed, but galloped on a few rods, dragging Bennett, before rolling into the ditch. Earle, his 17-year-old brother, was severely wounded in the head and shoulders, and his horse shot from under him. Earle managed to get up and run, but fell and lay unconscious, while Sory and his men went to Vaughn and identified him, but left him lying in the road. Earle came out of his faint and got up and went home, but said nothing about his brother. The next morning the dead boy was brought home.

They were the sons of J. H. Bennett, an Association warehouse prizer at Woodford. The Riders had not been within shooting distance of Clarksville, but had been on a small raid at Port Royal. There they had cut the telephone wires and whipped James Welch, one of Sory's spies. When fired upon they were homeward bound.

There had been a hue and cry at Hopkinsville about the killing of young Gray. Down at Clarksville the outcry was a burst of genuine indignation. Association members were furious, and Felix Ewing said, "This man Sory deserves nothing but to be shot down like a dog." So intense was the feeling against ruthless "police" action that Sory hid out for days, and Hunt and Gardner left their families and ran away. When they appeared they surrendered themselves to the sheriff and took refuge from mob violence in jail. Men shouted that Sory had no right to patrol the country. He had no business on flimsy reports to load up automatic shotguns and rifles and shoot passing horsemen from ambush. If he could do anything at all, he might have arrested the Riders. But this thing of killing young men!

In retaliation the Association brought business to a standstill in Clarksville by its old weapon, the boycott. Saturdays there were no wagons hitched around the courthouse, and the stores were mostly empty. The town gradually awoke to the fact that it faced ruin, and after about a month the businessmen began to demand something be done about Sory. A raid by Night Riders could not have hurt business like the boycott. The result was that Sory was stripped of his authority. His disused factory at Adams, which he had left when he moved to team up with Hayes, was burnt by Night Riders. Word went out the Silent Brigade was going to get him. Sory went about with a personal bodyguard and a harried expression on his gross face. Governor Patterson sent in a company of militia to reinforce the local police. Night and day the soldiers tramped the streets, and the police redoubled their vigilance. Sory's work, and the soldiers and police, undoubtedly preserved the Queen City from the most spectacular raid of Night Rider history.

After the wars were over Sory took credit for saving the city. "One strong man," he quoted Andrew Jackson, "makes a majority."

Chapter Nineteen

Ban-the-Bomb Boys

Storm clouds lay heavy all over the Black Patch. Soldiers were everywhere. Uneasiness ran deep. Talk went on about killing Ben Sory. Talk went on about killing Dr. Amoss. Nobody knew where the Night Riders would strike next. Out of this welter of fear and terror there rose a new movement called the "Day Riders." Their slogan was "Let us have peace." It was a good battle cry, for even the American Tobacco Company was in favor of it.

The Day Riders were really members of Society of Equity, an agency that was established firmly in parts of Kentucky, a branch of a much larger type of farmers' marketing association that had been established in 1902 by James A. Everett, of Indianapolis, to sell not only tobacco through pooling, but wheat, corn and hogs in Indiana, Ohio, and Illinois. The movement had drifted across the Ohio River into Kentucky, and for some time rivalled the Night Riders and Protective Association. It had strong lodges in the Ohio River towns, and had spread as far south as Bowling Green. Owensboro was the home of a famous wagon factory, and

Bowling Green was a quaint place of old-fashioned buildings, forgotten history — an ancient structure still stands
that housed the Confederate Government of Kentucky as it
fled ahead of the advancing uncouth Yankees. Dr. A. L.
Crabb of *Dinner at Belmont* and *Supper at the Maxwell
House* fame, wrote a charming novel about the provincial
tobacco mart; and one walks the court-house square staring
nostalgically at the four faces of the buildings that were
quaint even when the Night Riders had a hasty look at the
place. It was Equity country.

Yet the Equity idea did not catch on, mostly because it
was persuasive instead of forceful. Now it was Day Riding.

The first massive Day Riding took place in August, 1907,
just as the tobacco was drying at the base ready for cutting.
The wide fields lay under the dusty sun. Men remarked that
sweat felt gummy on hairy sunburnt arms, and the skin
tingled. In a few days of idleness before cutting started
John M. Rice, county president of Equity in Christian
County, rode ahead of some two hundred men.

"We are the 'Army of Peace'," he told the farmers, as
they rode up to the gates. "We ask you to pool your new
crop of tobacco with us. There will be no flogging. No barn
burnings. No plant-bed scrapings. We are honest and open
Christian farmers. You'll not be driven into the pool. If
you join up and later want to pull out, you'll be free to go,
and no hard feelings. Just brothers and neighbors under our
leathery hides." And he would laugh a big haw-haw.

The farmer on the other side of the rail fence might
covertly examine the leathery brothers and neighbors, but
even without masks they didn't seem very different from
Night Riders, and besides men not now in some kind of
association were apt to be the kind who were not joiners.

"I was never a hand at letting somebody else tell me when

I could sell my tobacker. I always figgered I was a free-born American, and I could do with my own what I liked. I'll study over it. I'll let you know."

The Day Riders would shrug and the long column would move away, going down the dusty road.

When their crusade was local, toward sundown the riders would disperse for home. When they moved more deeply into enemy territory, they carried along provisions and cooking utensils, and after a day's pleading with farmers they would fry their hogmeat and bread, and lie around on the ground smoking, chewing, dipping after eating. They would always be visited by nearby suspicious farmers. "Who you fellers? What's a big mob of you doing riding like this? You some them goddamn Night Riders I been hearing about?" If the farmer carried a shotgun it was for killing owls. "Well, just don't bother nothing around my place."

Rice then would go through his routine of explaining this "Army of Peace." He'd give his pitch for the farmer to join the Equity.

The Riders would buy eggs for 5c a dozen, and maybe a hen for 50c. They got sore sleeping on the ground, and more than one crusader muttered, "I sure as hell miss my feather bed and my woman." As their provisions gave out they would buy the little country stores barren of sardines, cheese, crackers, salmon, and other edibles. It grew harder by the day to get corn for their nags, for new corn was not yet dry in the shuck and old corn was growing scarce. What was worse, their travel money was running low. In this general situation of semi-starvation they arrived at Bowling Green, and pressed on some miles out to Horse Cave, where the Trust buyers were out in force. News of the "Army of Peace" had preceded them. But the Trust boys, no doubt egged on by the higher ups, called the sheriff and a dozen deputies and took the whole drove into custody, charged them with disturbing the peace, intimidation and seeking to coerce the independent tobacco men into a distasteful combine. Circuit court was in session at Bowling Green at the time but the judge said his docket would not permit hearing the cases until the following week. The jail wouldn't hold all two hundred Day Riders, so an arrangement was worked out whereby the culprits could stay in hotels and boarding houses for the week, and be under technical arrest. The men groaned. Tobacco was yellowing for cutting back home. They had scant money for board and rooms and provender for their beasts, and none for legal fees. If they had to go to jail or pay fines, in case they lost their case, they would indeed be, as one said, "in one goddamn hell of a fix."

Somehow it punctured their sense of crusade. The judge heard their case and dismissed it. "Not sufficient evidence." But the Trust boys won the round, and sadder and wiser the Army of Peace turned homeward.

Victualing their retreat was even harder than their advance. It wasn't exactly starvation that would cause them to turn from the big road back on the hillsides and eat pawpaws. Wild grass was all their horses had for forage. Back in Owensboro they made one last gesture of defiance. Travel-stained and disgusted, they formed a parade, with banners hoisted high. "Peace Today, War Tomorrow."

"If you don't heed us (pool your tobacco with Equity) another army will follow for whose actions we will not answer, and you must take the consequences."

Did Rice mean the Day Riders would turn into Night Riders, or that the Night Riders would be invited to move in and take a hand? He never answered the question. Then the crusaders dispersed for home and began cutting their tobacco.

Actually resentment was running high against the American Tobacco Company, the British Imperial, and Gallaher, chief buyers of Burley tobacco. In the back country, as tobacco was barned and men had time to meet, there were secret lodges at churches and schoolhouses similar to the Silent Brigade. Dr. Amoss and Guy Dunning found time to meet with some of these and instruct them in the techniques of flogging, barn burning, and other methods of coercion. Once in Owensboro three hundred infuriated farmers made up a mob and were about to attack three different warehouses, with sticks, stones, and maybe guns and the torch, but were driven back by the sheriff and chief of police and a score of deputies and police. The upper burley area was prime for Night Riding, and Governor Willson had another hot spot to ship soldiers to in case he was called on.

Perhaps what helped settle the froth was the price American was at last offering for tobacco. The Owensboro market in 1903 had been paying 2.81c a pound. Now the average was 7c, and for fine British leaf, 8.75c.

In New York James Duke and his able attorneys, DeLancey Nicholl, of New York, and John C. Johnson, of Philadelphia, were down on the mat with the United States Justice Department, and the gouging and chewing and cracking of bones drifted down into tobacco land, while barns began to burn all over Dark Kentucky.

Chapter Twenty

Wild Fire in the Blue Grass

THE BLUE GRASS OF KENTUCKY AND TENNESSEE IS A
fabled land. Merely mention "Blue Grass" and instantly
you invoke in your listener visions of mansions, bourbon
and belles, proudly galloping horses, glittering social carrying on; stately swains and haughty ladies in swishing crino-
line and technicolor, and all the fringe benefits of perfume
and bosomage and sex and noblesse oblige and duels. There
is no such uncouth thought as chewing tobacco and dipping
snuff and spitting on the floor or in the fireplace. In these
latter depraved days the region had fallen into the clutches
of absentee millionaires who bred fine horseflesh for the
Kentucky Derby and other great racing downs. Back in the
Night Rider epoch, burley tobacco was the chief root-crop,
and strangely enough, outside of horses, it remains that
today. Drive from Nashville to Bowling Green, to Horse
Cave and Bardstown and Lexington, and on and on to
Flemingsburg and Maysville on the Ohio River, and you'll
see a thousand stately barns packed in the fall of the year
with golden leaf. You'll drive through undulating farmlands

of soft fertility and ancient beauty. You'll stare in wonder at
the lovely little towns that seem to have been seeded in old
Virginia, or Maryland, or Tidewater. None of the crude
utility architecture of the raw western towns. We know Lexington. It's a clean-limbed little city with tobacco warehouses, the yards of the Chesapeake & Ohio railroad
sprawled about, the campus of the University of Kentucky
sprawled elsewhere, and an air of stateliness that could
come only from legend, culture and learning — and fine
liquor and warm women and burley smoking. I think of
Flemingsburg, a quaint little child of the Blue Grass, and
how, driving through the town, I thought I was once more
going through Fredericksburg, Virginia. There were the
old fashioned brick rows with front doors stepping out into
the sidewalks and those adorable windows with arches or
over-drapes of bricks; the old-timey narrow-waisted glass
fronts of the shops, the streets where dwellings thrust their
beautiful doorways into your face and the veiled windows
look down at you secretly in passing; and deep into the
oaks and elms the mansions. Bricks burnt by black slave
hands and mortar distilled from tobacco sweat through
black hides. And in the outlands always the solemn tobacco
barns and the amorous rolling farmlands. And Old Kentucky Homes.

It was Burley Tobacco Society land. Night Riding had
not yet arrived, but in 1900 burley prices were declining
and the American Tobacco Company captured the tobacco
market, and by October 1907 the growers were becoming
desperate. There was a huge rally in Shelbyville, a town
between Frankfort and Louisville, just 22 miles from where
Governor Willson was posting $1000 rewards and promis-
ing to pardon any man killing a Night Rider, and directing
his augmenting army of occupation out in the heathen prov-

inces. At this rally the redoubtable tub-thumper Colonel Joel Fort was to make history by his famous remark, "No state raises more tobacco and *less* hell than Kentucky," and he aided in inspiring the tobacco growers to adopt the slogan, "No Crop For 1908." It was the opening battle cry of speakers, organizers and hell-raisers who fanned out in the Blue Grass to force adoption of the pledge. Governor Willson should have been present at this gathering. He was surely invited. But he chose, as always, when he had a chance to hear the growers' side, to remain aloof.

The general effect of this campaign was that some men, instead of aligning themselves with the boycott, held back, planned larger acreages and waited to get rich at the sacrifice of their neighbors.

The neighbors didn't take to this idea very cordially. Back in May they had already toyed with barn burning, when they fired the barn of the Shirley Brothers, in Sanders, Carroll County, and burnt 200,000 pounds of fine tobacco valued at $30,000. After the Shelbyville rally the Riders began to bestir themselves in earnest. Dr. Amoss and Guy Dunning made flying trips to their secret lodges and instructed them, and drilled them. There was no close-knit underground like the Silent Brigade, but anger was just as violent. After the great Hopkinsville raid the Burley Riders decided if the Night Riders could do it, they could do it too; and they wanted to spit in Governor Willson's face as well. Soon groups of horsemen, sometimes hooded and sometimes not, carried the warning abroad. "Join the Burley Society. Heed that 'no crop' order." An unknown artist painted great portraits of gallows on barns. After the highly successful Russellville raid, a hundred Riders moved on A. T. Robertson's warehouse, in Bath County, 50 miles from Lexington, and burnt 60,000 pounds of tobacco. The flames got out of hand

and burnt a nearby general store. The squad went six miles north into Fleming County (seat Flemingsburg) and destroyed another 100,000 pounds. The visitation looked so ominous that all the Trust buyers and independents fled the locality, and guards were stationed at all the important warehouses.

After six weeks of quiet another squad of Burley Riders fell upon the warehouse of Dave Snell in New Liberty and destroyed 25,000 pound of burley. The same night they burned 10,000 pounds belonging to John Garney, two miles away, and shot out the windows of the Bond Brothers' store. March 25, they were back at one in the morning and burned warehouses and tobacco valued at $30,000. Three days later another squad moving horseback and in buggies burned the barns of three people and left notes on the gateposts, "No Crop For 1908." George Graddy, one of the victims, rebuilt his barn, and in hope of catching Riders placed sticks of dynamite around it. His hogs rooted around and seven of his fall-meat porkers were blown to hell and gone. On the night of March 22 another band of 50 Riders moved in on Hiram Hedges, who lived six miles from Carlisle, not far from Flemingsburg, called him to the door and at the point of guns forced him to promise not to put in a crop. Who fired the shotgun that killed Hedges was never known. Three men were accused of the crime but were freed after a preliminary hearing. March 27, a small body of Riders, nine in number, demonstrated that huge spectacular raids, while getting wide publicity, were not essential to spectacular results. They fired the warehouse of T. S. Hamilton, in Covington, Ky., and burnt 300,000 pounds of tobacco valued at $70,000, and destroyed an adjoining block of buildings used as offices of buyers, valued at $200,000. On April 17 sixty Riders fell upon a wagon train of tobacco going to market, flogged the drivers, scattered the mule teams, and dumped the cargo into a flooded creek. The sheriff got wind in time to chase this band, captured four of them, and put them them in jail. But when their trial came up the jury acquitted all four.

It began to appear there was as closely knit an underground here as on west in the Black Patch, though no "brains" were ever discovered. But Bracken County was the hotbed of this activity. On March 9 Riders burned Bob Staton's last-year's crop and flogged him. On April 8 they captured Augusta, a small town on the Ohio flat not far from Maysville, pinned down the inhabitants with gunfire, and burnt $10,000 worth of Trust tobacco. They crossed the river and burnt a string of barns in Brown County, Ohio, just to show the Yankees how their hearts still beat. Then they came back and whipped an independent buyer and made him promise on his life to buy no more "independent" tobacco.

On May 7 Augusta staged a great rally, with five thousand marching in the mile-long parade. "Two floats attracted considerable attention and vast applause. One showed a masked Night Rider guarding while others scraped a plant bed. The other showed a prominent local man being hung in effigy."

By June 15 there was not a sprig of tobacco growing in the county. This was saturation raiding. To these Riders "No Crop" meant no crop. They began subsistence-living off the land. After the Shelbyville rally they returned home and instead of depending on tobacco they planted food crops, bred more sows for meat, raised chickens, and big gardens. Butter, milk, eggs, ham, now and then a yearling beef, became the staple food at every farmer's table. One farmer was heard to say, "I never had enough fried chicken

till this year." Clothing could be made to last another year.
A patch on the seat of a man's overalls was his badge of
fidelity to the cause.

It was not all sugar and spice. Men who refused to join
burnt their neighbors' barns, and set fire to all their vacant
tenant cabins. They put Paris green in the springs and poisoned Society men's stock. The few that had tobacco to sell
sent their leaf to Lexington and Maysville under heavy
guard; and Trust buyers toted heavy hardware in their dealings. There were killings on both sides. In addition to Hiram
Hedges, there was the case of Newt Hazlett, a farmer near
Jackson, who was found dead in the big road on the night
of May 22 clutching a revolver and wire pliars. Two uniden-
tified men were discovered in a strawstack, their throats cut.
Some growers like Dr. Sam Halley in Fayette County put
in a crop under guards day and night. But many farmers
solved the problem by leaving the state, moving up into
Indiana or down into Tennessee, where Night Riding seemed to be held under control by Ben Sory and troops. Those
who quit the state carried burley tobacco seed with them
and so the Burley Belt began to widen. The Burley Society
numbered at its peak 35,000 active members, and rivalled
the Black Patch groups.

Governor Willson's headache kept getting worse, as he
called up more and more troops, dispersing them more
widely in the Black Patch, and sending them here and there
in the Blue Grass as sporadic Riding went on. The trouble
was that when soldiers reached a spot, things quieted down,
and nobody could say who rode or who didn't. And Willson had no idea where things would break out again.

Meanwhile James Duke was being pinned down more
and more closely by the Justice Department. James Mc-
Reynolds, from Tennessee, was stuffing his brief case with

facts and figures and asking Duke the most embarrassing
questions. McReynolds was a man of parts. Besides coming
from Tennessee, he was later to become a justice of the
U. S. Supreme Court, and Attorney General under Wood-
row Wilson. Was Buck Duke breaking the law? *Breaking
the law!* Horrors, no. Law-breaking was for that poor bastard down in the jungles of Kentucky, with his wife's petti-
coat cut with holes for eyes over his head and burning the
wind nights to burn tobacco poor Mr. Duke had bought
with his little bright gold dollars. The slow-motion lawsuit
was swinging into high gear; and in the end there would be
a score of volumes of testimony, covering thousands and
thousands of pages.

Chapter Twenty-one

He Who Rides and Runs Away

WHERE THE SOLDIERS WERE, PEACE REIGNED. GOVERNOR Willson was busy chasing Riders in the Blue Grass. Governor Malcolm Patterson down in Tennessee kept his militia alerted around Clarksville and Springfield. But tension persisted between citizens and soldiers. There was much roistering, considerable thieving, and always the secret attack of cornfed youths on the budding flowers of the country girls. Willson had standing rewards of $500 for any Night Rider captured dead or alive, and $1000 reward for any of the leaders. Soldiers were heard discussing the rewards on the streets of Princeton one Saturday. A trooper said, "I'd as soon collect that money, me. It'd buy a little tobacker farm and there's a gal out Wallonia way I'd marry, and who could ask for a better deal than that?" The word was carried to Dr. Amoss. He shrugged, but he did not ignore the ominous threat. He and Guy Dunning, while things were quiet around Russellville and Hopkinsville, plotted a movement up into the northern provinces, that as yet had scarcely felt Night Riding.

228

Meanwhile, as the militia increased, Goveror Willson found difficulty in billeting his soldiers. The problem was that of camp grounds. People knew if they harbored the hated soldiers the Night Riders would descend on them. There'd be whippings, barn burnings, house burnings, mysteriously poisoned stock. At the very least there would be warning notes at gateposts and bundles of dogwood switches. Merchants and farmers refused to sell feed for the horses and food for the men. Up in the burley belt men said they hoped the military would have to eat the bark off trees. When the overflow of militia from Hopkinsville came to Gracey hunting campground, men refused to accommodate them. "Move on. You're not needed, you're not wanted, you get no ground nor shelter. You get no grub for yourselves and no forage for your beasties." The soldiers finally found ground on the I.C. railroad right-of-way. Reprisal against the railroad was swift and costly. Three parties of Night Riders, moving quickly in the dead of night, swooped down upon the railway stations at Gracey, Otter Pond and Cerulean Springs and burnt them to the ground. The guests of Cerulean Springs Hotel saw the show of a lifetime when after midnight they were wakened by the lurid glow of the huge blaze through their windows. Most of the guests got ready to vacate the hotel, supposing it would be fired next; but the band of hoods took off in the night. At Gracey the squad trundled two boxcars of tobacco up to the station and fired them both. Soldiers rushed in — when the fire was beyond control — and fired a few shots. The Riders had already escaped. When the railroad placed a boxcar at Otter Pond as a substitute station, Night Riders moved in and burnt that.

Governor Willson's annoyance increased. He wired Major Bassett, "Get in there and capture those scoundrels!"

He made a public statement that was widely reprinted in
Black Patch papers. "The Night Riders are a lot of cowards. Any man who goes around at night wearing a mask is
a coward. Twenty men of our militia could whip 500 of
them. They have worked great havoc, destroying property
and even responsible for loss of life, but every power at the
command of the state authorities will be used to check them.
The power of the law will soon be restored and the guilty
ones will be punished." On June 14 in the Cincinnati *En-
quirer* he said further, "The tobacco laborer, most of whom
are white, are a distinct class in themselves. They generally
live in huts, work very hard, as do their women and children, whom they compel to go to the fields and, as a rule,
are lawless and violent. Troubles are certain to follow where
a region is given over to the production of tobacco."

"A baser libel was never uttered against the people in the
history of the state than the above!" O. J. Jennings, editor
of the Murray *Ledger,* shouted. His ball-bearing pen reached red hot. "Governor Willson is owned body and soul by
the Trust, and every utterance emanating from him . . . is
dictated by the Trust."

The effect of such statements was to make the Night
Riders more determined, and to stimulate the Hillbillies to
sell the Trust and plot some Riding of their own. There
were some 200 farmers around Crider, Fredonia and Farmersville, villages north of Princeton, who, under a leader
named Henry Wilson, organized a raid on Princeton, knowing the law was on their side. They'd give the Night Riders
a dose of their own medicine. After the raid on Princeton
the Night Rider faction was in full control of marketing
there. The Hillbillies were forced to wagon their leaf round-
aboutly to Paducah, and they moved in long trains, a dozen
vehicles, and every man armed to the teeth. They wanted

to ship from Princeton. On March 13 word reached the chief of police in Princeton that one hundred Hillbillies were gathering at Farmersville, seven miles distant, to capture Princeton, burn the court house, whip Ward Hadley the Association attorney, and burn all the Association tobacco they could find in the warehouses. The place was bulging with leaf, for the 1907 crop was going to market and cars were going out daily with Association tobacco. If this scheme worked, they would go on seven miles south of Princeton and whip John W. Hollowell, Robert's cousin, to avenge his dastardly act. They still professed great indignation that Mary Lou Hollowell had been scourged out of the country.

There were soldiers about, but the Hillbillies knew they would give no trouble. They had Willson's promise. "I will immediately pardon any man who kills a Night Rider." And there were those rewards.

The Night Riders kept spies abroad, and listening posts brought in the word the moment the scheme was plotted. The alarm went forth and scores of Night Riders without hoods galloped into town, deployed at every street corner, climbed up on roofs of buildings. The roof of the Odd Fellows Hall, the highest in town, was covered with armed men, who asked for nothing better than an open battle with Hillbillies. Squads marched out the north road and took battle station behind barns and trees. Spies eased out ahead. They waited.

It was late in the morning and nothing happened. Spies for the Hillbillies had sneaked down to get the lay of the land. They reported, "The place is reeking with guns. They'd kill a man down there." The raiders dispersed, and the Night Riders at Princeton ground their teeth in frustration and cursed. But guards patrolled the town for a week afterward, and a heavy guard took care of Hollowell till danger blew over.

Most of this was shadow boxing. But it made nervous wrecks of many good folk. The killing of Orbie Nabb, a young Night Rider from down in the Nabb Schoolhouse locality, and the brutal whipping of Henry Bennett, on February 4, were the real articles. Nabb had grown prosperous enough to move to Princeton, where he engaged in prizing tobacco for the Association at Stegar & Dollar's factory. A leg show entitled "The Isle of Spice," was delighting the yokels and sending the baldheaded row into hysterics at the Henrietta Theatre. So juicy was this performance by what might be called a squad of female Night Riders — they were mostly chippies in disguise — that thunderous applause kept the show going till past midnight. The dancer by today's standard of nudity were naked except for their armor plate corsets and thigh-length can-can skirts with enough foliage to bluff even an amorous senior citizen. Before the final curtain sweat was filtering through the paint on their faces, and their armpits oozed a kind of amber. Orbie Nabb had an after-show date with one of the chorus girls. Henry Wilson, the same young fellow who had planned to lead the attack on Princeton, was at the show. Nabb and Wilson had been at outs a good while and words had passed between them not yet taken back. Threats had been made to shoot on sight. The two met on the steps of the theatre. Wilson was coming out; Nabb was going in to get his girl. Both were armed and Wilson reached his gun first. "Take that, goddamn your soul!" he shouted and fired and Nabb turned crying, "I'm shot," and staggered back, rolled down the steps to the sidewalk, where he died before the horrified eyes of the folk coming from the show. Wilson ran for his horse and galloped out of town, hiding in the upper

country and eventually quitting the country, pretty certain
the Night Riders would kill him. Governor Willson in due
time pardoned him.

The Bennett affair was even more important and uglier.
Dycusburg is one of the small tobacco towns on the Cumberland River. There Henry Bennett was an enterpriser of
some substance, operating a large tobacco business where
the river facilities for shipping were good; and back against
the river bluff where a cold spring poured forth, he had a
whisky distillery. Some miles back in the hinterlands he
operated a big tobacco planting. Bennett bought tobacco
for the Trust warehouses in Paducah and Clarksville. He
added no small income to his tobacco money by selling
whisky to the captains and passengers and crews of passing
Cumberland packets, as well as local trade among the back-
landers. His brew was prime and he had a way of paying
his Hillbillies gold dollars for their leaf. O. J. Jennings of
the Murray *Leader* complained bitterly of this extra lure to
the Hillbillies. It was bad enough to buy bootleg tobacco.
It was a sin and shame to use American Tobacco Company
gold to glitter the sin. He said it was just another one of the
Trust's subtle efforts to crack the Association. In a way,
times were critical. With Willson's army operating farther
afield, riding by night to scatter bands of Riders and break
up their lodges, and this blinding of the yokels with the
glitter of gold — and worse yet, Bennett's daring Amoss
and Dunning to do anything about it — well, the time had
come for the Night Riders to act, danger or no.

There was another influential citizen and farmer and
Trust buyer living between Dycusburg and Marion, near a
village named Salam on what is now Highway 60. The region there was lovely rolling valleys, and vistas stretching
for miles across fertile tobacco fields; and A. H. Cardin had

named his plantation View. His home was the most impressive in the locality. The mansion was situated on a knoll, and was surrounded by fine trees and an iron fence — status symbol in that day and time. Cardin had once been a candidate for governor, and in the beginning had been active in the Protective Association. But he had broken with Felix Ewing's outfit, and this secession made him a marked man; for there was no sin more heinous than for an Association member to backslide and take up buying Trust tobacco. He too had ready gold dollars to attract the growers who were pledged to the Association. It was time to break this business up. Dr. Amoss' warriors had been inactive since the Russellville affair, and were champing to ride once more.

Orders went out and on the night of February 4 a hundred Riders moved in a body on Henry Bennett's factory and distillery and burnt them. The barrels of whisky made weird blueish flames, by the eerie light of which the masked raiders hauled Bennett's factory foreman, W. B. Grove, from bed and lashed him; and going to Bennett's house, shouted him out. They carried him a way from the house and tied him to a tree, and laid on his back the most brutal flogging inflicted upon any man during the troubles. There was a thorn tree nearby, and the Riders broke off limbs and tore Bennett's back with thorns. "His shirt and underclothing were punctured like a sieve." A long thorn tore his cheek and broke off in his flesh. Someone shot at close range and the bullet went through one of his ears. "He was roweled with a steel spur which broke off in his thigh." Later the excessive brutality was explained by the Riders because Bennett emerged from his house with his pistol, and would have used it but for his wife's tears and pleading. It seems a lame explanation. Riders expected their victims to use guns if they could. There was something else here; and one surmises it was vengeance of a very personal nature. There is no evidence that either Amoss or Dunning were present on this night; for though these men were leaders of the underground, they did not encourage excessive brutality. But the band was made up of Trigg, Caldwell and Lyon men, the home area of Amoss and Dunning. A crowd saw the Riders returning through Eddyville, and a voice called, "What you fellows been up to tonight?" A voice already gruff with remorse answered, "You'll have to ask Henry Bennett."

Bennett came close to dying. He was removed to a hospital and the man, who lived only two years longer, never again was able to walk upright. His wife had carved on his stone, "Killed by the Night Riders."

Five nights after the Bennett raid the same squads rendezvoused a few miles from Lamasco before dark and moved through Eddyville, 12 miles away, and then on to Fredonia, another 12 miles, and fell upon the village about one in the morning, capturing the telephone office, covering the manager Oscar Scarberry, who was also night operator, and cutting the outside wires. They left a rear guard and the main body rode six miles to View, other Riders joining until the force was perhaps two hundred. That they were able to move in such force, and from scattered lodges, indicated how ineffective the Guardsmen were in preventing Riding when the lodges were determined. They arrived at View about two o'clock, shooting heavy volleys into the house to rouse Cardin. It developed that the man and his family had gone to Evansville to attend a funeral and had left the home unguarded. Men fetched kindling and rails from nearby fences, piled them around both the mansion and the warehouse, packed almost to the rafters with fine leaf — $20,-000 worth, it was reputed — poured kerosene and struck matches, and stood back as both buildings rose in magnificent spirals of flames. The time was winter and one Rider remembered afterward how welcome was the warmth till the heat drove them back. They loitered to enjoy the spectacle. Some men quaffed from bottles. One man put his cigar on a long fishing pole, eased in and got a light from View. He said it was one of the nicest fires and finest smokes he'd ever enjoyed.

Down the long valley the lurid glow brought sleepy watchers from their beds. "Goddamn it's the Night Riders!" But none showed their faces as the column of horsemen strung past along the winding road. At four o'clock they picked up the rear guard at Fredonia, and squads began breaking away. By the time they arrived at the original meeting the Riders had made sixty miles over roads deep in mud, and now and then spits of snow cut their lips.

This, men said who knew, was the work of veterans.

One more raid was projected on Marion. These smaller towns had no Association warehouses, and they thus became the object of attacks. This time they had the audacity to send word ahead they were coming. Their target was the Trust warehouse of R. H. Kemp, the leading trader in town. Kemp had been intensively brainwashed by Association pleaders but it hadn't taken. He could have pooled with the Henderson Stemming Association, but he disdained that. A small squad of Riders suddenly appeared at Kemp's yard gate and shouted for him to come out. Instead Kemp fled out the back way, telling his wife to say he had gone to the warehouse. He hid under a wagonload of tobacco in his barnlot. He heard his wife say, "My husband's gone to the warehouse." For a moment Kemp was sure his life hung by a thread. Would they know she was lying and come gunning for him? It would be like them. Riding had become more and more brutal as the battle lines were joined. He almost had a heart attack when the band reined around and trotted off into town for the warehouse. He crawled from the wagon and went into the house and lay down on the living room couch till his faint passed. He'd been warned the raid would be made Monday night. Tomorrow would be Saturday. The following afternoon he joined the Stemming Association. After this he did not remain long in Marion, fearful that the Riders would get him yet. He sold his home and business and moved away.

Chapter Twenty-two

The Moving Finger Writes

FOR MORE THAN THREE HUNDRED MILES STRETCHING from Maysville on the Ohio River in a long semi-circle to Murray, in western Kentucky, Governor Willson had troops moving, guarding, prowling, arresting. No exact number is now available. But they ran into the thousands. Friction increased as police action became more ruthless, and often lawless in itself. O. J. Jennings, of the Murray *Ledger,* kept up a running feud with Governor Willson and Judge A. J. G. Wells, who requested that troops be sent into the Murray area when a raid was threatened. Jennings wrote, "County Judge Wells did make the request, but the attack was not founded on facts." The very idea, he snarled, of "soldiers riding into Murray, great strapping six-foot mountain boys . . . armed with Kreg-Jorgensen rifles and army Colts!" He went on: "I contend that the presence of armed troops is not only destructive to the business interests of the town, but conducive to greater unrest in the country. Their presence is a galling yoke upon the good citizenship of the County." At the remoter end of the half circle, at Owings-

238

ville, Bath County, Judge Allie Young frothed at the mouth because soldiers were sent there. At the time there was a law in Kentucky: the governor could not send in the military unless county officials requested police help, on the basis of being unable to handle a situation with their own power. Judge Young had made no such request. He called up a Grand Jury instead, and charged them, "Indict Governor Willson himself for sending in troops without official orders." He went on to denounce Willson. "Any Governor who will promise to pardon a man killing a Night Rider would establish himself as a dictator and rule by means of the military."

A lonely voice from Madisonville, Kentucky, wrote to the Louisville *Evening Post,* "The question of whether or not the governor is going beyond his rightful powers in sending troops into counties where they have not been called for is one that should be investigated and settled. Has the governor the right to transgress or manufacture law in order to enforce law? Is the state under martial law? Is the present state government of Kentucky a military despotism in alliance with the American Tobacco Company?"

Henry Waterson may not have been answering this question directly when he editorialized, "The dispatching of troops . . . was merely preparation against mob violence. Policing . . . with military arm of the law will result in no permanent benefit unless the doors of the pentitentiary close behind the backs of a few men who have held to the erroneous theory that they have the right to lay waste the countryside and burn and bully towns because somebody has failed to obey the law. At great expense the state has offered protection. Now let the people . . . do the rest."

The county judge at Princeton gave orders, "Any man arrested by state troops . . . [who do not show a civil warrant] shall be within his legal rights to shoot the soldier down like a dog."

It began to look as if the time were ripe for open civil war over the tobacco belt. From Maysville through Fleminsburg, to Lexington, Bardstown, Bowling Green, and on west, the pots were seething. But Governor Willson pushed his troops in closer; soldiers made arrests and didn't get shot; they broke up Masonic and Odd Fellows meetings, thinking they were Night Rider Lodges; they vandalized churches; they rode high. They did not drive the Night Riders wholly from the saddle, for one night one hundred Riders swooped down on Eddyville, but paused at the city limits and contented themselves with shooting the posters of Barnum & Bailey Circus off a Hillbilly barn. They scattered before the troops could catch them. Here and there would be a burning barn; now and then there'd be a midnight whipping. On the whole things had reached a point where something had to give.

It gave first on two abortive raids — on Marion and Murray. Marion nearly wet its pants in terror when a mob of strange men in civilian clothes entered town and began loitering, filling the court house square and staring curiously at the store window displays, and the shapely women who happened to be inside shopping. Females hoisted their lacey skirts and with muffled shrieks took off for refuge in nearby homes; and two were seen to hide in a privy back of a drygoods store. The first reaction of the town was this was some kind of "day raid." People still shuddered at the lashing given Henry Bennett, and the burning of View. Tension increased rather than diminished when the strangers identified themselves to the county judge as guardsmen, sent in answer to his request, since threats kept floating about the Night Riders were going to attack and burn every Trust leaf in the place. Instead of Night Riders here was the Army. They'd be ready to rape any old or young woman caught on the streets; and by night forage down among the whorehouses for any sex garbage they could pick up. They'd raid the Negro chippie joints, and there would be a flood of incoming prostitutes. It had been like that at Hopkinsville, Russellville, every station where the military had been posted. There were plenty of townsfolk who would have connived with a Night Rider raid, if the soldiers could have been got rid of.

The Murray raid was never pulled off, because of the troops. Murray had an active Trust buying market; the hotels were usually full of buyers for the American, Imperial and Regies. On a spring night when there was a train of loaded tobacco cars on the siding at the N.C. & St.L. depot, Riders gathered to the number of an estimated two hundred fifty, ready to swoop down and burn the big Trust factory and cars under the very noses of the soldiers. The plan, as it seems at this remove to have been worked out, was to send in spies reporting the Riders at a point some miles out, to toll the troops from town. Then they'd gallop in and in ten minutes have the fires going. Murray was too well guarded to risk it. The Riders dispersed. But rumor said the buyers at the hotel had their upstairs windows open so they could leap out on the roof of the kitchen and dining room and escape lashings.

The actual crackup came from two unexpected directions. Guy Dunning had been prizing Associated tobacco at Stegar & Dollar in Princeton when a Night Rider spy came to him to report. "You'd better see Dr. Amoss as soon as you can. I picked up something. One these goddamn soldiers, Bud Kelso's his name, has somehow been in touch with Governor Willson and has agreed to kill Doc on sight, for $1000 reward, a pardon, and guards just in case. The feller's been courting old Dink Marshall's girl down there around Wallonia, or Cadiz, and he aims to buy a tobacco farm with the money and marry the girl. Doc Amoss had better get the hell out of the country."

"I'll see him tonight," Dunning said.

The other news was even more disquieting. Dunning picked up the rumor that Mary Lou Hollowell and her husband and son were back in Paducah, and had retained John Miller, probably the best lawyer in the Pennyrile, to take the case in Federal Court, and even at this moment the names of all the Riders in that whipping were being processed for arrest. Dunning and Dr. Amoss had not been in that party. But the significance could not be escaped. This word had to be got to the General. Dunning wound up his day's work in midafternoon and galloped out of town to see Dr. Amoss. He met Dr. Amoss as dusk along a country road, and hailed him. "General! General!"

Dr. Amoss reached for his army revolver. Then the voice registered. They turned off the road into a bit of sheltered wood, and there Dunning gave the reports. They sat long moments in silence. "We're in for trouble!"

"Yes, I'm afraid so," Dr. Amoss agreed. "Well?"

"You get the hell gone."

"They'll only get you."

Dunning shrugged. "I can take care of myself. It's you they want. I'd waste not one minute. I'd take off tonight."

"Leave my practice? Leave my folks?"

"If somebody kills you for blood money, you'll leave your practice and your folks."

Dr. Amoss sighed. His age was beginning to tell on him. "Y-yes, I reckon you're right."

"I'll go back home with you. Pack up and get out. Don't tell me where you're going. A fine doctor like you can make a place anywhere. Then send back for your family. I'll see nobody tries to burn you out." He got on his horse, Dr. Amoss crawled awkwardly into his buggy, and they moved away in the night. At Dr. Amoss' house he told his wife, and she packed. They had supper and Dunning drank coffee and they worked out such plans as they could. Dunning was to keep close watch on that developing law suit. Dr. Amoss instructed him to see all the men involved in the Hollowell whipping and have them work out air tight alibis. They must employ the best lawyer available. Maybe in the end they could beat the case. But Federal Court — now, that was different. If it had been circuit court they could have controlled the situation.

So Dr. Amoss took his luggage and a bottle of whisky and rode off in the deep night to no place Dunning could name.

Chapter Twenty-three

We Fear No Judge Nor Jury

WHEN THE HOLLOWELL CASE REARED ITS UGLY HEAD above the tobacco fields of Kentucky land, after the Night Rider hierarchy had figuratively laid Mary Lou by, it upset the emotions of scores and hundreds of brave horsemen. And the retaining of "Judge" John G. Miller — the honorary appellation of Judge is still used in Kentucky for its distinguished barristers — did not help matters.

Miller was born and raised around Princeton. He was something of a poet at heart: He loved to go out in the country frosty nights when woodpeckers were migrating and listen to their elusive transient cry, "Ch-e-ir-ar." He had a fine nose for hickory smoke issuing from a log barn. He was a shrewd lawyer and before long was waxing fat and prosperous. He wore dark suits with vests, and a gold watch chain across his fine abdomen, with a Masonic charm. He had a gold pin with the effigy of a galloping horse in his fashionable cravat. Another status symbol was a gold toothpick with removable quill and a small scoop at the other end for removing wax from the ear. One veteran tobacco man once said he never saw Judge Miller in a dirty shirt, and another said, "I reckon he was as well-set-up a man as the Pennyrile ever seen."

Success led him far afield from the tobacco patches, which he quit in 1874 and he ended in Paducah with two partners, where they did an assembly line practice. His gold coffers fattened and his reputation cast a long shadow. He still practiced in the Circuit Court at Princeton. One morning he was standing in front of the bank waiting for the up train, when the sheriff joined him with the news of the Hollowell flogging.

"Johnny," the sheriff said, "there stands the Hollowell house, riddled by bullets, windows and doors smashed, fences broken, stock wandering through the growing crops. Bob and his family run out of the country and can't even come back to see his old sick mother. Sad, sad." He shook his head. "They were an industrious family. They're at the depot now, taking the same train you are."

"Well!" Judge Miller said.

"I had to guard Mary Lou from the hotel. I got a deputy there now."

The train whistled. Miller said some word of sympathy. In the waiting room Mary Lou and Bob and the boy were guarded by the deputy. Judge Miller had a discriminating eye for an attractive woman, for he later reported, "She was dressed well, was tall and well formed, made a handsome appearance, and had associates in the towns. She was high-spirited and likely to express her opinion with freedom." He was thinking of her report to the Grand Jury, and she had more than plenty to say about the men who whipped her husband. Her brother, living a few miles from Nabb School-house, had refused to join the Association, and his plant beds had been scraped. She had more to say about that. Miller realized hatred for her was intense.

They boarded the train and after a few miles he caught her eye and joined her. She remembered him with a gush of words. "They were shooting up the tenant cabin. That woke us and we got up and tried to dress. Then the bullets crashed through the windows and doors. I heard Bob's brother shout, 'Close up, close up!' Then a shot hit me." She showed the bandage over her eye. "They yelled for us to come out. Bob said 'No they'll kill you,' but I went. Bob and Price came along. They grabbed Bob and carried him down behind the barn — O my God!" She covered her face and wept. Bob sat a few seats away, hunched up like a man who would never face the world again. "I want to law 'em. Judge Miller, will you law 'em for me?"

Miller considered. Down deep he wasn't anxious to get mixed up with any of this Night Rider stuff. "You come to see me when you get settled, and we'll see."

She kept sobbing. "They kicked me. It was a young man. I heard a woman scream, 'This is sweet revenge to me!' That was Lula Hollowell, Bob's brother's wife. I screamed right back — I'd come out of my faint — I'm going to law you!' Some man shouted, 'We fear neither judge nor jury!' I can name most of them, even men living over in the other counties."

It was puzzling and confusing. Here was an attractive woman being kicked by a young man. The flogger was a blood brother, member of the Baptist Church, a leader in the community. And this sister-in-law giving a hideous laugh of revenge! Miller wanted to ask a lot of questions, for he sensed there was much more here than would come out in any indictments and lawsuits. He left Mary Lou still in tears and went on to his office uptown. There he laid the business before his partners. They heard him with horror. "I'm running for office down there," one excused himself. "I need every Night Rider vote I can get. If I messed up with Mary Lou I'd be snowed under."

The other said, "We could make a case. You say Mary Lou can name 30 men and this woman? But I own a house in Princeton and run a tobacco farm out in the country, and they'd burn me out the minute they heard we'd been retained. It would be futile, Johnny. No judge or jury would find those Nabb neighborhood Baptists and pillars of society guilty."

Mary Lou came to consult Miller before she removed to Oklahoma.

She appealed to me with intense emotion personally to take charge of the claims of herself and her family for damages. I told her the decision of the firm was irrevocable though we sympathized deeply with her. But it was highly important for me to know with absolute certainty what connection if any she had directly or indirectly, may have had with the commission of the offense she was charged with in the indictment (that she had master-minded the plant-bed scrapings that Choate and Pettit were already serving time for, after testifying in their trial that Mary Lou had paid $10 for the job;) that she might confess everything to me as her counsel and that I could not under the law violate her confidence.

A full confession might be of the utmost importance to herself and family. "She fell upon her knees, held up her right hand and said, 'I swear to you that I had nothing to do with the scraping of that plant bed, have no knowledge of who did it and am innocent of that charge as an unborn child — so help me, God.'"

Miller at least was convinced, though the jury that convicted Choate and Pettit accepted their own testimony. It did not seem plausible that two uncouth tenants would seek revenge on three neighbor planters. Here was Mary Lou on her knees before God pleading she knew nothing about it. It's one of those puzzles in Night Rider history where you lay your cash on the barrelhead and take any opinion you like.

Judge Miller promised to take the matter up in a few months, and Mary Lou and her family went to Oklahoma. Out there Bob found the work he could pick up was too straining and they returned to Paducah. Mary Lou once more called on Judge Miller. Miller meanwhile had dissolved his partnership with the candidate and business man and had taken into the firm his son, John Goodrum Miller, Jr. Now he could consider Mary Lou's case. He'd done a lot of meditating on it since he last saw the woman, and no doubt the image of her well formed person, and maybe memory of her hot biscuits, had had weight in his decision to represent her.

"Move to Evansville, Indiana," he told her. "Establish residence there in good faith. Bob can find work. We'll keep in touch."

The time was late in November, 1907. Miller's plan was simple and legal. A civil case would have to be tried in Princeton. The courts and juries there were in complete control of the Night Riders. Conviction would be impossible. There was one small thing he had been meditating on all along. Mary Lou was more than just *popular* with men. Any defense would seek to make more of this than perhaps there was; and maybe there was plenty, too. That would weaken her case. The Hollowells moved to

Indiana and Miller began preparing the case for the April term of Federal Court in Paducah.

When the twenty-eight subpoenas went out, there was great consternation among the lodges in Caldwell, Lyon and Trigg Counties. Night Riders took it as lick in the dark, and they quickly enough decided they'd have a pound of flesh from old Johnny Miller's tail. If they got within reach of Mary Lou they'd kill her. A petition was circulated and signed by scores of prominent citizens in defense of the accused Night Riders. "We believe they are wholly innocent of the charges brought against them by the Hollowells . . . as citizens of the good Commonwealth of Kentucky we deem it our duty to so certify to all the world."

Among the signers were the cashiers and assistant cashiers of the two banks, the county judge, mayor and chief of police of Princeton, two Baptist ministers, four doctors, a dentist, a horse doctor, and lesser citizens presumed to be Night Riders themselves, or coerced into signing by Night Riders.

The suit, filed March 2, 1908, was for $50,000 for Mary Lou, $50,000 for Bob, and $25,000 for Price. John E. Hollowell, Bob's brother, was named first; John W. Hollowell, a cousin, was named second; and Lula Hollowell, Mary Lou's sister-in-law was named third in the list of defendants.

The suit caught the defendants, as one person remarked with wry earthy humor, "with our britches down and no corncobs handy." When good neighbors met in town Saturdays they'd stare at each other and break into nervous laughs. "Well!" one man said. "So Mary Lou and her man and that brat want $125,000 damages for that licking we laid on Bob! Well, if she thinks she'd going to buy one

of those gas buggies to drive around in and wear silks and
satins and lace pants while our women settle for flour sack
pants, she's got another think coming. We'll show her, by
God, we will, now!" Their laughter faded thinly. There
might not be time for mirth and laughter when Johnny
Miller had shot his legal wad.

Besides his son, Miller engaged to assist him George Du
Relle of Louisville, who had been United States District
Attorney and formerly Judge of the Court of Appeals.
The defendants retained Ward Headley of Princeton,
W. H. Yost and Ruby Laffoon of Madisonville. Headley
felt they could beat the case, saying, "The plaintiff is a
woman indicted for having two tenants scrape the plant
beds of her neighbors, and the tenants are now in the
penitentiary, having pleaded guilty. This suit is brought
for revenge, and the defendants anticipate no trouble in
showing their absolute innocence."

Miller recognized instantly the first move of the defendants would be an assault on Mary Lou's character.
There was the indictment; there was the confession of the
tenants. There was this background of vague gossip about
a buxom, attractive women with a fine figure and a sharp
tongue. She lived apart from Bob for months, and people had their opinions about any good wife that would
do that. She knew all these men in three counties, and
could call them by name. A banker said, "They will tear
the jail down and take her out and kill her," were she to
come to Princeton. There she was in Judge Miller's
office on bended knees denying the testimony of Choate
and Pettit. If all this innuendo could be got to a jury
it was going to be hard on Mary Lou.

Miller began working the angles. There was the jury.
More than one likely would be summoned. By law the

first would have to be drawn from the Black Patch "peers."
He hoped an alternate jury could be drawn from, say,
Louisville, 275 miles distant, and a town out of sympathy
with lawlessness. Such a jury would be reasonably dis-
passionate, though probably in favor of awarding Mary Lou
damages. He legal acumen told him the most spectacular
show he could stage was the case of Mary Lou. On paper
it looked perfect: "Beautiful woman shot by Night Riders;
driven out of the state by hate and jealousy; falsely accused
of high crimes; pleading now only for justice."

All this while the Night Riders would not be taking this
lying down. There was a chance a dedicated Night Rider
would shoot him or knife him in the dark. Miller was not
too uneasy, but when a close friend fetched him an army
pistol and a villainous hunting knife, he did not refuse
them. He knew he was protected against bodily harm by
the very intensity of the known hatred for the Hollowells,
for the Riders would be instantly accused of his murder.
Governor Willson was sending in five hundred troops,
to counter the five hundred Night Riders that rumor said
was going to come to Paducah and deliver the defendants.
The army thought well enough of the threat to station
soldiers at all the roads entering the town. They tramped
the streets, their Krag-Jourginsons clanking dully. But
Judge Walter Evans gave it out ahead of time he would
have none of Governor Willson's troops in his court room.

There was no doubt of the tension as the day of trial
drew on. Slinking tobacco figures might very well have
been Night Rider spies, sent in ahead to get the lay of
the land. Certain other characters wearing coats and
ties might be agents of the Tobacco Trust, patrolling the
scene with gold to grease the palms of jurymen. Mary
Lou and Bob and the boy did not come into Paducah

directly or even risk a boat ride down the Ohio. Instead
they took train through Illinois and Indiana to Brook-
port, on the north bank of the river, and a ferry over,
well guarded by plain clothes men employed by Miller.
Mary Lou wore a heavy veil and Bob had grown a
scraggly beard for disguise. They were hustled from the
closed carriage into their boarding house. The next morning the court convened, and the jury was drawn from jury
lists from Lyon, Graves, Livingston, McCracken and
Carlisle Counties. Mary Lou and her family were then
fetched to a juryroom.

A fragment of drama was instantly enacted. The Night
Riders saw to it there was a warrant for her arrest for com-
plicity in the plant-bed scrapings in the hands of the sheriff.
He proceeded to serve the paper. If she could not make immediate bond, she'd be hustled down to Princeton and
lodged in jail. Miller must have shrewdly foreseen this, for
he clapped his palms and a gentleman appeared and signed
Mary Lou's bail bond. The Night Riders were frustrated.
Twisting their waxed mustaches where amber trickled, the
Night Riders filed into court and readied themselves for
the killing.

Miller did not present Mary Lou's case first for the
showpiece. He presented Robert. He told his sad tale of
being wakened by the shooting, the Night Riders moving
around and around his house like wild Indians at an attack, the shot that struck his wife, almost ruining her vision,
(people craned to see Mary Lou, who had covered the scar
discreetly with rice powder, which a lady might wear and
not be labeled a whore), how Bob had been taken down
to the lot and made to strip and was flogged, and how
he almost died from loss of blood. When Mary Lou had her
inning as witness she corroborated all of her husband's

testimony, adding that she had been kicked — she named
the kicker — and Lula Hollowell's cry, "Ah but this is
sweet revenge to me!" The defense protested this and
the evidence was stricken from the record. Just the same
the jury had been let in on what happened, and then the
defense went to bat. All twenty-eight defendants had per-
fact alibis. Sick children. Sick horses. Visits of friends
and relatives. Out of town, out of the state. Each defendant had two or three witnesses to corroborate. How
they kept straight faces is hard to see. In any case for two
days this hog killing went on, then came the dramatic
speech of Judge Miller, the speeches by the defendants'
lawyers; and the jury got the case. They deliberated for
hours. Ten were for conviction. Two held out to the bitter end. The jury foreman finally reported, "Your honor,
we are unable to reach a verdict."

Judge Evans declared a mistrial and named May 11,
three weeks hence, for the second hearing.

Miller's law partner once said to Miller, "Watch that
fellow," indicating a juror. "He's a Night Rider."

"How can you tell?" Miller asked.

"He's sweating like a plow mule in new-ground tobacco
and he's scrubbed that jury chair to the bone."

The juror proved to be one of two who held out for
acquittal.

Chapter Twenty-four

Thirty Pieces of Silver

GOING BACK TO THE FIELDS FOR THREE WEEKS, MEN who had helped with a flogging had time to meditate upon the ways of the transgressor. But here might be the proverbial second ring of the postman. The members of Nabb Schoolhouse lodge dodged the military to hold meetings, and they had present not only their lawyers but an expert from Louisville, who instructed them in the business of transferring their property into their wives' names and going into voluntary bankruptcy. It did not seem possible they would lose the case. Nor did it seem quite plausible they would win. Getting a Night Rider on any new jury to hang it for mistrial looked exceedingly dubious. So they deeded their farms and livestock and chattels to their wives, shuddered in fear, but hoped for the best.

That $50,000 damages meant, if awarded, that each defendant must pay some $2000. In that day such a sum would buy a fair-to-middling tobacco farm of seventy-five or one hundred acres, with a decent house on it. A committee was set up by Guy Dunning, acting now as

"General" to assess each member of the lodge some share he could pay, and he himself made a trip to Glenraven for a conference with Felix Ewing for the Association out of its reserves to underwrite some percentage of the damages. It was agreed that if the Hollowells won, a precedent for scores of suits would be set, against the innocent as well as guilty.

The first trial had held interest mostly for the defendants. But as the second trial approached, men were aware of the threat of the suit, and prepared themselves to be there. On the given day hundreds crowded into Paducah, from booted tobacco farmers to spies of the American Tobacco Company, to reporters and an artist from *Leslie's Weekly*. The state militia tramped their beats but once again Judge Evans declared no soldiers should darken the door of his court room. Men remembered other years, other excitements. There were the great rallies and barbecues, as at Guthrie; the bands, the parades, the fine ladies, the horsemen, the gay darkies ("DOWN WITH THE TRUST OR WE NIGGERS BUST"), the clanking wagons bringing whole familes to town to sit around the fair grounds and guzzle cold drinks and listen to the orations, the speakers sweating as they spilled their eloquence: the pomp and circumstances of hope.

It was mid-May and the day was clear and fine. Long before the crying of court the place was crowded. When the bailiff opened the doors the people jammed in, the last comers crouching clear up to the railing. Those who could not get in tried to hear from the street.

Then the proceedings opened. One might have supposed Judge Miller would use Mary Lou for his first act since the jury was made up of "furriners." He offered only Bob and Price. Later Miller in an offhand way explained why he did not use his star witness: "On the second trial the court declined to allow the wife to testify for the husband — or, possibly, *we did not offer to introduce her as a witness.* While this forced us to rely upon two witnesses, plaintiff and his little son, it eliminated the only doubtful legal question (of a wife testifying in her husband's defense) and at the same time *relieved us of all necessity to defend the character of the wife,* and left the defendants' artillery for this attack useless in their hands; and as the court had required us to prove that each defendant was not merely an aiding and abetting conspirator, but an actual participant in the alleged attack, and had charged the jury accordingly," the verdict and judgment would be unassailable. (Emphasis mine.)

The Riders were outwitted. They had hoped to slaughter Mary Lou. Worse yet, the prosecution produced a surprise witness in shape of Sanford Hall, who lived a few miles from the Hollowells, and was one of the Rider recruits who came into the Silent Brigade immediately after the flogging to save his own hide. While his testimony so far as the Hollowell case was concerned was hearsay, he recited the Night Rider oath, demonstrated the various challenges for identification; he named a number of lodges and great numbers of leaders; he stated that Dr. Amoss was the "General" and Guy Dunning the "Lieutenant." He knew much about the network of spies the Inner Circle kept busy; and stated that he was present at the meetings when the defendants' lawyers met to assist in creating bankrupts. Hall simply let all the cats out of the bag. He was not a heroic figure, sitting there mumbling this fatal information — it was the first time that Dr. Amoss and Guy Dunning had been named officially and publicly; and his furtive look around the court room, a mixture of 'wise-guy' and frightened animal, showed that he understood very well certain clauses of the Oath meant what they said; he'd be killed at the first chance. Then came the long list of alibis. If they had hardly rung true during the first trial, they now sounded as hollow as dried peas in a pig's bladder. Nevertheless the rote had to be recited, and men muttered with bloodless lips and taut faces as they chanted "sick children," "sick cows," "visiting kin folks," "out of town, out of the county, out of the state." "The court was rigid with dignity but very alert," Miller later said. "At times as the trial and interest grew intense [it] fairly quivered with that suppressed excitement whose silence means much. People pressed up as close as they could, some crouching even on the judge's stand. On tiptoe in the corridors they strained ear and eye to hear and see all they could as the struggle neared the climax."

Judge Miller when his turn came to speak was in form. He realized he was the incarnation of Justice, Avenging Angel, and the most successful lawyer in the Pennyrile. He launched his tirade with shouts; he sank his voice to a hoarse whisper, full of sobs, when he rehearsed the bloody details of the night of the flogging — that helpless man, that distracted wife, that innocent child! And then those alibis! He gave a hideous insane laugh. It was the most preposterous mess of lies ever an intelligent jury was asked to accept as truth. His simulated laughter was echoed by the jury, and though Judge Evans rapped for order, twenty-eight Night Riders dropped their candy in that moment. Somebody was going to have to raise $50,000.

Judge Evans instructed the jury. "The defendants rely on the alibi." The alibi, he said, was the most satisfactory defense but the most easily fabricated. The defendants

would say they were not present at the time and place of
the outrage; they would be elsewhere and have witnesses
to corroborate them. He reviewed each of the twenty-
eight alibis. "There are all the elements here of the fabricated alibi. It was a most fortunate circumstance that each
of the defendants had a friend or relative with him and
they talked on such and such a subject at a particular
hour on this particular night." The outrage took place
May 2, 1907, and suit was not brought till March 2, 1908,
ten months later. The defendants had not been aware of
any suit until it fell upon them. "Yet each, with two or
more witnesses, could remember what he was doing at a
precise hour in a precise location, on a precise day, and
all testified positively to the facts." Then he added his
dry understatement, "Such a memory is remarkable and
beyond my powers."

The jury promptly found the defendants guilty and
awarded the plaintiff $35,000 of the $50,000 demanded.
The editor of the Hopkinsville *Kentuckian* said, "It was
all railroaded through so rapidly as to take one's breath
away."

Judge Evans let it be known that those voluntary bank-
ruptcies would not count. The defendants would pay off
or go to jail. The threat did not sound too empty to the
stunned ears of the Night Riders, though throwing twenty-
eight good citizens in jail would not sound too good for
Justice; and the sullen faces of Night Riders indicated if
it came to this, there might be a storming of the jail
by thousands of infuriated Riders. In other words if the
law was too tough there would still be a riot. Judge Miller
knew this, as well. So negotiations opened out of court.

Guy Dunning had followed both trials closely, and he
acted as spokesman for the defendants. He pointed out

to Miller that Hall's testimony was bought, probably by
$500 of Governor Willson's reward money; the man was
a known liar and his testimony could be impeached; there
was nothing to keep the defendants from appealing the
case to the state Supreme Court and eventually to the
U.S. Supreme Court; that it was all involved with the
fight of the tobacco farmers on the Trust. These men were
desperate and they had plenty of fight still in them. This
dialogue took place in the lobby of the hotel where the
Hollowells were lodged, and later in the room with the
family. There was Mary Lou, triumphant one moment,
sullen the next, and Bob Hollowell in the corner his face
streaked with tears. Miller asked Dunning, "What do
you propose to offer to settle the case?" Dunning said,
$10,000." Miller threw up his hands. "The very idea!
We won't settle for that paltry sum. We'll throw the last
defendant in jail first." Dunning asked him to name a
figure, and he named $20,000 as the very least he would
permit his clients to settle for. Dunning said, "We won't
pay it. We'll appeal. Before we're through it will cost
your clients more than they'll ever gain." Finally Bob
Hollowell quavered, "I wouldn't go through this again
for a million dollars!" In the end they reached $15,000
as a settlement. It would not ruin any Night Rider; Felix
Ewing would chip in $5000, and the other $10,000 would
be portioned out among the defendants and other Night
Rider lodges. It was a victory for the law but only half a
victory. Miller never did explain in the eighty-seven-page
book he wrote that he got only $15,000 out of the suits
for $125,000 he had prosecuted for; for the Hollowells
withdrew Mary Lou's suit and Price's in the compromise.

The whole affair moved back into history, and now the
Night Riders had the task of killing Sanford Hall.

Men debated how to do this; for Hall was immediately spirited away. A .44 bullet would do a nice clean job, but the trick was catching Hall. The suggestion finally adopted was to send Hall an infernal machine that would blow him to hell and gone. The bomb was duly manufactured and dispatched by mail to Hall at Paducah, General Delivery. It was reasoned that sooner or later the traitor would slip in Paducah and pick up his mail, and the crude device would blast him to perdition. The parcel lay around the post office for some weeks, uncalled for. The post master was unable to get a forwarding address. He finally grew suspicious. Calling the chief of police, he placed the parcel on a table and they gingerly began unwrapping heavy brown paper. There was a tab marked "Pull." They pulled with very great care, and discovered matches tied to the cord, so arranged that a quick jerk would scratch them on a file, which in turn would ignite blasting powder, and this would detonate three dynamite caps, and the stick of explosive would end the doomed man. They were unable to make out the post mark of the point of origin, but thought the blurred mark was Wallonia.

Eventually through their network of spies the Night Riders learned that Sanford Hall was living in a boarding house down in the tobacco slums in Louisville with the wife of one of his neighbors back in the Nabb neighborhood, Hall having abandoned his own wife and children. The Night Riders were not to be thwarted in their revenge. In the Lamasco neighborhood Sanford's younger brother Herbert, thirty years old, farmed a small tobacco place, and worked on the side for a neighbor. On the morning of June 7 he passed over a hill by a foot trail to work. He was ambushed and his head almost shot off at close range. Who was delegated to this job never came to light, but probably it was one of the men paying off Mary Lou's ransom. Young Hall's body was dragged to a swamp nearby during the afternoon where it was hidden until night. Then men in a buggy came — the tracks were afterward traced — and the body buried in a lonely eroded field three miles away. His people searched for him for days and weeks and at last gave him up as dead. They supposed his body had been thrown into one of the limestone sink holes in the locality.

Traitors began to spring up on every hand, stimulated to confession by the results of the Hollowell trial, but probably more so by Governor Willson's reward money that was being guardedly disbursed by Walter Krone at Princeton. One of these was an obscure fellow named Tom Stephens, who appeared before Krone and made a confession. What sum he received was not named, for these traitors were becoming so commonplace their testimony actually would carry little weight in any court. His confession was instantly relayed to Night Riders, and it showed the Riders were by no means unhorsed. That night twenty-five hooded Riders surrounded Stephens' house, hauled him out, chained rocks to him and got ready to drop him in his well. He cried and wept and pleaded, "It's a lie, I never told nothing, don't kill me, don't kill me!" His sobs gave the Riders pause. "We'll turn you loose, but if we find —" The following day they investigated his movements and verified the conference with Krone. That night they came back, surrounded the unpainted plank house, and shot the place up from comb of roof to dogtrot. They riddled the doors and windows. How Stephens managed to survive all this lead was a miracle. He crawled out through a loose board in the kitchen floor, and through the grass past the well where they were going to drown him, and along the bean-vine paling garden fence till he was in his crib lot. Then he ran crouchingly till shed of the premises. Once well away, he walked and ran most of the night till exhaustion stopped him, and he slept the following day in a straw stack. That night he stole ears of corn from a farmer's crib and in the deep woods well away he built a fire and roasted the corn in the hot ashes. He kept walking by night, hiding by day, except now and then when he would show himself to beg a cold biscuit or sweet potato to augment his diet of parched corn. He finally reached the Ohio River. There in Indiana he established residence, as had Mary Lou, and afterward brought suit in Federal Court at Paducah, craving $20,000 damages. This was the going price at the time for suits against the Night Riders. But even Federal juries were a bit fed up with such cases, and awarded him $200 judgment. A preacher named by Stephens as one of the defendants did not believe in law suits and refused to contest the case. He paid off the judgment, being a free-will foot-washing Baptist.

All this while the search for Sanford Hall went on, and in late August one of those excursion trains was run on the I. C. Railroad to Louisville, a dozen old soiled cars hitched to a sooty locomotive for cut-rate sight-seers to the autumn state fair. Among the five hundred riding the train were some score plain-clothes Night Riders, who looked like all the other rednecks out for a lark. Spies had located Sanford Hall down near the American Snuff Company plant. The Night Riders sneaked along the street to the soiled boarding house where Hall was shacked up with this other man's wife. Three men went to the house and knocked on the door. "We want Sanford Hall," they told the greasy-bellied landlady. "He ain't here," she told them;

and they asked, "Then where's he at?" The door was slammed in their faces. The Riders then began a vigil, walking up and down the street, peering up at the windows, spying furtively. Some people in the nearby houses recognized men from Caldwell and Lyon Counties, shrewdly guessed they were unhorsed Night Riders after somebody, and called the police. The cops came and scattered the Riders. But Sanford Hall had already sneaked out the back way, knowing his old cohorts were after him, and if they caught him they'd kill him. He took what money he may have had left from the rewards, crossed into Indiana, and for the time being disappeared from the face of the earth. The deserted paramour did not even know whether he was alive or dead.

The Night Riders kept hounding him, sending him warning letters when they could locate a post office where he got mail. "We aim to kill you if we ever catch you back in Kentucky!" Hall never returned to the Black Patch, so far as his old Rider confederates knew.

Chapter Twenty-five

Ghost Riders of the Past

IT SEEMED A PROPITIOUS MOMENT FOR THE AMERICAN Trust Company to move in and cut the tobacco growers down to their suspenders. The Night Riders were unhorsed. Damage suits were breaking out all over the Black Patch. The Association was fighting a two-front war — Governor Willson and his troops on the one hand, the Trust on the other. James Duke might have stepped in, depressed prices, and got a fresh retread of gold on his purse. The Hillbillies would have been hand in glove so long as they were paid an average of 8c for their leaf. There was a shortage of the crop, due to drought in some areas and shortage of labor and general unrest because of Night Riding.

With traitors everywhere drooling to tell all — for a part of Governor Willson's gold — Guy Dunning felt it was all the more necessary to maintain the image of the Planters Protective Association. Nothing cheered the unwashed denizens of the huts, to borrow one of Augustus Willson's good words, like a rally, barbecue, a couple of wind-lashed orators, barrels of lemonade and wagonloads of soda pop, and meeting old friends at the fairgrounds that one hadn't seen since the last warehouse fire or Night Rider trial. He knew very well why the Trust was not depressing prices. Actually the buyers were paying premium for choice leaf. Duke was fighting a two-front war of his own — the various tobacco associations, and the U.S. Justice Department. The moment was propitious for the Association.

The rally was held at the fairgrounds in Princeton on September 19, 1908. Dunning did his best with the publicity. The principal speaker was J. S. Ragsdale, of Hopkinsville. Dunning wanted Joel Fort or Felix Ewing but they were unable to make it. The Association stood the treats, for there was money in the treasury. It seemed a lifetime since September 22, 1906, at the great Guthrie conclave. And in the two years, nearly to a day, a kind of lifetime had passed. The way of life in the Black Patch had undergone an entire revolution. It was impossible, though Dunning tried, to bring back nostalgically the triumph of that other day.

Yet there were more than ten thousand people in town that day, by no means a bad turn-out. The weather was hot and dry, like September mostly is in Tennessee and Kentucky. The fairgrounds were gala and the speakers stand was decorated with bunting. At eleven o'clock the grand parade formed, many horses and buggies, all in bunting; one band instead of ten in the olden times; and three thousand footmen. Guy Dunning and Bradley Wilson headed the columns, with Lula Hollowell riding ahead of them. Dunning was chief marshal; Wilson, Association chairman of Hopkins County. Lula, you will recall, was John E. Hollowell's wife, who cried at the kicking of Mary Lou, "This is sweet revenge to me." There is no

certain record that the Hollowell family attended the great
circus at Guthrie two years earlier, though probably they
did; and if Mary Lou had, and she now could have seen
her sister-in-law trying to ape the supple, charming, graceful Mrs. Felix Ewing, rider after the hounds, winner of
Blue Grass horse shows for horsemanship, and social leader
of the rural section of Montgomery and Robertson Counties, she could have cried in her turn, "Ah but this is
sweet revenge to me!" Lula Hollowell was definitely growing feather pillow at the belly, and she looked dowdy
even in her riding habit. She did not ride well, and once
her horse shied and got her hat with its plume askew, and
she messed it up more trying to keep it on her graying
hair — that trial had aged Lula. Nor did Guy ride a
prancing stallion. His was the same old horse he had ridden
to scores of raids, great and small. The beast moved as
if trotting faithfully to some flogging back of a farm
barn. There were banners, but the chief one had inscribed:
WE ARE FOR LAW AND ORDER AND THE AS-
SOCIATION TOO. Another carried a crude picture of
twelve hogs and the caption, THE JURY FROM PADU-
CAH. There were floats with pretty girls nursing bundles
of fine dark-fired tobacco, and their sweating faces were
feeble facsimiles of Ringling Brothers lovelies. It was the
rank and file of marching men that impressed the observer
interested in the secret history of these men. There was
a rare military swing about them; they moved with the
pride of veterans home from the wars. They were the
flower of Dr. Amoss's and Guy Dunning's warriors and
probably not a hand but had set the torch or lifted the
cat-o-nine. The parade moved steadily up town, swung
around court square, made a detour out to the rebuilt
Orr and Stegar & Dollar factories, now buying for the As-

sociation; and then back at noon to the fairgrounds for refreshments. Folks nearby said Mrs. Hollowell grunted when assisted from the saddle.

There was a kind of sadness about the whole business. All the kings and princes and war horses were in other parts — Dr. Amoss was still in exile, though the rumor was abroad he was returning to Cobb to resume his practice; A. O. Stanley was up in Washington beating the drums for repeal of the 6c tax and belaboring Nelson W. Aldrich and his Senate Finance Committee without actually accusing the Senator of having been bought off by the Tobacco Trust, though all the circumstantial evidence indicates this was true; no Felix Ewing, and his ascetic scholarly speech, no lovely wife, not even Mary Lou Hollowell, who was in exile in Indiana, and might just have got herself killed if she had shown her face. Nobody but tobacco farmers and their wives and children, and footsore Night Riders. And soldiers. When Governor Willson heard of the rally, he shipped in another company of militia to overrun Princeton.

It was a built-in situation for a riot. From the early hour of the morning when people began to arrive, a feeling of tenseness developed and in the middle of the forenoon the hostility between the glowering farmers and the smart-aleck militia was showing at the seams. It was tacitly known that some considerable number of Night Riders had a secret plan to attack the soldiers, beat them up, chase them out of town and, if necessary, shoot a few of them. Men toted concealed hardware and surely the soldiers must have observed this. Night Riders started drifting up town after polishing off the barbecue. They slouched along in twos or at most threes and seemed to peer at everything but the soldiers. It was whispered that the signal for a general attack would be a gunshot at the back of Blue Goose saloon off Court Square.

Guy Dunning could not have been wholly blind to what was happening, though there is no evidence to indicate he was behind the movement. He had a good feed of barbecue under his belt as he and Ragsdale rode in the direction of the square. The sudden shot came as the men hitched their horses. All at once the streets were alive with shouting, yelling, swearing Night Riders, boys, dogs, and Hillbillies sneaking in to see the fight without mixing in it. The surprised soldiers hastily formed and presented a formidable array of bayonets. Their orders probably were to use powder and lead only as a last resort, but to shoot if they must. Any wholesale killing of citizens would become a massacre, and the Governor's position as riot queller would be weakened. The very idea of bloody-handed troops shooting down innocent Democrats! The belligerents were just about to mix it when Mr. Ragsdale rushed into the space between the infuriated Night Riders and militia. He raised his hands aloft, shouting above the hubbub:

"Gentlemen! Gentlemen!"

He faced first one faction and then the other. His big voice carried. "Men we must not have this!" He did make a splendid figure, knocking off his hat as he waved and gestured, his white hair shining in the noon sun.

A sudden frustrated hush fell upon the mob. "Let us have law and order! Let us not sully this day with bloodshed! Men, do nothing this day that you will rue the rest of your lives!" The mutter rose and fell, and Ragsdale stood there in a heroic pose, waiting till reason soaked into the embattled hosts. He knew how these men felt but he knew also they would feel worse after the bloody riot.

It was a demonstration once again how one strong man makes a majority. It was a credit to good sense that the wavering attackers began to draw back and then to dissolve gradually, some growling, some cursing, some sheepish. The soldiers had good enough sense to withdraw in the opposite direction. Only the Hillbillies were disappointed. They had hoped to see a first-class fight. They hated the Night Riders only slightly more than the militia. The crowds kept retreating till they reached the fairgrounds, where they listened to some more oratory and finished off the refreshments and toward sundown got ready to return to the farms. A few die-hards remained in town to frequent the grog shops and say what they would have done to the armed forces if they hadn't been interfered with.

What the thwarted riot did show was that the Night Riders were spoiling for a good knock-down-drag-out fight with law and order, and if in the passion of the moment somebody got killed, it might just be a hated soldier. In that case Princeton and Night Riding once more would make international headlines instead of innocuous editorials in the Cadiz *Record,* Princeton *Twice-a-Week Leader,* and some soothing rhetoric from Charles Meacham, commending the bravery of one of Hopkinsville's citizens.

It showed further the deep-seated hatred of the people for military rule. Maybe some of the farm girls were falling in love with some of the soldiers. Marriages were being announced. It was notable that no city girl had any time for the uncouth military. Parents longed for the day when the troops would be recalled. And presently this would come about, by Christmas, 1908; by then all but the detail policing the still festering sore at Eddyville would be withdrawn.

Dr. Amoss returned home, started riding in his buggy,

and the damage suits began to pile up. Henry Bennett, exiled in Jeffersonville, Indiana, filed suit for $100,000 on October 30, 1908. Alfred Cardin, master of View, living near Bennett, filed claim for $16,400, estimate of Night Rider destruction. C. M. Rucker of Metropolis, Illinois, filed for $50,000; Lura Toomey, of Metropolis, for $25,000; Lucile Wood for $25,000, these obcure ladies alleging the Night Rider activity had wrecked their lives and run them out of Kentucky. The total of all these varied suits was approximately a quarter of a million dollars — $241,400, to be exact. To make sure of collections a great number of reservists were named, Bennett naming 155, Cardin 182; the two ladies named 269 and 259. These lists without doubt were compiled from records supplied by Sanford Hall, and other men who turned state's evidence. And even Felix Ewing, Joel Fort, George Snadon, and the whole hierarchy of the Planters Association did not escape: it was assumed they were equally guilty with Dr. Amoss and his Riders. It was possible, then, if they could make cases, the plaintiffs could collect a large portion of their claims.

If the Army had not already made Night Riding unpopular these damage suits would have done so. Together they reduced the Black Patch to a reasonable facsimile of its former tranquility. But beneath smoldered the ancient hatreds, made all the more bitter by the chastisements of the law. Any time there might be an outbreak of lawlessness, flaming across the tobacco country. But agencies were at work. Following some barn burnings and a flogging or two, the *Black Patch Journal* made an eloquent appeal.

"Rider, turn the reins of your horse's head homeward and there dwell in peace. The human heart cannot condemn your zeal, but common sense and decency does your foolishness."

And the time was drawing down when the American Tobacco Company must answer for its sins and men could wait.

Chapter Twenty-six

The Mill of the Gods

THE TOBACCO WARS BETWEEN THE UNITED STATES Justice Deparment and the American Tobacco Company began in 1906, the year the Association held its great rally at Guthrie. A grand jury investigating Duke's tobacco empire issued subpoenas for the officers of the Tobacco Company and directed them to produce records and pertinent materials concerning the company. The officials refused and were promptly adjudged in contempt of court. Duke fought the Justice Department every step of the way, fighting bitterly, with that passionate parsimony that made him keep records down to the last penny of an enterprise like his Wonderland in New Jersey. The first sparring for position was a suit against two licorice manufacturers, MacAndrews & Forbes, and J. S. Young. The law won this round handily in January, 1907, and the makers of the root-goo that gave Star Navy flavor as well as gravy had to pony up fines of $8,000 and $10,000.

For months the head-butting went on, with officers, directors, heads of departments, almost everybody in authority in the main company and its subsidiaries trudging to the chambers with briefcases, and leaving behind half-bushels of cigarette butts and nervously chewed cigars.

Of all the statements James Duke made under the intensive questioning of James McReynolds, the one that looms out of the verbiage is, "The American Tobacco Company has not raised prices to the consumer *or attempted to depress prices on the raw product.*"

Yet down in Kentucky and Tennessee even in 1905 in the era of great rallies in the Black Patch, and the organization of the Association, "it became evident that many growers were not going to join willingly or lend their support, and that the Trust was going to continue its opposition in an effort to break it [the Association]." There is small point in reviewing the skullduggery of James Duke's Wall Street manipulations except to note that W. Duke & Sons, his own company, controlled half the nation's cigarettes, and Duke took in the American Snuff Company, to dominate the dipping business, the American Cigar Company for cigars, the American Cheroot Company for the cheaper forms, and the Continental and Consolidated, dominating the plug and twist markets. Duke contended he did not buy in these companies to control the market, but to get the services of great tobacco men like R. J. Reynolds. He insisted more money could be made by competition than monopoly. He felt, too, it was better to have competition in buying the raw product.

Felix Ewing, the Forts, Dr. Amoss and Guy Dunning, and thousands of tobacco growers living in huts would have been happy at this news had it been true.

The Government produced bales of evidence to support its contention that the American Tobacco Company had a virtual monopoly of the domestic and foreign trade, and it thus was outlawed by the Sherman Act. On November 7, 1908, in the New York Court of Appeals the case was decided against Duke and his American.

Judge Lacombe presented the majority opinion. Reading between the lines one gets the uneasy feeling that Judge Lacombe was not wholly in sympathy with the decision. The record in the case, he said, indicated no increase in the prices of tobacco products to the consumer, one great point stressed by the defense. There seemed little persuasive evidence that undue pressure or unfair practices had been used to dragoon the associated companies to sell out to the principal defendant. In fact during the existence of the American Tobacco Company many small enterprises with limited captial had been established and had been successful even in the face of competition like Duke's companies. The price of leaf — the raw material — *except for one brief period of abnormal conditions,* had steadily increased until it had more than doubled, while at the same time 150,000 additional acres had been planted to tobacco and the consumption of the leaf had greatly increased. Through the enterprise of the defendants, and at large expense, new markets had been developed in populous India and China and elsewhere.

The judge's arguments were based, of course, on the "facts" supplied by the American Tobacco Company. The brief period of depressed prices, no one mentioned, was the work of Duke and his buyers. Prices had more than doubled, due to Night Riding and the various pools and associations that kept tobacco off the market. Actually there is no evidence I can find to support the contention that 150,000 acres of additional tobacco had been planted. All the facts indicate heavy shortages.

It would almost seem that the United States Government was the culprit, for Judge Lacombe went on:

"But all this is immaterial." The Sherman Anti-Trust Act, as construed by the Supreme Court, prohibited every contract or combination in restraint of competition. "Each of these purchases of existing concerns, complained of in the petition, was a contract and combination in restraint of competition when it was entered into, and that is sufficient to bring it within the ban of this drastic statute."

Judge Lacombe must have winced when he used the word *drastic*. Didn't he like the law? Well, if a Night Rider was expected to obey the law, the Judge should manage to put up with it.

Meanwhile what was going on in the Black Patch? The army of occupation was patrolling the tobacco country, and had scattered the last of the Riders. There were clashes here and there and some shooting, but otherwise the land was tranquil. Mary Lou and Bob were using what was left of the $15,000 after paying off Judge Miller and other expenses to buy a farm in Kentucky that was better than the one they had abondoned. Dust had settled on the last great rally at Princeton. Though rumor had it Dr. Amoss was coming home, he was still doctoring malaria down in the swamps of Arkansas. There were bushleague lawsuits against obscure Riders, but juries would not convict. Sanford Hall was kept under careful guard against the day when the law could use him as witness against Dr. Amoss. Max Hanberry, a citizen of note in Cadiz, resigned from the Republican party, shaming Governor Willson in a widely published open letter.

You have been a friend of the Trust and an avowed enemy of the common people. You have been wined and dined (by the American Tobacco Company) by the plutocrats in the eastern cities. You pardon men for swearing falsely according to your bidding. You pardoned Sanford Hall. Do you know this man Hall? Are you aware he is publicly accused of stealing money from his old aunt, and has abandoned his lawful wife and is living in open sin with a Mrs. Dean, his accomplice in furnishing evidence against the Night Riders? Are you aware Hall is the most unholy liar of any man in the country?

Yet Hall would be one of the chief witnesses against Dr. Amoss.

In Washington A. O. Stanley and his confederates were hammering away at the 6c tax law like woodpeckers toiling at a sun-dried oak snag. Repeal would add 6c more to the price farmers were getting for tobacco. There was considerable potential local market for long-green and twist, just as with the Dukes when they first began to peddle cigarette tobacco. Fighting this market served Duke's monopoly. At last Stanley developed a scheme. The Payne Tarriff Bill was in process of being written and adopted. Stanley and James tacked the repeal clause on this bill. In this wise they could circumvent Aldrich and his Committee. "The trick was that even though the item might be stricken out in the Senate Committee, it could be reinserted on demand after the bill reached the Senate. The tariff bill with the rider passed the House April 9, 1909, and was promptly erased by Aldrich April 14. When the Payne-Aldrich bill reached the Senate the two Kentucky senators, Thomas Paynter and William O. Bradley, demanded that the clause be re-inserted. In due time the bill passed and was signed April 5, 1909, by President Taft.

The fight lasted from 1904 till 1909. Its repeal "was one

of the most difficult pieces of legislation ever to pass through Congress, and to do it cost far more than it was ever worth to the Federal Treasury. It reflected the tenacious forces that carried on the tobacco struggle on both sides."

A. O. Stanley put it eloquently and indignantly when he said:

No writer has ever taken the trouble to paint for you the story of the misery, the story of the want, of the utter destitution that visited the country when the tobacco farmers for two long years got less than twenty cents a day because the American Tobacco Company reduced the price of the raw materials from an average of 7c a pound, where it had been for half a century, to 3c a pound. But they have told you of the Night Riders and their activities and have greatly exaggerated their disorder and lawlessness.

We return to the hassle between the Justice Department and the American Tobacco Company. Neither the government nor the Trust was pleased with the decision handed down by Judge Lacombe. The government contended that the petition should not have been dismissed as to the individual defendants, naturally James Duke at the head of the list. The government contended that the two foreign corporations, Imperial Tobacco Company and the British-American Tobacco Company, should not have been excused, nor should the United States Cigar Company. The American Tobacco Company appealed as a matter of principle, because James Duke still vaguely hoped to find a rat hole to escape. He had plenty of money to fight the case and he proposed not to take any of this legal stuff lying down. The law? Hell, the law was for Night Riding, not tobacco trusting.

At last the Supreme Court, on May 29, 1911, handed down a sweeping decision against the defendants, holding

Riders in the Night

that the tobacco combination "in and itself as well as each and all of the elements composing it, whether corporate or individual, whether considered collectively or separately" was "in restraint of trade and an attempt to monopolize, and a monopolization within the first and second sections of the Anti-Trust Act." The American Tobacco Company was ordered dissolved, and the constituent elements separated so that competition could be restored. The high court remanded the case back to the Circuit Court of Appeals with directions on how to carry out its mandate and dismember the Trust. It's another story how James Duke got down to the unholy job of tearing apart the structure he had so painstakingly built, sweating pure nicotine in the butchery. One almost feels sorry for the poor fellow, with all his hundreds of millions, tearing apart his play-pretty. Lest the reader shed a tear, I pass hastily along on the other side of Tobacco Road with my face averted from the tragedy, and stare instead at the battered and beaten huts of the tobacco farmers.

January, 1911. Five long years. Marie Taylor, a graduate student in the University of Kentucky in 1934, wrote her master's thesis on *Night Riders in the Black Patch,* and on page 89 she has a chart of prices paid for tobacco from the year of 3-2-1, to 1910, just before the Supreme Court adjudged the American Tobacco Company a law-breaker, when dark tobacco was selling for from 9c to 10 to 12c. It was a long cry down through the dim avenues of tobacco. Small wonder that Felix Ewing, the Forts, Dr. Amoss, Guy Dunning realized the law would never save the tobacco growers from starvation. The mill of the gods may grind exceeding fine, but when men's guts are growling and their women and children are crying from hunger there isn't time to wait for the grist.

Chapter Twenty-seven

The Law and Evidence

NO ONE EVER ATTEMPTED TO COMPILE A RECORD OF how many men were killed during Night Rider times. There were killings that got wide publicity, such as Orbie Nabb at Princeton by Henry Wilson, young Gray at Hopkinsville, and Vaughn Bennett by Sory and his men. But there were dozens of killings, first and last, that made no special stir. Around April, 1908, Governor Willson gave out the statement that sixteen Night Riders had been killed by his soldiers in Western Kentucky to that date. He gave out no names nor the authority for his statistics, which presumably would have been Major Bassett. During the two most active years of the Silent Brigade a number of men, usually the hut-dwellers, simply disappeared. Some were killed for this or that reason, but many must have taken this chance to get away from their families. They walked out and were never heard of again.

By the beginning of 1908 the Black Patch had quieted down. This is not to say that peace was more than skin deep. For one thing, Dr. Amoss and Guy Dunning advised

men to wait; the Supreme Court decisions would be forth-
coming, and they had faith that James Duke would be
stripped of his bloated wealth and reduced to the ranks of.
ordinary millionaires. But back on the land, old grudges
smoldered on, and now and then they'd flame in a torching
or bed scraping or ambushed murder. "The vicious influence of the unlawful organization," Judge Miller said, "was
still active where it dared to be, [and] was plainly effective
upon courts and juries for several years in some places, and
perhaps has not entirely disappeared [1935]. It will not die
with this generation, which saw its birth."

Dr. Amoss had returned to his home in Cobb in April,
1909. He had that mass of damage suits to deal with.
While he went up and down at his old medical practice he
found time to work out compromises with most of these
suits, probably paying something on the damages as token,
with Felix Ewing and the Association assisting materially —
though this was never a matter of public knowledge. Only
one case got into court. This was that of C. W. Rucker,
where a $10,000 judgment was decided against Amoss.
One of the important suits was that of the widow of John C.
Latham for burning the Hopkinsville warehouse, $50,000
damages demanded, from Dr. Amoss and 256 other Night
Riders, the names again being furnished by Sanford Hall
and certain other renegades. The matter dragged on for
years and was never settled till after Dr. Amoss's death.
The Federal Court suits against the fourteen hundred-odd
Night Riders sued with Dr. Amoss were dismissed for lack
of actual evidence. The prevailing joke during this while
of shaking down Night Riders was, when one Rider met
another and asked, "Haven't seen you lately, Sam, what you
doin these days?" and the answer, "Worming tobacco for
Mary Lou."

One last effort was made by the law to bring Dr. Amoss to taw. In March 1910, Dr. Amoss, Guy Dunning, B. Malone, Newton Nichols, John Robinson and Irving Glass were indicted by the Christian County Grand Jury charged under the old Ku Klux law with "wilfully and feloniously confederating, conspiring, and banding together for the purpose of molesting, injuring, and destroying property of other persons," the specific molesting and destroying being the burning of the Latham factory on the night of the great raid.

If the Hollowell trial had created consternation in the ranks of the Night Riders who had waited upon Bob and Mary Lou, this new threat stirred the previously somnambulant torch-bearers down to the saddle scars of their great battle nights. If Dr. Amoss and Guy Dunning could be clapped in jail for from one to five years, and fined up to $10,000, who really was safe from prosecution? It was well known that Sanford Hall was one of the State's star witnesses, and there were others, perhaps even more dangerous: Milt Oliver and Art Cooper, Art's brother Carl, and a traitor from around Clarksville, Tennessee, by the name of Robert Warfield. If the Night Riders could have got to these traitors they would gleefully have killed them. All were kept carefully under wraps, and no one but the law and close members of their families knew their whereabouts. Sanford Hall was seen once on the streets of Paducah, armed with heavy-calibre hardware sufficient to stand off any army; but he was also guarded by Governor Willson's soldiers and the Night Rider that saw him had no chance to kill.

On March 6, 1911, the trial opened in the old court house in Hopkinsville. That building still remains a noble pile, with its classic columns, its austerity, its associations.

You go up Main Street, climbing a rise to the summit of the hill, going through the shallow canyon of old-timely business houses where only now and then a face has been lifted to add black marble and create the illusion of modernity. But antiquity shows through in the upper windows, some arched, some in modified Tudor. Here and there one can see faded signs of former establishments, and at corners where the telltale round windows high above the sidewalls betray old-time saloons, one can guess the denizens liked their mint julips. In one place I remarked the long shaled-off portrait of Blackwell's huge bull, which made Durham famous and caused James Duke's mouth to water and he stuffed a half ounce more of granulated tobacco into his Duke's Mixture to put the Bull out of business — if you can't lick 'em, push 'em against the wall and buy them in.

Along this avenue that moonless fateful night about one A.M. Dr. Amoss, Guy Dunning, and their avenging hosts marched with military precision and with the sure touch of trained arsonists put the torch to the Latham and Tandy & Fairleigh factories. You walk along the same route with eyes half closed and all your senses shut to everything but memories, and the people moving by you are the infuriated angels of vengeance out to burn Trust tobacco. Up at the court house where Dr. Amoss goes on trial for his sins and high crimes, you find on closer observation that a lot of modern wings and additions have just about crowded the noble pile of justice out on the sidewalks to make room for the new hutments of bureaucracy. Bedrock has been blasted for comfort stations to replace the dingbats used by a population accustomed to back privies and woods and bushes and barns and corncobs. You know, thus, that the creeping socialism of sanitation has caught up with you. There is a kind of square, not a formal public square, back of the court house, and the old brick structures remain which once housed the lawyers' and doctors' offices, and emporiums where books as well as bourbon could be bought — for Kentuckians not only wrote books, they now and then read them. But over it all still clings the musty beauty of a time long ago, and a dream that even to this day stirs the old-timers to recollections if you stop them on the street and start talking. The problem is not to hear about Night Riding. It's to escape the ancients who remember. And curiously, when I'd meet a pretty girl and look directly into her eyes, her fresh Kentucky face would break into a smile and in her lilting Kentucky voice she would say, "Howdy."

But the Amoss trial — that day Hopkinsville was filled with outlanders: booted and bearded farmers, most if not all of the 500 that stormed the town; reporters from the Nashville and Louisville papers, with pencils back of their ears, and a hopeful gleam in their eyes that there would be killings of traitors as they sat in the witness chair; that a great riot would break out and Dr. Amoss would be hustled out of the clutches of the law; that maybe even the torch bearers would saturate the courthouse with coal oil and Justice would snatch off her mask. In this atmosphere of suppressed excitement and threat the trial got under way.

Sanford Hall, upon whom the State relied so heavily, was early placed on the stand. He said he was present at Cedar Grove schoolhouse at a lodge meeting when Dr. Amoss said he was general of the Night Riders — grandaddy, father and all. He heard the plans for the Hopkinsville raid outlined. When asked, "Were you a member of the raiding party," Hall said, "No, I was home sick in bed that night." It is noteworthy that Hall had a way of being home sick when the heavy jobs were to be done. But he named hosts of men who were in it. Milt Oliver was called, and when asked, "Milton Oliver, were you present at the Hopkinsville raid on the night of December 7, 1907?" Oliver answered, "I was." "Were you a Night Rider?" "I was." "You took the oath that bound you to their secrets?" "I did." "Was Dr. Amoss leader of the raiders?" "He was." "You are positive that you saw him that night giving orders?" "I am." Then Arthur Cooper was called to the stand and he gave about the same answers to the same questions. He added that he was being groomed as an understudy of Dr. Amoss, to lead the projected raid on Murray. The night of the Hopkinsville raid he was immediately under Guy Dunning's command and had charge of the squad that captured the Home telephone office. "And did you see Dr. Amoss when he got shot?" "I was standing close by, no piece at all." "You knew he was shot?" "I seen him bleeding." When Carl Cooper was questioned, "Did you take part in that raid?" he said, "I did." "Was Dr. Amoss the leader that night?" "He was the 'General.'" "Mr. Cooper, were you at the meeting at Cedar Grove Lodge on Tuesday night before the raid?" "I was." "Did you hear Dr. Amoss outline the strategy for the impending raid?" "I did." Robert Warfield testified that he was present at the Guthrie Lodge when Dr. Amoss, after Hopkinsville, visited and showed the fresh gunshot wound on his scalp.

Through the days this damning evidence piled up. The Commonwealth established the facts beyond apparent dispute that on a night a few days before the great raid the Night Riders some five hundred strong met at Cedar Grove school house and Dr. Amoss and Guy Dunning — not yet brought to trial — had worked out minute instructions for every phase of the night's activities. They had sent spies in to check the police station, the two telephone offices, the fire station, the office of the *Kentuckian,* and naturally the exact lay of the land with reference to the two big Trust warehouses. Certain men were assigned to buying the dynamite and kerosene and transporting these needments to town for the night. The amount of tobacco in Latham's and Tandy & Fairleigh's was checked. So minutely was all the strategy worked out that even the men to strike the match had their assignment.

Through the days of taking testimony, Dr. Amoss sat quiet and impassive, and if any fear of the ultimate outcome of the trial troubled him he did not show it. Men remarked, observing him closely, that there was more gray in his hair and beard. Since he had quit the country this change increased rather than diminished his strength and masculinity. When he walked from the hotel to and fro from the court room his step had that old elastic firmness that gave him a military carriage. One man whispered to another, "I'll bet the old boogar could rut a fresh wench every night for 30 days." The women in the court room who knew the good doctor probably could have agreed. Amoss was known as a ladies' man — in the best sense of the word.

The court room was crowded at every session, and scores and hundreds were turned away by the bailiffs. The people were tense and quiet. The town itself was tense and quiet. There was a prevailing rumor that somebody was going to get killed before this was through, and Sanford Hall was the most likely witness to stop a bullet. Sometimes when Hall came in there was an escape of pent breath from the hundreds that hated him. The guards that attended him were unobtrusively careful to get between him and certain windows in the upstairs of an old hotel above the grog shops. The Honorable Judge J. T. Hanberry presided, and he was alert for any show of trouble. Hanberry was Circuit Judge of four counties, Christian, Trigg, Lyon, and Calloway; and there had never been any positive association of his name with the secret clans of the Night Riders. His conduct of the trial remains still an impartial record of almost one thousand typewritten pages. Yet there is no evidence there of any bullying of the accused or the witnesses. In fact, nearly all the questioning was courteous almost to the point of friendliness. Eventually the Commonwealth finished its case, and the defense had its turn. Charles Fort was one of the character witnesses in Dr. Amoss's behalf. In Fort's book the good doctor was a gentleman through and through and a man of integrity. He added, "This witness Robert Warfield is a liar from the ground up."

At last came Dr. Amoss's turn to testify. He had four prosecuting attorneys to cope with: Commonwealth Attorney Danny P. Smith, of Cadiz, J. C. Sims of Bowling Green, County Attorney J. C. Duffy of Hopkinsville, and S. Y. Trimble and Douglas Bell. They were all able lawyers and anxious to secure conviction of this famous Night Rider General.

To counter these determined prosecutors Dr. Amoss and his Night Rider crew had retained C. H. Bush, Thomas P. Cook, and W. T. Fowler of Hopkinsville; S. T. Hodge of Princeton, and John W. Kelly of Cadiz. It is interesting to note that the jury consisted of eleven farmers and one carpenter.

Against this background Dr. Amoss testified in his behalf, the Honorable C. H. Bush questioning him.

"Doctor, where do you live?"

"In Cobb, Caldwell County, Kentucky."

"Doctor, were you living in Cobb the sixth of December, 1907?"

"I was."

"Doctor, were you ever, are you now, a member of a group known as the Night Riders, or an organization going by that name?"

"Sir, I am not a Night Rider nor have I ever been a Night Rider."

"You are aware there are Night Riders?"

"You hear of such things. I would not know one if I saw him."

"Do you know these men?" Bush pointed to Sanford Hall, Milt Oliver, Art and Carl Cooper, and Robert Warfield.

Dr. Amoss bent a penetrating glance at the Commonwealth's witnesses and shook his head. "I guess I've never seen them in my life, though of course I see a great many people, and I could have passed them on the street not knowing."

"Doctor, I will now ask you to tell the jury in your own way where you were the night of December 6, 1907, from the time you ate supper that night until the next morning."

Dr. Amoss studied some moments, to give the illusion of recalling with an effort, as if he had not carefully rehearsed all this beforehand with the Honorable Barrister Bush.

"I had a late supper at home. I'd been twice to see a patient — W. H. White's wife who lives three hundred yards from my place. I found her suffering from double pneumonia. I made four visits during the day, thinking the disease would be fatal. I left the White's about nine or nine-thirty. There was a call then for me to go see White's sister, five miles over at Wallonia." He had to saddle up his horse and get some medicines, and this took a few minutes. Then he got in his saddle and began the five-mile visit. "When I got back home it was around 3:00 A.M. Along the way I crossed the railroad and passed in front of Lee

Sizemore's store, and Lee and Walter Wadlington were
standing out there staring at a light in the direction of Hopkinsville. I saw the light but had no idea what it was.
Hopkinsville is about 20 miles from home. Well, I went
on home and retired. I heard of the raid the first time the
next morning at breakfast."

"And that was the first time you heard of the raid?"

"Yes, the first time I knew of it."

"Doctor, you have heard the testimony of Sanford Hall,
in which he stated you were at Cedar Grove schoolhouse
and outlined certain plans for the 'capture' of Hopkinsville.
You said you were the 'Granddaddy of the Night Riders,
father and all.' I want to ask you if you were the 'General'
or if you had any connection with this organization?"

"None whatever."

"Doctor, did you ever say at Cedar Grove or anywhere
else that you were the 'General of the Night Riders,' or that
you were in any wise connected with the Night Riders, in
the presence of Sanford Hall or any one else?"

"I never have. I've never been at Cedar Grove schoolhouse in my life."

"Did you ever talk in the presence of Arthur Cooper
about wanting to assassinate Judge Wells?"

"I never did."

"Did you ever want to assassinate anybody?"

"Never had that desire."

"Doctor, did you order any lawlessness or burning of
property at Hopkinsville?"

"I did not."

"Were you ever shot?"

A sudden movement crossed the courtroom. Somewhat
testily Dr. Amoss answered, "No, I have never been shot."

"Are you willing to strip and let the jury see?"

The room became quiet. "Yes, sir, absolutely willing." There were many ladies present and there was a muffled titter. The idea of this iron man, oozing masculinity, stripping before the jury and demonstrating that he had never been shot was funny enough that under less tense circumstances there would have been a howl of ribald laughter. Judge Hanberry reached for his gavel to forestall it.

The questioning was resumed.

"Now, then, Doctor, did you help to set fire to the Latham warehouse or any building in Hopkinsville that night?"

"I did not."

"Did you shoot into any of the buildings, the Methodist parsonage, police headquarters, any bank, or the *Kentuckian* office? Did you have anything to do with running the Honorable Mayor into the Baptist Church? Did you shoot into the house where Lindsey Mitchell was?"

"I did not."

"Doctor, why did you leave home?"

"I was shadowed everywhere I went by soldiers and plain-clothes men. Soldiers would meet me at the train I came in on and follow me everywhere I went. Drug stores, business houses, everywhere. When I went back to the train they would be following. I got information from the chief of police at Princeton that a soldier boarded the train that morning and in the presence of Bob Pepper, another policeman, said he had orders to shoot me on sight. I knew I had no law in this state to protect me. I left because my life was threatened."

"Doctor, did you also receive information that if you were killed the party who did it would be pardoned by Governor Willson?"

"I did receive such information. I left home about June 1, 1908, and returned in the spring of 1909."

"Did you leave to escape persecution?"

"No. I left because I was satisfied, with conditions as they were, I would have been killed for the rewards still out."

Harvey, Dr. Amoss's attractive daughter, and his wife testified to Dr. Amoss's alibi that night. Also the White families, Dr. Hayon, who was also attending Mrs. White, and Sizemore and Wadlington also corroborated his testimony. The case went to the jury at the close of the afternoon session March 16, 1911. Judge Hanberry charged the jury as to the law and evidence.

"If you believe that Dr. Amoss entered the conspiracy to destroy the warehouse of John C. Latham and did carry out this object, you shall find him guilty. *But you cannot convict him on the unsupported testimony of accomplices.*

"The law presumes the defendant innocent until he is proven guilty, and if the jury has any reasonable doubt as to the defendants' guilt, it shall acquit him.

"If you believe from the evidence in these cases that the witnesses Milton Oliver, Sanford Hall, Arthur Cooper, and Carl Cooper did conspire and confederate with the defendants, or any one of them, for the purpose of destroying the tobacco warehouse of John C. Latham, as charged in the indictment, *then the jury cannot convict the defendant upon the testimony alone of such accomplices.*"

Judge Hanberry reached for his gavel. The jury took one poll and the foreman reported, "Not guilty."

The court room could have torn the ancient edifice down with their applause, but that stern gavel halted them. When court was adjourned the mob rushed up and almost smothered Dr. Amoss, his wife and daughter weeping as they clutched him. For a time Dr. Amoss was likely to be carried out on the shoulders of a hundred stalwart Night Riders. But everybody scattered and had a good chew of Brown's Mule, a good cigar, a deeply inhaled Lucky Strike, a relaxing dip of Bruton's Snuff. (James Duke once said, "Tobacco is the poor man's comforter.") The indictments against Guy Dunning and the others were dismissed. Later the traitor witnesses were spirited out of Kentucky and ferried across the Ohio River, and it would be their necks if they ever came back. There is no record any of them did.

The greatest trial the Black Patch ever saw was in March. In May the news broke that the Supreme Court of the United States declared the American Tobacco Company a monopoly in restraint of trade and therefore a law-breaker, James Duke and his associates being named as *de facto* criminals.

The tobacco wars were pretty much over. Charles Meacham, always the master of understatement, remarked, "Some regarded this as a victory for the Night Riders." But he added thoughtfully, "The lessons learned were that the American people will not tamely and permanently submit to injustice, nor will they permit a reign of lawlessness to go on unchecked. The whole deplorable business had in the end its benefits. It is doubtful if the problem could have been handled any other way [than by Night Riding]."

Chapter Twenty-eight

Envoi

KENTUCKY: YOU TOUCH ITS HILLS; YOU TRAVEL ITS valleys. The warm winds off its wide-leafed tobacco — the graciousness of the blue distances — the dreaminess of its harvests: all the magic of this fair land remains. Along the old-time forgotten roads the four-mule wagons rumble by night, and you listen thinking it's the wind; ghost horsemen gallop past, hooded and menacing, and you think the fall of their hoofs is autumn rain in the dead leaves and sassafras bushes in the darkness. It is fertile earth and only the old men remember. Yet I like to think that over the land and its cities hovers this nostalgic atmosphere of those tragic and stirring times I have here taken delight in recording; and I take leave of writing the book, and these fading memories, with a kind of sadness at parting.

THE END

Note on Sources

I have in no sense tried to write a Ph.D. dissertation, with a footnote for every statement. I have respected facts without calling attention to where I found them. When I set out to write *Riders in the Night* I made a firm resolve to do a book after my own heart. I grew up in the fringes of the Black Patch, and when I came back to the Martin Branch of the University of Tennessee as professor of English, back in 1936, I returned to my interest in the tobacco wars and my sympathy with the growers. In the years between I had taught school in Kentucky and Tennessee, and Night Riding was still sporadic. So books have not been my only sources. Through the years, the past quarter century, I have talked with men who rode by night, and because they trusted me, they gave me much information that never came out in the newspapers of that day or the books and articles since written. This sort of folklore is woven all through my narrative. It would be difficult to find a page where material of these confidences is not implied. Thus I wanted to write a social history in human terms, rather than a dissertation.

But books have been tremendously helpful, and I name as of first importance to me James O. Nall's *The Tobacco*

Night Riders of Tennessee and Kentucky. Hardly second to Dr. Nall's fine book was Marie Taylor's *Night Riders in the Black Patch,* a Master's Thesis from the history department of the University of Kentucky (1934).

Next was John G. Miller's *The Black Patch War,* University of North Carolina Press (1936), in which Judge Miller gave a record of the trial of the Night Riders for flogging Robert Hollowell in Federal Court, in Paducah, Ky. Chapters 23 and 24 are mainly built from this book, plus records of the trial, and folklore of the results.

Of equal value has been Charles Mayfield Meacham's *A History of Christian County, Kentucky,* with its detailed chapter on the Hopkinsville raid covered in Chapter 14.

I was fortunate in having at my disposal for two years the bound volumes of the *Murray* (Ky.) *Ledger,* for the years of the most active Night Riding. Though a county weekly, the Ledger, edited by O. J. Jennings, who was a partisan of the tobacco revolt, had complete coverage of the events, in the most usable form.

In addition to these basic sources, I got important information from the Kentucky Historical Society, the Filson Club Quarterly, and the Tobacco Institute of New York.

The material on James B. Duke was drawn from *Dictionary of American Biography,* and *James B. Duke, Master Builder,* by John Wilber (Doran). In addition I journeyed to Duke University to look up materials on him in the university library. There was not much. All of Duke's personal papers were destroyed at his death.

Sections of the book are written in fictional form. Where this occurs they are usually founded on folklore and interviews. The chapter "Law and Evidence" was built around the court records — Commonwealth vs Dr. D. A. Amoss, 1000 pages, bound in the office of the Circuit Court Clerk,

Hopkinsville, Ky. Little liberty was taken with the actual words of the lawyers and witness.

Individuals have been of inestimable worth to me. Among these I take pleasure in naming Dr. Hensley Woodbridge, of the Murray State College Library, Dr. Lawrence Thompson of the University of Kentucky Library, A. W. Wood, publisher of the *Kentucky New Era,* and Harvey Amoss Moore, Dr. Amoss's daughter, who furnished me important information concerning her father. To all the anonymous Night Riders, now mostly dead and gone, I fervently offer my thanks to their ghosts, who now ride no more.

Bibliography

NEWSPAPERS

The *Bowling Green (Ky.) Messenger,* 1908.
The *Clarksville (Tenn.) Journal,* 1909.
The *Daily Leaf Chronicle,* Clarksville, Tennessee, 1906-1908.
The *Daily New Era,* Hopkinsville, Kentucky, 1906-1908.
The *Lexington (Ky.) Herald,* 1906-1908.
The *Louisville (Ky.) Courier-Journal,* 1906-1908.
The *Murray (Ky.) Ledger,* years 1906-1908.
The *Twice-A-Week Record,* Cadiz, Kentucky, 1906-1908.

GENERAL WORKS

Connelley, William E., and Coulter, E. M. *History of Kentucky.*
New York and Chicago: American Historical Society, 1922.
Ewing, Felix Grundy. *The Tobacco Situation in the Dark To-
bacco District of Kentucky and Tennessee.* Clarksville, Tenn.:
W. T. Titus, 1915.
Meacham, Charles Mayfield. *A History of Christian County,
Kentucky.* Nashville, Tenn.: Marshall & Bruce Co., 1930.
Miller, John G. *The Black Patch War.* Chapel Hill, N. C.: Uni-
versity of North Carolina Press, 1936.
Ogilvie, Frances. *Green Bondage.* New York: Farrar & Rine-
hart, 1931.
Robertson, Charley. *Send for Miss Cora.* New York: Reynal &
Hitchcock, 1948.
Warren, Robert Penn. *Night Rider.* New York: Random House,
1930.
Wood, H. C. *The Night Riders.* Chicago: Laird & Lee, 1908.

THESES

Kilpatrick, Elmer James. *The Changes in the Market Demand
for Tobacco.* University of Kentucky, 1929.
Taylor, Marie. *Night Riders in the Black Patch.* University of
Kentucky, 1934.
Wrather, Stephen Elvis. *Tobacco Marketing in Western Ken-
tucky.* University of Kentucky, 1933.

ARTICLES, DOCUMENTS, MANUSCRIPTS.

Beach, H. L. "The Great Tobacco War," *Saturday Evening Post,*
August 3, 1908, and January 18, 1908.
Documents of the American Tobacco Company, New York.
Documents of the Tobacco Institute, New York.
"Driven to Desperation," *Up-To-Date Farming,* Indianapolis,
Indiana, April 1, 1908.
Killebrew, J. F. "Tobbacco Report," July 1, 1911, U. S. Depart-
ment of Agriculture Circular 22, Washington, D. C.
McCulloch-Williams, Martha, "The Tobacco War in Kentucky,"
Review of Reviews, February, 1908.
Manuscript of "Dr. Amoss," by Harvey Amoss Moore.
Manuscript of the Kentucky Historical Society, Frances Cole-
man, Librarian, on biographical materials of Governor Augus-
tus E. Wilson, governor of Kentucky during the Night Rider
epoch.
United States Senate Document: 58th Congress, March 21-April
18, 1905; 59th Congress, March 4, June 30, 1904; 59th Con-
gress, December 3, 1906-March 4, 1907; 60th Congress,
December 2-May 30, 1908.

Index

299